Research Centre for the History of Religious and Cultural Diversity
(Meiji University, Tokyo)

Memory and Narrative Series 10

The Life Story of Dr Dorothy Francis, MBE
An African-Caribbean Business Woman in Leicester

Edited and written by **Kiyotaka Sato**

Foreword by Jenny Holt

In Jamaica, March 2012

The memory and narrative series is published by Kiyotaka Sato, Professor of European History, School of Arts and Letters, Meiji University, Tokyo. The purpose of the project is to enable the UK's many and various ethnic minority communities and indigenous groups to record and preserve their memories, life experiences and traditions, and to ensure access to this rich inheritance for present and future generations. The project is established with financial support from the Meiji University as well as the Ministry of Education, Culture, Sports, Science and Technology (Japan) and other organisations.

First published by RCHRCD, June 2019

Copyright © 2019 Kiyotaka Sato

Research Centre for the History of Religious and Cultural
Diversity (RCHRCD)
Meiji University, Tokyo
1-1 Kanda-Surugadai, Chiyoda-ku,
Tokyo, 101-8301, Japan
Email: satokiyo@meiji.ac.jp

All rights reserved. No part of this publication may be reproduced, stored in a retrieval system, or transmitted in any form, or by any means, electronic, mechanical, photocopying, recording or otherwise, without the prior permission in writing of the author. Enquiries concerning reproduction outside these terms and in other countries should be sent to the editor at the address above.

Outside front cover:
  Dr Dorothy Francis
  (Reproduced with the permission of Dr Dorothy Francis)
Inside front cover:
  Dr Dorothy Francis
  (Reproduced with the permission of Dr Dorothy Francis)
Outside back cover:
  Dr Dorothy Francis and her family
  (Reproduced with the permission of Dr Dorothy Francis and her family)

ISSN 2185-6079

Published by the Asia Printing Office Corporation
Address: 1154 Miwa araya, Nagano-shi, Nagano, 380-0804, Japan

Acknowledgements

I wish to thank the following people and organisations who assisted me with my
  work:
Mrs Delia Baker
Mr Richard Bettworth (former Editor, Leicester Mercury)
The late Emeritus Professor Richard Bonney, University of Leicester
Dr Margaret Bonney (former Chief Archivist, Record Office for Leicestershire,
  Leicester & Rutland)
Mr Kevin Booth (Editor, Leicester Mercury)
Mrs Cynthia Brown (former Project Manager of the East Midlands Oral History
  Archive [EMOHA], University of Leicester)
Mr Nick Carter (former Editor, Leicester Mercury)
The late Mr Steve England (former Archivist, Leicester Mercury)
The family of Dr Dorothy Francis
Professor Jun Fukushi, Okayama University
Mrs Yoshimi Gregory (Chair, Leicestershire Japan Society)
Dr Jenny Holt (until recently, Associate Professor, Meiji University)
Mr Asaf Hussain (Chairperson of the Society for Intercultural Understanding)
The late Mrs Freda Hussain (former Principal of Moat Community College)
Mr Colin Hyde (Researcher and Outreach Officer of the East Midlands Oral History
  Archive [EMOHA], University of Leicester)
Dr Shuichi Kurosaki (Research Associate, Meiji University)
Emeritus Professor Werner Menski, School of Oriental and African Studies (SOAS),
  University of London
Emeritus Professor Eleanor Nesbitt, University of Warwick
Mr George Oliver (Editor, Leicester Mercury)
The late Mrs Sonia Spencer
Dr Pippa Virdee, Senior Lecturer, De Montfort University
The Crescent in Leicester
De Montfort University
Leicester City Council
Leicester Mercury
Record Office for Leicestershire, Leicester & Rutland
Leicester Central Library
Stoneygate Baptist Church
University of Leicester

Above all I wish to thank Dr Dorothy Francis, both for the interviews she gave in
preparation for this booklet, and for all the other information she has given me
regarding her life story.

Foreword

When I worked at Meiji University and took part in Prof. Sato's activities with the Research Centre for the History of Religious and Cultural Diversity, I became curious about the people he had interviewed, and hoped that a chance would eventually come to meet some of them in person. Finally, in 2014, he called me down to Leicester and introduced me to Dorothy Francis, who was to feature in the latest of his studies. We had dinner with Dorothy and her extended family, and the following year, she invited me, with my son, to attend the Leicester Caribbean Carnival, after which she regularly holds a party for extended family and friends. I found her warm, engaging, interesting, and sympathetic – the kind of person you can happily talk to for hours, and still have room for more.

Kiyotaka asked me to write the foreword to Dorothy's biography because we had significant life experiences in common. We were both in mixed-heritage partnerships, with mixed-heritage children, and, as a European living, at that time, in Japan, I was an immigrant, and as such, I had glimpsed how unrelenting and insidious the grip of systematic, institutional racism could be in a society. On my journey down to Leicester in 2014, I read Dorothy's narrative, which was enthralling. It was also, at times, horrifying. Although I was familiar with the depths some individuals sink to in order to denigrate or even endanger others purely because they look different, sound different, or happen to have been born in another country, individual stories never cease to shock, especially when they involve children. The shameful treatment meted out to African-Caribbean people when Dorothy arrived in Britain was calculated to grind them down and ensure they never rose out of menial positions. However, Dorothy was not prepared to submit to this, and she has tackled obstacles placed in her way with a deep determination, a strong sense of justice and fairness, and a desire to improve the situation for all who have faced injustice and marginalisation. Her success in the field of ethical business is now recognised nationally, and one of the most uplifting things of the last few years has been seeing her receive accolades which have been so justly won and so hard fought for.

It would be nice to be able to situate Dorothy's story within a general narrative of progress and enlightenment, and to portray Britain as a country learning to deal with difference positively as a society which valued individuals as individuals. Unfortunately, however, this year, 2018, has proved again that the UK is still torn between embracing and rejecting minorities. The year began with celebrations to mark the seventieth anniversary of the arrival of the Empire Windrush in 1948. A series of Black history documentaries told the story of how families strove to succeed through the ensuing decades in the face of immense prejudice, how they worked twice as hard to achieve half as much esteem as their white counterparts, and of the long road to equality legislation. Then, in March 2018, the 'Windrush Scandal' hit the headlines. It emerged that there had been systematic attempts to deport UK citizens born in Commonwealth countries who had lived legally in Britain for decades, many having contributed years of their lives to keeping the country afloat by working in essential sectors such as the National Health

Service (NHS). This was part of Theresa May's 'hostile environment' policy, designed to cut net migration figures by any means possible – by making it very difficult for anybody but the wealthy to enter the country, and by finding excuses to threaten legitimate residents with deportation for pettifogging bureaucratic reasons. This resulted in some people losing their jobs, their homes, and also their health. This came as a shock to the public, but it revealed what many of us knew already – especially those who had struggled through the tortuous visa process. Like many governments with a tenuous mandate, ours has garnered support among certain sectors of society by stirring division, and they have worked with the tabloid press to encourage the mistaken belief that the interests of 'white' people (particularly working-class white people) are opposed to those of minorities.

It shouldn't be like this, because the majority of people in the British Isles, of whatever origin, have every reason to feel solidarity. While the landed elite rampaged across the globe during the 18th and 19th centuries, pursuing ill-gotten gains through the slave trade and Imperial projects, they were also busy disinheriting those closer to home. They implemented the Highland Clearances, perpetuated the injustices that led to the Great Famine in Ireland, and used the Enclosure Acts to rob villages of the common land on which many low-waged labourers depended for food. These policies led to displacement, starvation and death, and arguably brought about much of the inequality still present today in Britain, where more than half the land still belongs to less than one percent of the population, and where vested interests come first. The majority of people in the UK have ancestors who were affected by those traumatic social policies, either on the British Isles or in the Empire. Whether they are the descendants of slaves, the colonised, the dispossessed or the displaced, these people should not be at odds with each other. It is in all of their interests to work together for equality, a fair division of national assets, decent wages, ethical business practices, and a just economy – precisely those values which Dorothy has spent her life promoting.

Jenny Holt
Storth, Cumbria
30th August 2018

Dr Dorothy Francis

Delivering my response the orator by the public orator Mr Nigel Siesage at Doctorate ceremony.

Contents

Acknowledgements   **5**

Foreword   **6**

Ⅰ. Introduction   11

Ⅱ. The life story of Dr Dorothy Francis, MBE   17

     1 My country of birth and my family background   18

     2 Moving to England — from an 'extended family network' to a 'nuclear family'   25

     3 Good memories from my early days in England   31

     4 A new life in Coventry   38

     5 My school experiences and incidences of racism   60

     6 Four generations of our family in the UK   66

     7 My higher education and career   88

     8 Moving to Leicester, my marriage, my children and their education   104

     9 My religion and faith   109

     10 My love of cooking, favourite writers and cultural influences   115

     11 The notion of 'home'   121

     12 Awards   129

     13 The EU Referendum and Brexit   139

     14 Reflections on Japan and Japanese culture   142

     15 Reflections on the 'Memory and Narrative Series' (No.1 & No.6)   144

Ⅲ. Kevin's contribution to Dorothy's story   155

Ⅳ. Appendices   159

     Appendix 1: Photo memories of Dorothy and her family   160

     Appendix 2: Dorothy and Kevin's wedding, 17th September 1994   192

     Appendix 3: Gathering Dorothy's extended family in Jamaica, 2015   200

Appendix 4: A celebration of International Women's day
at Stoneygate Baptist Church, 2015   211

Appendix 5: Dorothy's annual carnival party at her home, 2017   219

Appendix 6: Dorothy's work and her business awards   223

Appendix 7: 'Day trip to Rochdale'   251

Appendix 8: Account of Honorary Doctorate of Laws, Graduation Day 253

Appendix 9: Dorothy's experience and 'Working together to end
strip searching'   259

Appendix 10: The Windrush scandal (Extracts *from Leicester
Mercury*)   268

Appendix 11: Ethnicity and religion in the UK, Coventry and
Leicester   272

Appendix 12: Maps of Jamaica with Caribbean Sea, Coventry and
Leicester in the UK   280

Appendix 13: Select bibliography and websites   284

Appendix 14: Message from Dr Dorothy Francis, MBE   294

I
Introduction

I Introduction

Between April 2001 and March 2002, I spent a sabbatical year in Leicester. While living there, I became very interested in the history of this city, which, since the Second World War, has become what many consider to be a shining example of a harmonious multi-ethnic, multi-cultural community. As a result of my developing interests in the history of immigration to Leicester, I subsequently began to visit two to three times a year. Although visits are short, I make every effort each time to conduct as much local research and carry out interviews with individuals who have made Leicester and its surrounding areas into their home over the last sixty or so years.

In October 2010, I established the Research Centre for the History of Religious and Cultural Diversity (RCHRCD) at Meiji University. The support I have received while doing so has enabled me to record many of the findings I have gathered from interviews and other types of research in a collection of booklets entitled the 'Memory and Narrative Series'. [1]

My first booklet featured Mrs Elvy Morton, who was born on the small Caribbean island of Nevis (then a British colony) in 1935, and who migrated to Britain in 1958. Among other events, the narrative tells how Mrs Morton became the first Chair of the Leicester Caribbean Carnival, founded in 1985. [2] I have fond memories of the time when I was working with Mrs Morton on our booklet.

This time, for my tenth booklet, I am very pleased to be able to present the life story of Dr Dorothy Francis, who like Mrs Morton, made that long journey from the Caribbean to the United Kingdom. She was born in Jamaica in 1961, when it was a member of the West Indies Federation, still partly under British control; however, Jamaica gained its Independence the year after. In 1962, Dorothy's parents moved to England and settled in Coventry. Dorothy followed them in 1966, when she was five years old. Except for a short interval, she lived in Coventry until she was in her early twenties, but by the mid-1980s had moved to Leicester to work. This is where she married Kevin, who was originally from Birmingham.

Dorothy gives a frank account of her life story, which spans from her childhood to the present day, of the experiences she encountered, and her feelings about these experiences. Here, I will briefly summarise some key points which are essential to understanding her narrative.

One particularly outstanding issue which has made a great impact on Dorothy's life has been the racial discrimination she has been forced to endure, particularly as a small child at school in Coventry and, later on, during one notable incident in 1987, when she was subjected to severe harassment by immigration services at Heathrow Airport when travelling back home to the UK from Jamaica. [3] When we read this narrative, we can understand the magnitude of the pain and suffering such incidents inflict. However, rather than retreating into a corner, Dorothy has spent her life campaigning both against racial discrimination and many other forms of entrenched social injustice. This is reflected in

I   Introduction

the way she fosters awareness of the negative impact the British Empire had on many lives, and the fact that its legacy still continues into the present day. In addition, her pro-active response to her experiences in Britain have contributed greatly to the formation of her identity, which places much importance on her African-Caribbean and Jamaican heritage.

The next thing I want to mention here is the vivid way in which Dorothy tells her story, not only of her relationships with the 'host society' she has encountered in Britain, but also with her own African-Caribbean family and culture. This includes the issue of mov-ing from being within an extended family network in Jamaica to being in a nuclear family unit after arriving in Britain. Dorothy also talks about the continuance of her extended family relationship across the Atlantic Ocean throughout the period she has lived in Brit-ain. I hope that her story will help readers to gain a perspective on the lives of African-Caribbean people who have made their homes in the United Kingdom. In order to help readers to develop a picture of life in this community, I have included photographs at the end of the book. [4]

Thirdly, I want to talk about Dorothy's work and the number of awards she has received due to her achievements in her work-place. Currently, she is Chief Executive Officer of the Leicester-based Co-operative and Social Enterprise Development Agency (CASE). CASE is a workers' co-operative specialising in delivering advice, training and business growth for co-operative and social enterprise, mainly in Leicestershire and the East Mid-lands. Dorothy has worked for CASE for over thirty years, since 1985. Her work has achieved recognition and she has been presented with a number of awards. Apart from the 'Student of the Year' award on completion of her Chartered Institute of Personal and Development (CIPD) course, her awards have been: the Leicestershire Business Wom-an of the Year Award 2011 (presented at the Jubilee 'Enterprising Women Awards Cere-mony' at the Curve Theatre, 19 November 2010); the Woman of Achievement Award 2014 from Leicester Asian Business Association (LABA); the Queen's Award for Enterprise Promotion (Lifetime Achievement), awarded on 20 June 2016 in celebration of H.M. the Queen's 90th birthday; the Companion of the Chartered Management Institute (CMI) [awarded to selected leaders who manage successful organisations and demonstrate ex-ceptional management skills]; Member of the British Empire (MBE), for the promotion of enterprise, in 2017 and an honorary Doctorate of Laws from the University of Leices-ter in 2018.

During interviews Dorothy has frequently mentioned her parents, in particular, her mother, in terms of her work, discipline in bringing up children, etc. Through this I be-gan to appreciate a sense not only of her mother's love for her daughter, but also Doro-thy's affection and sense of gratitude towards her mother. As I mentioned above, Doro-thy received an MBE in 2017, and at the time of receiving the honour, she remarked:

I am delighted to have been recognized for my work, and it's a great honour to receive an MBE, although I had to think long and hard about whether or not to accept. An

I Introduction

MBE commemorates 'empire', and as a person of colour, with Jamaican heritage, that is not something that I particularly wish to celebrate… I accepted as I feel it's not just an award for me, but for my community, my family and my colleagues, past and present, at CASE. The deciding reason why I accepted is that I knew that it would have tremendous significance for my mother and would contribute, in a small way, to repaying the courage and faith that she showed in leaving Jamaica to make a life in Britain so that her children could have a better future. I'm pleased to accept on her behalf and gratified that thirty-three years of doing a job that I love has been recognized in this way. [5]

I first met Dorothy on the eve of the Leicester Caribbean Carnival, which is held on the first Saturday in August each year. She was holding a party at her home for family, relations, work colleagues, and neighbours. My Irish landlady, with whom I lodge while I am studying in Leicester, asked me if I wanted to go to this party, because she knew I was interested in the personal life stories of individuals who lived in Leicester. At the party, I had a chance to ask Dorothy if I could interview her on some other occasion, and she willingly replied, 'yes!' A little while later, I visited her at her home, arriving at about 6 pm, and interviewed her. Initially, we were both nervous and self-conscious, but in the middle of the interview, she started to tell me her story while answering my questions. I had anticipated that the interview would last for one hour, but when I realised what time it was, it was already past 9 pm, and we had been there for over three hours! I am deeply grateful that she trusted me with her life story and responded to my many questions.

However, when I discovered that the family had arranged to eat out that evening, I felt guilty for detaining her for so long, and still feel bad about it now! As her home is close to my lodgings, I visited her more or less every time I went to Leicester, and I asked her all sorts of questions regarding her story, and interviewed her again. All in all, I interviewed her nine times (August 2010-March 2017). [6]

In the meantime, my administrative work and my role at the University have intervened, and the publication of this booklet has been greatly delayed. However, during this time she has received a number of awards, and I have been able to mention them here. Indeed, she has received so many that I am only able to include the MBE on the front cover of this volume, otherwise the title would be far too long!

I am delighted to be able to publish Dorothy's booklet at last. I also asked her husband, Kevin, to write a paragraph about how they met, and this is included in the booklet. I would like to thank him for his contribution, and I am sure that his recollections will enhance the volume.

The foreword to this work has been written by Jenny Holt who was, until recently, a colleague at Meiji University. [7] Her specialist field of research is English literature of the Victorian period, in particular children's literature and Anglophone literature about Japan. When I mentioned that I had been interviewing Dorothy in Leicester, she was very interested to hear her story. She was particularly interested in her experiences of racial discrimination in Britain and about the harassment she suffered from British immigration authorities at Heathrow Airport. Jenny herself has been subjected to discrimination from Japanese society, which can be seen in hurtful behaviours such as labelling all foreigners as 'Gaijin' ('outsiders'). Dorothy's experience of the immigration authority's harassment at Heathrow Airport reminded Jenny of her own Japanese husband's experience with British airport immigration. Jenny saw Dorothy's experience of racism and harassment as being, like her husband's, part of a more pervading atmosphere of racial prejudice which persists in Britain, and also in many other countries.

In order to write this Foreword, Jenny visited Dorothy in Leicester twice. Both times were in early August around the time when the Leicester Caribbean Carnival is held. The first time, I introduced them and we all had dinner at an Indian restaurant with Dorothy's family, and the second time she went with her son and attended the party which Dorothy always organises after the Carnival at her home. Dorothy welcomed them warmly on both occasions. I would like to take this opportunity to thank Jenny for making the trip to Leicester and conducting extra research in order to write her Foreword. Finally, I would urge readers to peruse the Appendices to these volumes, which include the many photographs which illustrate Dorothy's story.

Dorothy's mother fell seriously ill in late December 2018. She died on Christmas Eve, and was buried on 25th January. I wish to conclude this Introduction with my heartfelt condolences to Dorothy and her family.

Notes

1   I have already published nine booklets. These include the life stories of a Caribbean woman, a Jewish woman, a Sikh woman, a Sikh artist and his wife, a Muslim businessman who came to Leicester via Uganda in 1972, a man of mixed heritage, a Lativan man and his wife, a Hindu man, and an Indian Classical Dancer. I have embarked on publishing a second series of Memory and Narrative biographies, in addition to the nine booklets which constitute series one. The first volume focuses on the life story of an adherent of the Hindu faith who resides in Coventry.

2   *Life Story of Mrs Elvy Morton: First Chair of the Leicester Caribbean Carnival*, edited and written by Kiyotaka Sato, Tokyo: Research Centre for the History of Religious and Cultural Diversity (Meiji University), 2010, 96 pp.

3   See Appendix 9: Dorothy's experience and 'Working together to end strip searching', pp. 259–267.

4   See Appendix 5: Dorothy's awards in business, pp. 223–250.

5   See Appendix 5: Dorothy's awards in business, pp. 223–250.

6   My interviews with Dorothy were: 26 August 2010, 14 March 2011, 10 August 2012; 17 March 2013; 3 March 2015; 11 March 2015; 16 March 2016; 14 August 2016; 16

I   Introduction

March 2017.

7   Dr Jenny Holt was, until recently, Associate Professor in English Literature at Meiji University in Tokyo. She has published a book entitled *Public School Literature, Civic Education and the Politics of Male Adolescence* (Aldershot: Ashgate, 2008), and a number of papers and articles. She is currently working on a monograph entitled *Utopians and Samurai: Representations of Meiji Period Japan in English Literature*, which examines works written between 1850 and 1920 by British, European and Japanese writers. She is also currently constructing an internet project entitled 'Tracking Isabella Bird'. The project consists of an online critical edition of *Unbeaten Tracks in Japan* (1880), with hyperlinks to information and illustrations.

II
The life story of Dr Dorothy Francis, MBE

II The Life Story of Dr Dorothy Francis

1 My country of birth and my family background

Dorothy was born on the Caribbean island of Jamaica[1] **in 1961. Here, she recalls Jamaica and talks about her family background.**

Jamaica, my home country

I was born in Jamaica in the parish of St Catherine in 1961. I spent my early years in a small village called Peartree Grove, which is in the hills of St Mary, one of the parishes that adjoins St Catherine.

Jamaica is situated in the Caribbean Sea and is a beautifully verdant and hot country. The island is divided into three counties, Cornwall, Middlesex and Surrey, and these are further divided into 14 parishes, which are similar to counties or districts.

A view of Caribbean sea from Jamaica.

In terms of topography, Jamaica is a very mountainous island: over fifty per cent of the land lies more than 1,000 feet above sea level and there are numerous mountains, rivers, hills and valleys. The land is very green and fertile, and many different foods are grown across the island. Indigenous plants include cassava, sapodilla (called naseberry in Jamaica), avocado pears and star apple, and crops include yams, bananas, mangoes and sugar cane. Jamaica is famed for its citrus production, which includes oranges, grapefruits, tangerines and mandarins. Jamaican growers have created a number of hybrids, including the ugli fruit, a type of tangelo which is a hybrid of the grapefruit, orange, and the tangerine. Another citrus fruit developed in Jamaica is the ortanique, which is a cross between an orange and a tangerine. The name is derived from the words 'orange', 'tangerine' and 'unique'. The sight and smell of citrus groves is a feature of certain areas of Jamaica, especially Manchester, St Elizabeth, Clarendon and St Mary. There are a number of citrus processing factories in Jamaica, and the resulting juices are enjoyed across the island and exported across the world.

The Jamaican climate lends itself well to crops and many new foods were introduced to the island from other countries. These include breadfruit and the otaheite apple, which were both introduced from Tahiti by Captain William Bligh (1754–1817), famed as the captain who was deposed during the mutiny on the *Bounty* in 1789. Bligh had been promised a huge amount of money to bring breadfruit plants from Tahiti to England so that they could be bred and established across the Caribbean islands as a basic foodstuff for the enslaved people. It is said that Bligh's careful treatment of the 1,000 breadfruit plants that the *Bounty* carried contributed to the mutiny, as the plants occupied a great

II The Life Story of Dr Dorothy Francis

deal of space and caused severe overcrowding on the long voyage; and because, in addition, Bligh gave the plants water whilst denying rations to the sailors. Bligh survived the mutiny, returned safely to England and eventually set out on another journey which was successful in bringing breadfruit plants to the UK, and from there to various botanical gardens across the Caribbean. The result of this is that breadfruit trees are now one of the most common trees across the region.

Many other plants such as yams, ackee, bissy, coco yam, watermelon and gunga peas were brought to Jamaica by Africans, whilst sugar cane was introduced by the British as a cash crop. Most of these foods have been integrated into Jamaican cuisine and are now seen as essentially 'Jamaican'.

The Jamaican climate is tropical, and so does not support foodstuffs such as apples, pears, strawberries and potatoes, which are commonly grown in temperate regions and demand a cooler climate. The overabundance of other fruits means that these rare imports are a treat rather than a necessity.

The original inhabitants of Jamaica were a sub-grouping of the Arawak people called the Tainos. They were skilled navigators and farmers with complex social systems, art, music, and poetry. They travelled from South America around 2,500 years ago seeking new land on which to settle, and they named the island Xaymaca, which meant 'land of wood and water'. The Tainos were peaceful people, who caught fish and farmed crops such as cassava, sweet potatoes, maize, fruits, vegetables, cotton and tobacco. Many of their words, such as 'cassava', 'canoe', 'hammock', 'hurricane' and 'barbeque' found their way into the English language and are still used today.

The Tainos did not survive long after Christopher Columbus (c.1451–1506) landed on the island in 1494. The Spanish tortured and killed the Tainos to obtain their land. Many Tainos took their own lives to escape the misery; others were overworked and ill-treated, and died within a short time of Columbus's arrival. The process was hastened by the introduction of European diseases, such as measles, to which the Tainos had no resistance. So within a very few years, only a few Tainos survived in isolated communities.

The British grabbed Jamaica from the Spaniards and began a new stage in the island's history when they introduced sugar cultivation, bringing enslaved Africans to work the sugar plantations that were established across the country. At one point, it was estimated that there were ten African slaves for each white person in Jamaica, and these enslaved people were controlled by a vicious and severe regime. The planters lived in fear of uprisings, as they were so greatly outnumbered, and they therefore used a multiplicity of techniques, including divide and rule, to control the enslaved population.

Following the abolition of slavery, Chinese and Indian people were brought to the island as indentured labour. Europeans – particularly from Ireland and Scotland – joined the English immigrants in settling on the island, and Syrians and Lebanese arrived to trade.

II The Life Story of Dr Dorothy Francis

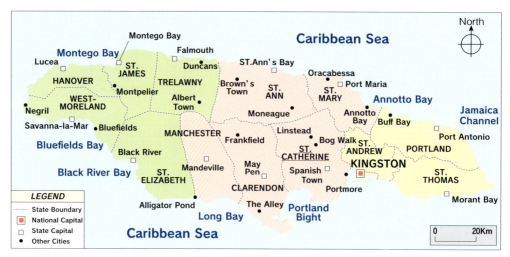
Jamaica

People also arrived from various Jewish communities, and a large group of Germans settled on the island. The result of this history is a fusion of people from across the world of all skin tones and shades, all of whom identify as 'Jamaican'. The Jamaican national motto is: 'Out of many, One people', because the population has been formed from many diverse ethnicities but has melded into one people.

After many years of slavery and colonialism, Jamaica achieved independence from Britain in 1962.[2]

My grandparents

My grandparents on both sides were subsistence farmers. They were excellent cultivators, who worked the land to feed their families and sell their crops. My father was an exceptional farmer, and my brother has inherited the family 'green fingers', displaying a natural affinity for growing plants.

My grandparents farmed various crops, including yams, bananas and cocoa. They kept pigs, goats, chickens and sometimes a cow, and sold eggs and chickens for the pot. They raised their family in that way, selling what they could at market and bartering with neighbours.

My grandmother on my mother's side was Loretta Walker, and my grandfather was Luther Walker. They were born in the early 1900s in St Mary, which is a region of Jamaica. My grandmother was usually called 'Sis' or 'Miss' Loretta and most people called my grandfather 'Daddy' or 'Mas' Luther. In Jamaica it is common to give everyone a title – it is not usual to call people, especially elders, by their first name so we usually affix a title such as 'Miss', 'Mr', or 'Mas', which is a shortened version of 'Master'. I simply knew my grandparents as 'Daddy' and 'Sis' – they are the first people that I remember and I loved them very much.

My grandparents were popular and well known in the area and much respected. My grandfather was primarily a farmer but he had a lot of other skills. He was a master basket maker with skills much in demand for weaving baskets of all types for use in the home, fishing, in farming and as panniers on donkeys. My grandmother was a skilled herbalist and understood the use and application of a wide range of herbs and plants. When people were sick or injured, they would come to her and she would prescribe herbal remedies. My grandparents were a good team and they worked alongside each other to bring up five children and a host of grandchildren, great grandchildren and adopted children.

My parents left me in the care of my grandparents when they emigrated to England, and I spent my early years with them. In fact, I don't know if I was aware that they were not my parents. I had little understanding of family structure as our household comprised my grandparents, me, my niece, a cousin, and an adopted cousin, plus, 'floating' members. Everyone, young and old, called my grandparents 'Daddy' and 'Sis', so I was unaware of the concept of 'parents'.

I don't know my grandmother's name on my father's side because she died when my father was very young and he didn't really talk about her. My paternal grandfather was called Ezekiel Francis, but I didn't know him well as I only met him once when I returned to Jamaica on holiday when I was twenty-one. I have always been closer to my mother's side of the family, and when I recall my grandparents I primarily think of my mother's parents.

My parents and their historical background (British Empire)

My mother worked as a housekeeper and domestic help for a while, but she needed more flexibility so turned to self-employment, buying and selling fruit, primarily oranges. This was her employment at the time that she met my father in the late 1950s. My father worked in the local citrus canning factory, and they met through that connection. My mother would have been in her early thirties and my father about twenty-eight or twenty-nine at the time, and they married in 1961. My father had already spent some time in the United States of America on what was called 'farm work', which involved picking crops in southern states, and had enjoyed being abroad. He had returned to Jamaica but opportunities were few and far between and he was already

My mother and father, taken in late 1963.

II The Life Story of Dr Dorothy Francis

considering emigrating to England when he met my mother.

Jamaica was still a British colony when my parents met each other in the 1950s. Like most people brought up in colonial settings my parents had little concept of Jamaica as a separate country – for them Jamaica was an extension of Britain and they were proud to be British. The 1950s in the UK was a time of great change and prosperity with full employment and labour in very short supply. England was still suffering after the Second World War and was in urgent need of labour to rebuild the economy. Jobs in England were plentiful and British people were able to pick and choose. However, the indigenous population did not want to do what they considered to be menial jobs – such as cleaning, road sweeping and working as conductors on buses or orderlies in hospitals, and so the government sent to the colonies to obtain labour to undertake these jobs.

The British government held big recruitment drives across the Caribbean colonies, inviting people to come to England and appealing for their help in rebuilding the 'mother country'. Major British institutions, including the National Health Service (NHS) and British Rail, set up stalls wreathed with posters and glossy leaflets to recruit labour. In return for the passage money, workers guaranteed to give a certain number of years' commitment to the firm that they signed up with. The recruiting drive was beseeching, frantic and urgent and many young people were caught up in the frenzy. Government ministers often went to the Caribbean to encourage people to sign on and John Enoch Powell,[3] as Minister of Health, was instrumental in recruiting hundreds of nurses from the Caribbean for the National Health Service.

Life in Jamaica and other Caribbean islands was difficult and people were looking for a different way forward. I suppose for young people like my father it was a bit of an adventure. They thought that they could go to England for a few years and then return with their earnings to resume life in Jamaica, but this did not prove to be the case; most of them never returned to live in Jamaica. The joke amongst the Caribbean community is that if you speak to anyone who came at that time they will tell you that they only came for five years – some have now been here for 55 or 65 years!

The economic situation contributed to my parents' decision to come to England; they wanted to seek a better life for themselves and their children and believed that emigrating to the mother country would allow them to do so.

People wishing to move to the UK required sponsorship from someone who already lived in the UK. A family friend, Mr Glen Morgan (whom my parents had known well in Jamaica), sponsored my father to come to England. Mr Morgan had settled in Coventry,[4] so that is where my father came when he arrived in 1961. This is the way that communities were built – people who were already in the UK sponsored others to come and built small networks around themselves. So communities remained tight knit, as many people knew each other from 'back home'. Once my father had settled he sponsored my mother to come to the UK, and she arrived in 1962, having left me in the care of my

22

II The Life Story of Dr Dorothy Francis

grandparents. My father came to the UK while Jamaica was still a British colony. Independence came on 6th August 1962, as my mother was preparing to leave for England.

My mother has been in England for over 55 years and is very settled here, but she still talks about Jamaica as 'home' because that is how she sees it. Like most Jamaicans she loves the island and if she had had other choices she would never have left. However, life was hard. She and others of her generation were promised opportunities of work, education and housing in the UK and were pressurised to serve the 'mother country', so they accepted the inducements and moved thousands of miles from home.

Many people have said to me: 'If Jamaica is so lovely, why did you leave?'. I feel that such questions belie their lack of knowledge regarding colonial history and the influence of the British Empire. Most Jamaicans loved their country and did not leave by choice. It was very difficult to live in Jamaica at the time my parents emigrated; they had little choice but to leave. I think that they were very brave to leave everything to move to another country almost 5,000 miles away. They relocated to a place which was so very different in terms of climate, culture and attitudes and I think people have to be subject to a certain level of desperation to do that. If they had been richer or had access to resources and assets they could have afforded to stay in Jamaica and they would probably have done so because they loved the island and never truly stopped pining for what they had left behind.

The British Empire promoted itself as a mother to the world; however this was a lie told in order to make colonialism seem acceptable. A mother is someone who nurtures her children and keeps them safe and it sounded so much friendlier to proclaim the empire as a 'mother' rather than as a rapacious conqueror. The British peddled the myth of the mother country in order to exert a form of social control with the intention of engendering a sense of 'belonging' and to hide the fact that the whole purpose of colonialism was to enrich the mother country by exploiting copper, bauxite, gold, silver, sugar and other valuable resources, using slavery and indentured or poorly paid labour. The riches generated by the rape of resources were channelled to the UK, enabling the Empire to enrich great cities such as London, Bristol, Liverpool, Manchester, Glasgow and Birmingham, and to build edifices such as Rochdale Town Hall and the Houses of Parliament.

Many of the great buildings and edifices that we see around us in the UK were built on slavery, but this is usually unacknowledged and the myth of the munificent mother country is still deployed. People from former colonies are often told that they are 'lucky' to be allowed to live in the UK but such comments make no reference to the fact that the resources of colonial countries, as well as unpaid, or poorly paid labour, drove the UK in its industrial and economic revolution. It is galling that so few British people understand the legacy of colonialism and its contribution to the lives that they live today. This is one of the reasons why the International Slavery Museum in Liverpool[5] was welcome, as it clearly outlines the debt that the UK and cities such as Liverpool owe to slavery, indentured labour and colonialism. It does not change history but at least it recognises and

II The Life Story of Dr Dorothy Francis

acknowledges a significant part of UK history.

The myth of the mother country was a way of keeping people loyal by encouraging them to think that they were British and that they were valued as such. The story was that even if they lived 5,000 miles away from the motherland in Jamaica, Barbados or Antigua they were still part of England. They spoke the language, understood British customs and were schooled and cultured to believe that their country was simply an offshoot of the UK. This sense of belonging to the mother country was an important identifier and was a contributing factor to the willingness of colonial people to relocate to the UK when called upon to rebuild the nation after World War Two. However, the people from colonial countries who responded to the call did not realise that they would be offered dirty, tedious, poorly paid and low-level employment that British people didn't want to do. A surplus of jobs meant that British people could pick and choose, and most of them had no incentive to accept work that was seen as dirty or menial. In short, Enoch Powell and other ministers sent to the colonies and appealed to the 'children' of the empire for help to rebuild the country with their labour, and the people of the Windrush generation [6] responded, travelling thousands of miles only to find that the embrace of the mother country was cold and harsh rather than the warm welcome pictured on the recruitment brochures.

Many felt rejected by the UK and were desperately unhappy but by then it was too late. They had sold their farms, smallholdings and houses, given up rented accommodation and had sometimes cashed in life savings to pay for the passage. They had burnt their boats and couldn't go back. Some were trapped in the UK by pride and an unwillingness to let their families in their home countries know how desperately hard life was for them. The recruiters who were sent out to persuade people to relocate to the UK painted a rosy picture and presented the country as a land of opportunity. They implied that anyone and everyone would be able to make it in such a land of abundance, so when people got to the UK and found themselves struggling to eat, never mind to save or live a good life, they were too proud or embarrassed to reveal this to family back home and just toiled on. Some – to their shame – severed ties with all family and ceased to answer letters or send remittances because they were so embarrassed and disappointed by their reduced circumstances. A great many never returned to their homeland, not even for a visit, and lost contact with parents, siblings and friends as a consequence of moving to the UK.

Many other people failed to settle in the UK and returned to the Caribbean as soon as they were able. I remember attending farewell parties for some of the families that we used to socialise with as they packed up their belongings and returned with glad hearts to Jamaica, Trinidad and Barbados because the UK had not lived up to its promise. However, the greater majority remained and worked hard to put down roots: it was not easy, but their efforts prevailed, most often because they had no choice.

II   The Life Story of Dr Dorothy Francis

My parents' brothers and sisters

My mother had four sisters but no brothers. My father had three brothers and two sisters – most of them, including my father, are now dead. My father's family stayed in Jamaica; none of them left the area where they were born so they were surprised when my father emigrated. Of my mother's family three of her sisters stayed in Jamaica, while Mum and her sister Esme, emigrated to England.

My sisters, brother and other relatives

I have three sisters and one brother. I had another sister, Joy, but she died a few days short of her first birthday, a year before my youngest sister, Lorna, was born. Three of my mother's sisters had no children, so all my maternal cousins are the children of my mother's youngest sister, Eula, who has eight children. Mum and Eula produced fifteen offspring between them and we are very close – I see my cousins as additional siblings.

The majority of my nuclear family live in Coventry, apart from me and Lorna; I live in Leicester and Lorna in Burbage, which is midway between Coventry and Leicester. My sisters, Sharon and Hortense and my brother, Steadman, live within two miles of my mother, and my cousin Trevor – who is like a son to my mother and a brother to us – lives just three miles away. Lorna and I are the furthest away, but it is not a big distance and we are able to visit and maintain contact easily.

We don't have many relatives in the UK. We have some second cousins in Coventry and a small number of cousins in London, but we do not meet often. My father had family in Birmingham and we would visit them regularly when we were young. However, that branch of the family moved back to Jamaica in the late 1970s, and we lost contact with them. My UK family is essentially my brother, sisters, Trevor and my mother, with brief appearances from distant cousins.

2 Moving to England—from an 'extended family network' to a 'nuclear family'

Dorothy spent her early years living in Jamaica with her grandparents, but she came to England in 1966. Here, she describes moving from an 'extended family network' to a 'nuclear family' and the adjustments that she had to make.

Living in Jamaica in an 'extended family'

I spent my early years living in Jamaica with my grandparents and have this in common with many people of my age group. It was standard in the 1950s and '60s for men to leave the Caribbean for England, America or Canada in search of better lives and once they were established they would send for their wives. If they had children they would

25

II The Life Story of Dr Dorothy Francis

be kept with grandparents. Once both parents were working in the new country they would save and send for the children one by one to join them. This process sometimes took ten years or more. I know many people who, like myself, arrived in England to be faced with parents they barely remembered and siblings that they had never met. Sometimes children were left in the Caribbean when they were toddlers and didn't see their parents again until they were fifteen or sixteen. By that time they had quite forgotten their parents, and this caused a lot of estrangement. Many of us were brought up by our grandparents, and treated them as parents. Our grandparents were the ones who loved, disciplined and schooled us. Our mothers and fathers were people we heard of in tales that were almost like fairy stories; people who lived in a strange place called 'England', where it was cold and white stuff called 'snow' fell from the sky. I had no idea of the concept of cold weather and could not imagine this mythical 'snow' that my elders spoke of.

It was a great wrench for children of my generation to be torn away from our grandparents and sent to a cold grey country to live with strangers, albeit they were our parents. Almost invariably the parents would have had more children in the meantime so the new arrival not only had to get used to new parents but also new siblings. Perhaps the new arrival would know that they had siblings but often they did not know and would struggle to fit into the family. I think that these enforced separations of the 1950s, '60s and '70s fragmented families and many never really fitted back together. Parents and children tried to get to know each other again but it was difficult. The newly-arrived children struggled to adjust to living in the UK but their parents were also struggling as they had only been here a few years themselves and were still getting used to living in England. It was a period of great instability for everyone concerned and a difficult time all round.

I grew up under my grandparents' roof with my niece and two cousins and lived just a few hundred metres from two of my aunts, three great aunts, a great uncle and various other family members. In reality I don't think I ever thought about my family set-up and did not realise that I lived in an extended unit – it was just the way things were. We have a very strong tradition and culture of the extended family in the Caribbean and it is not unusual for four generations to live together within the same household or for members of the extended family to live in close vicinity so my domestic life was not out of the normal.

This close family set-up means that young and old do not live separate lives as they often do in the UK. In Jamaica and other parts of the Caribbean grandparents often bring their grandchildren up whilst parents are working. At the end of their lives the elders are cared for by younger members of the family and live in the family setting until they die. When she arrived in the UK Mum was shocked and horrified to find that elderly people were consigned to homes when they became too much for families to look after. This was not her experience of old age and she found it strange and sad. In fact she found it so scandalous that she wrote at length to tell her parents about it and to let them know that they were safe from this barbarous practice!

II The Life Story of Dr Dorothy Francis

Once my parents had settled they sent for me to come to England. I hated leaving Jamaica, and can still recall the horror of being plucked from all that I knew to make the transition to England. I had an idyllic life in Jamaica and was pampered and cherished and I was quite spoilt. I was especially nurtured and loved because, although I am my mother's second child, I arrived 16 years after my sister which was an unfeasibly large gap. Mum was in her mid-thirties when I was born, more than a decade and a half after my sister, and I was seen as a 'little miracle' and was much cherished. My grandparents doted on me, as did other members of the family, and my elder sister Hortense acted as a surrogate mother to me. Hortense became a mother herself just over one year after I was born, so I became an 'auntie' when I was fifty-four weeks old, and have never known a time when I was not an aunt. My niece is called Velma and we both lived with my grandparents for a time when my parents were in England and Hortense moved to the capital for work.

Perhaps my birth acted as a catalyst because having had a sixteen – year hiatus my mother went on to have four more children in quick succession; in total she had five children in seven years. The upshot of this was that in Jamaica I had been the pampered baby of the family but I arrived in England to find I had a brother, Steadman, and two sisters, Sharon and Joy. Another sister, Lorna, followed two years after my arrival. Suddenly, I was the eldest child of the family (my older sister remained in Jamaica) and expected to hold responsibilities that had previously been unknown to me in terms of looking after my siblings and undertaking household tasks.

I hadn't known until the point when I moved to the UK that I had younger siblings and it was a novel, and not entirely welcome, experience. I knew that I had an older sister but in reality Hortense was an adult with a child of her own so she seemed almost like a mother rather than a sister. The generations had slipped with the result that my niece was a scant 12 months younger than me, and we were brought up like sisters. In addition, everyone called my sister 'Sister Mac', as adults in Jamaica are rarely called directly by their given names and usually have a title such as 'Sister', 'Mas' or 'Aunt'. So I did not think it unusual that everyone called Hortense 'Sister' (Mac was a nickname) and I also called her 'Sister Mac'. I don't think I really computed that Hortense was my sister, Velma my niece, Sis and Daddy my grandparents, and so on, because I had never had cause to think about it and because it didn't really matter. In reality, they were simply people who loved and cared for me and that was all I needed to know.

Moving to England – a 'nuclear family'

When I arrived in England to find that I was the oldest of four children it was a great shock to me. I did not like my siblings at first and I fought almost daily with Steadman and Sharon. My mother still reminds me of my shocking behaviour towards them and tells me, 'You bit, kicked, pinched and pushed your brother and sister and did so many bad things to them'. Her words made me feel ashamed but it is true that I resented the younger children because they seemed secure and comfortable within the family dy-

II The Life Story of Dr Dorothy Francis

Left to right: Sharon, Steadman and myself at our house, 12, Ashburton Road, Coventry in approximately 1967/8.

namic, whereas I had been uprooted from Jamaica and felt like a cuckoo in the nest. I did not feel like a family member. I was a stranger living in a strange household many miles away from my true home and in my loneliness I lashed out at everyone around me.

I didn't know my siblings but neither did I know my mother or father as they had both departed Jamaica when I was a baby. When it was my turn to travel my parents paid someone who was also travelling to England to escort me on the airplane and my father picked me up from the airport. However, I always comment that practically any Jamaican man could have picked me up because I had no idea what my father looked like as he had left Jamaica when I was months old.

On arrival my father took me to a strange and cold house, introduced me to a woman and informed me that she was my mother. I remember that I simply stared at her because she was a stranger to me. My mother was crying with joy because she had not seen me for years and I think she expected me to run to her with hugs and kisses. But I did not, as I didn't know her. It was a very sad and disjointed reunion as I was desperately unhappy and cried inconsolably. My parents were sad that I was upset but were nonetheless very happy to be reunited with their child who they had not seen for such a long time.

It was my first experience of living in a nuclear family and I didn't enjoy it. I did not know the man who called himself my father nor the woman who said that she was my mother nor the three children with whom I lived. I simply wanted to go home and I cried night and day for months to go back to Jamaica. I could not be consoled and refused to eat; I thought that if I manifested my unhappiness by starving myself I would be sent back to my grandparents.

We have a good family friend, Mr Glenton Morgan, who returned to the Caribbean in the late 1970s and when I met him a few years ago he recounted his memories of this time. Mr Morgan and his family lived in the same house as us and he saw me on a daily basis for my first few months in England and at least twice weekly for the next few years. He said to me, 'I didn't know that it was possible for a child to exist in such misery or to be so deeply unhappy and for such a sustained period of time. I didn't know that such a young child could grieve so deeply for home and family'. He reminded me that I had starved myself for many months and commented that he had never met a more resolute child. He had not thought it possible for a little girl to starve herself the way that I did and it had upset him deeply to see me in that condition. His reminiscences and descrip-

II The Life Story of Dr Dorothy Francis

tion of that unhappy time brought my own memories back with startling clarity and reduced me to tears even after 50 years.

Mr Morgan was like a father to me and was immensely kind and thoughtful. My own father was cold and uncaring and dismissed my unhappiness, doing nothing to assuage the loneliness and grief that I felt. My mother was busy with my small brother and sisters and did not have enough free time to devote to a small, unhappy person who refused to be comforted. Mr Morgan spent endless hours with me and never tired of my tears or flinched at my tantrums. He sat me on his lap and wiped my face when I cried. He told me stories, took me into his living quarters with his own children and kept me away from the wrath and scorn of my father, who could not understand why I refused to settle. I remember sitting on Mr Morgan's lap whilst he fed me small morsels of food from his fingers, almost in the way that a parent bird would feed a fledgling. I owe a debt of love and gratitude to Mr Morgan because he eased my transition into the UK and has showed me unflagging love and kindness throughout my life.

I was desperately, deeply unhappy during my first months in England. I hated it with a passion. Even now, just talking about it makes me want to cry and I can feel the tears brimming at the memory. In 50 years, I have rarely managed to talk about the experience of moving to England without crying. Coming to the UK was horrendous; I could not understand how people could live in such a cold and grey place and all I wanted to do was to go home to my grandparents and to the life that I had left.

I should note that as a child I only saw things from my own viewpoint and perhaps did not consider the unhappiness of those around me. In later years, my mother described her recollection of that time. She recalled how heartrending it had been to leave her baby in Jamaica and to travel 5,000 miles to a strange country. She said:

'I cried every day that I was away from you and bent down on my knees to pray for you. I cried myself to sleep nightly and missed you so dreadfully that it hurt. I saved every penny that I could to bring you here even though it was difficult as we had numerous expenses and a new baby each year. I counted the days until you arrived in England and then when you arrived you cried endlessly to go back. You don't know just how hurt I was and how unhappy it made me to see you in tears all the time. Having cried every day because you were far from me I now began to cry because I couldn't stand the pain of seeing you so unhappy'.

It was sobering to hear of the experience from her perspective and it made me realise what a deeply unsettling time it had been for all concerned.

Things got to the point where, after more than a year, Mum wrote to my grandmother, and said, 'Dorothy will not settle, can I send her back to you? I cannot bear seeing her so unhappy and I know that she will be happy with you'. My grandparents wrote back and said, 'Put her on the plane and send her back to us; we will be so happy to have Dorothy

29

with us again'. So my mother started to save money for the airfare to send me back to Jamaica and resolved herself to do what was best for me. So that would have been my future. I was destined to go back to Jamaica and to grow up there rather than in England. However, something momentous happened to keep me here and it changed my personal history.

When I was seven my youngest sister Lorna was born and my mother was inspired to delegate responsibility for the new baby to me. She appealed to me saying, 'You are the eldest; I know that you are only small but you can help me to feed the baby, play and talk to her and rock her to sleep. I have a household to run and can't spend as much time with the baby as I would like so I am asking you to help me'. I was fascinated by the new baby and delighted to undertake such a serious task. I learnt to make up Lorna's bottles and I fed her and changed her nappies. I spent many happy hours playing with Lorna and I read books to her and rocked her to sleep in my arms and in her cradle. Lorna rooted me to England and she is the reason that I am here now. The pleasure and attachment of a new baby helped me to climb out from my grief and to take an interest in my new found family. Lorna was the only sibling that I knew from birth and this forged a special connection. Had she not been born I would have returned to Jamaica and my life would have been very different, but Lorna's birth was the anchor that I needed to stabilise me in this country.

People sometimes comment that surely I can't remember coming to England as I was not yet six but I actually remember it with great clarity. I was deeply unhappy for a long time and in fact I don't think I ever fully settled. This was instrumental in me leaving home at sixteen years of age as I never developed a sense of belonging. The experience of being displaced and being forced into a new family was at the heart of me and I was always unsettled. I had a confrontational relationship with my mother, who practised a very disciplinarian method of child rearing, and my father was a cruel, unbending and cold man who was physically and mentally abusive and who seemed to actively dislike all of his children. By the time I reached my teens I could not stand to be in the same room as him. I loved my brother and sisters dearly but this love could not compensate for the arguments with my mother and the active dislike that I endured from my father. Shortly after I finished my O-Levels, I packed three small bags of possessions and walked out of the door. I didn't know where I was going or what I was going to find in the outside world, but I was not afraid as I was confident that I could make it on my own. I never returned to live at my parents' home; I have been responsible for my own wellbeing since the age of sixteen.

It was only after I left home and I could relate to my family on my own terms that relationships became better and closer. My mother was shocked that I had walked out at just sixteen years of age and this forced her to take stock. Our relationship improved once I no longer lived under her roof and we willingly spent time together. Mum changed her childrearing methods with the effect that my younger brother and sisters were allowed a lot more freedom and respect than I had experienced. For instance, I was never afforded a key to the house but all my siblings were given keys once they could be relied upon not to lose them. She also allowed them to attend parties, visit the cinema and go on days out with their friends, all of which had been denied to me and had been a source of conflict between us.

My mother loved us greatly, but she was very contradictory and sometimes difficult to live with and my father was cold and distant and threw a pallor of misery over the house. He and my mother divorced when I was twenty-one and the atmosphere became immensely lighter. My siblings and I experienced a lot of shared adversity as children and this helped to make us a stronger unit. I have an excellent relationship with my siblings; they are my best friends and we share a lot of experiences together. We use any occasion to spend time together and take a week-long annual holiday each May which involves lots of eating, talking and laughing!

3 Good memories from my early days in England

Dorothy's early days in England were not unremittingly awful. She had many good and interesting experiences. She recalls her good memories here.

My first English breakfast

My early days in England were not unremittingly awful and there are many good or interesting experiences which have stuck in my mind.

My very first breakfast in England is a case in point and is something that brings a wry smile to my face when I remember it. The breakfast was toast made from sliced white bread – probably Sunblest or Mother's Pride which were popular brands at that time – with marmalade. Next to the plate of toast was a small bowl of yellow fragments which I learnt were called 'cornflakes'. These were topped with sugar and covered with milk. My mother sat me, Steadman and Sharon around a table and I watched as my siblings tucked into their food with a hearty appetite. I merely stared at the food as I had no idea what it was, never having seen such stuff before. I tried to eat but did not enjoy the pappy texture of the industrially produced bread nor the strange bitter-sweet taste of the marmalade and I disliked the soggy cornflakes soaked in milk. My mother encouraged me to eat, but after a few mouthfuls I burst into tears and sobbed that I wanted a real breakfast! I remember her telling me that this was a real breakfast and I stared in horror at the thought of eating this food on an ongoing basis.

Fortunately this was not the case. Mum had served such a particularly English breakfast to welcome me to the UK and it was unfortunate that it was so badly received. I was relieved to discover that breakfast in our household usually had a more Caribbean slant, with fried dumplings, Jamaican hard dough bread, fried plantain, cornmeal porridge and occasionally liver and onions, or ackee and saltfish, all of which I was happy to tuck into.

II   The Life Story of Dr Dorothy Francis

Eggs of all types were often served for breakfast – fried, boiled, scrambled – and were sometimes accompanied by baked beans, which were another oddity that took me a while to get used to. Occasionally, especially if she was in a hurry, Mum served toast and cereal, but this was not the norm. I eventually became accustomed to English foods such as toast, marmalade, jam and breakfast cereals, but that first breakfast was a shock.

Waking up one morning – a wonderful and magical day

About four weeks after I arrived in England I remember waking up one morning to find the world in muffled quietness and an absence of the usual street sounds of cars and buses and high heels clipping along the pavements. My mother opened the curtains and I gazed out in wonderment and awe as soft white flakes whirled past the window and fell with delicate lightness onto the ground, where they formed a thick blanket which muted all sound. I stood by the window for hours watching as the snow transformed the bleak inner city landscape to a glistening and dazzlingly white fairy landscape. This wonderful and magical day was my first experience of snow and is a memory that always brings a smile to my face.

Going to a local dentist

Another strong memory is of having all my front teeth removed in one go by Dr Lal, the local dentist! I was about six years old and it became apparent that my second set of teeth was coming through but my first set remained strong and refused to fall out. I therefore had a double row of teeth, which was uncomfortable and crowded my mouth. One of the reasons I remember going to the dentist was because it was my first excursion with my father who usually paid very little attention to me. I had not been to a dentist before so I was fascinated by the surgery, the tools and the man in the white coat. I wasn't so pleased when he gave me a series of injections to numb my mouth nor when I suddenly found myself without eight front teeth! We returned home after the extractions and Mum gave me a big hug and wiped my tears. She then made me a jam sandwich because she knew this had become a favourite food and I tried to eat but couldn't as my jaw was numb and I was unable to bite due to my lack of incisors. Never one to let food go to waste, my mum took the sandwich from me, cut off the section that I had bitten, cut it into two and shared it between Steadman and Sharon, who ate it up gleefully whilst I watched on. This story always makes me smile when I think of it and I can still see Steadman and Sharon tucking into my sandwich while I surveyed them dolefully!

My first day at Annie Osborne infant school

I remember my first day at Annie Osborne infant school with clarity. I started at midterm, having recently moved from Edgwick Road to Henley Green, so the other students already knew each other. My class teacher was Mrs Woodhams and I think she also went on to teach Steadman and Sharon. She was a rounded motherly woman whom I liked instantly and she was a lovely teacher. Mrs Woodhams put me next to Susan

Williamson (now Susan O'Sullivan) and asked her to show me the ropes and to be a good friend to me because I was new. My first task at school was a 'join the dots' exercise designed to test our numeracy whilst also being creative fun. Susan helped me to join the dots and the picture that emerged was of a fox which I then coloured in rather badly. I remember that Susan's picture was very neat but mine was scribbled and untidy! I wasn't sure what a fox was, but Susan enlightened me and I came to realise that this small dog-like mammal featured in many stories. 'Brer Rabbit and the Fox' became a favourite and Mrs Woodhams would read us different stories that featured wily foxes.

Mrs Woodhams asked Susan to be my friend and she took this to heart and was my closest friend throughout infant and primary school until we were parted when we went to different secondary schools. We met again some years later via Facebook – I am easy to find as I did not change my name on marriage – and we have maintained contact. Susan was a loving and kind child and has remained the same in adulthood. She works within the care sector and has won awards for her contribution and service. It is odd to think that I am still in contact with the person who I sat next to on my first day of school, more than 55 years ago!

Visiting the library – one of my favourite childhood pleasures

I was a very shy child and it took me a long time to adjust to school. Learning to read was an uphill battle and I remember watching as Susan and my other class-mates romped ahead of me as I struggled to get my head around the English language and puzzled to understand how disparate letters became words. I had begun to think that I would never learn when one day, almost as if by magic, the words tumbled into place and began to make sense. Learning to read was one of the most magical experiences of my life and it opened up a whole new world for me. I became a voracious and insatiable reader, devouring all the books in our class library and then moving on to the school library. I soon read my way through these and hankered after further books to read. Our next-door neighbour, Mrs Palmer, loved to read and realised that I was thirsting for books. She asked my mother if she could take me to the public library at Bell Green to enrol me so that I could take out books. My mum gave her permission and I soon found myself standing in the public library looking around as if in a dream at the thousands of books that lined the shelves.

Visiting the library was one of my favourite childhood pleasures. At first Mum or Mrs Palmer would take me but as I became older I was allowed to go by myself. We lived in Henley Green and the library was over a mile away in Bell Green which is a considerable distance but one which I covered by myself – or sometimes with my siblings in tow – most weeks from the age of eight. The library was six bus stops away and Mum would give me the bus fare if she was able to afford it; otherwise I would walk. Sometimes she gave me the bus fare but I still walked so that I could spend the money on sweets. It is perhaps difficult to comprehend nowadays, when children are routinely accompanied on even the smallest outing, that an eight year old would be allowed to walk over a mile,

II   The Life Story of Dr Dorothy Francis

spend hours in a library and then walk home by herself carting an armload of books, but we had much more freedom in those days and it was not unusual at all to have such liberty to roam.

Armfield Street Church

Mrs Palmer introduced us to Armfield Street Church shortly after we moved to Henley Green and we worshipped there throughout my childhood. The church was about one and a half miles from our home but Steadman, Sharon and I walked the distance to Sunday school from an early age, with Lorna joining us when she became older. The number eight bus ran between Henley Green and Bell Green, which was the first mile of the journey, and we walked the last half-mile or so. If Mum did not have the bus fare she would simply send us out earlier to allow us time to walk the whole journey. Sometimes, we deliberately set out early so that we could walk and spend the bus fare on sweets. Finding money for sweets was an overwhelming theme of our childhood!

Crossing bridges

Another thing that I remember is that Sharon hated crossing bridges. This made getting to church or the library very difficult as there were only two routes to either of these places and both involved crossing the River Sowe. Most often we walked along the Henley Road towards Bell Green. Steadman and I would become tense as we approached Henley College as we knew that a few metres later we would have to cross the bridge over the Sowe and that Sharon would dig her heels in and refuse to cross. There were many occasions when we literally pulled her, kicking and screaming, across the bridge and would be forced to explain to concerned passers-by that we were not harming her but simply sought to get her across the bridge! Sharon grew out of this phobia after a few years, for which Steadman and I were eternally grateful.

Exploring Tile Hill Wood

We used to love exploring Tile Hill Wood when we went to visit Mum's friend Marsha and her husband Ted. Tile Hill Wood is quite small but to us it was a huge forest where we had swashbuckling adventures with local children, climbed trees, waded in small streams, built dens and defended forts and castles. In the autumn we picked blackberries and occasionally Marsha baked these into blackberry and apple pies which we took home with us. Visiting the woods was one of the simple pleasures of our childhood and we always jumped to get ready when Mum said that we were going to Tile Hill. Most of these childhood escapades took place out of sight of either our parents or Marsha and Ted; we were left to our own devices with the only instruction being that we came back at an agreed time.

II   The Life Story of Dr Dorothy Francis

One day in the first year of primary school

Another strong memory is that one day in the first year of primary school Miss Briggs advised that we should wear stout shoes and bring a packed lunch the next day as we would be visiting a farm. The trip took place on a bright summer's day and we walked from Annie Osborne to Woodway Farm, which is now covered with a housing estate but at that time was next to Woodway Park Comprehensive School. This was a distance of almost two miles so was quite a long way for small children, but we chattered the entire time and the miles went quickly. I recall that the teachers took turns carrying Clive – one of our school friends who had a hole in his heart and tired easily but who had not wanted to be left behind. Such a trip would be undertaken by bus nowadays, as I doubt many parents would be happy for their children to walk such distances and neither would schools have a whole day to devote to a single school trip. I also suspect that the teachers would not be allowed to carry a child, in the way that they carried Clive, either. At the farm we saw cows, horses, chickens and a few lambs and learned how meat is produced, eggs are gathered and cheese and butter made. The farmer fed us homemade cheese and gave us glasses of milk and afterwards we walked back to school.

At that time all infant and primary school children received a one-third-pint bottle of milk each day courtesy of the government as a drive towards building healthy teeth and bones. The milk was full-cream, known as 'silver top', and had a thick layer of cream on top which children either loved or hated. The day after the visit to the farm Miss Briggs asked us all to save the cream from our milk and told us that we were going to make our own butter. We poured the cream carefully into a large clean coffee jar until it was half full and Miss Briggs added a little salt. We sat in a circle on the floor and each child shook the jar vigorously for about thirty seconds before passing it onto the next pupil. We did this for what seemed like hours but was probably no more than twenty minutes, until the cream solidified into butter. We opened the jar and to our delight found that we had made a pale coloured and very fresh butter which we spread on cream crackers and quickly devoured. This was one of my favourite lessons and I liked the way that the activity tied in with the farm visit. Making butter was not a spectacular undertaking nor one that needed many tools beyond the cream from our milk and an empty coffee jar, but it is an episode that has remained with me as one of the most interesting and fun lessons that I had at primary school.

Parties, including a 'blues' party

My parents loved parties because Mum loved to dance and my father to socialise. He had two left feet and couldn't move at all. I often wondered how my dance-loving mother ended up with someone who could barely shuffle his feet; it was excruciatingly embarrassing to watch him on the dance floor. However, they made the best of it and Mum was never short of a dance partner as she was an exuberant and skilful dancer.

We often held 'blues' parties at our house, sometimes every weekend for months at a

II   The Life Story of Dr Dorothy Francis

time. My parents liked the parties because of the socialising element and also because they were money-making opportunities as we sold food and drink. My parents would visit wholesalers to buy alcohol and sold all the popular drinks of that time such as Fosters and Breakers, which were two brands of lager, and BabyCham and Cherry B, which were sweet alcoholic drinks sold in small bottles. They cooked and sold rice and peas with curry goat, which was always a great seller and turned a good profit. We had a very large living room which ran the length of the house and it lent itself well to such gatherings.

One year my parents threw a party in mid-January to celebrate Steadman's birthday. We took up the carpet, put it along with as much of the furniture as could fit into the utility room and covered the rest under tarpaulin in the garden to leave the living room completely empty. The party went well so my parents decided to hold another party the next Saturday. That also went well so they threw another one the following Saturday and the next and the next... We lived with bare floors and limited furniture for more than three months as they had a party every Saturday from January through to April. I think we must have had very tolerant neighbours to put up with car doors banging and music playing for so many weeks.

I loved helping out at these parties and would serve plates of food and collect empties to be stacked into the wooden crates to be returned to the wholesalers. It was at one of these parties that I became drunk for the first time. I did not like the taste of beer or spirits but I very much liked BabyCham, which was a sickly sweet pear perry, and Cherry B, which was syrupy thick and tasted like distilled cherry drops. They were mainly drunk by women and I suppose they were the 'alcopops' of their day as the sweet flavours disguised a heady alcoholic kick. I had the highly unhygienic habit of draining the bottles as I collected them; sometimes guests would leave half a bottle or more of Cherry B or BabyCham and I would knock them back, not realising that I was consuming alcohol as they were very sweet and fruity. We were always dispatched to bed at a reasonable hour while the parties continued in full swing beneath us. On this particular occasion I found that the bed was too soft and the room was whirling around my head so I chose, to the consternation of my brother and sisters, to rest on the floor and I lay there gently moaning whilst waiting for the crazy motion of the room to subside. Sharon ran downstairs and told Mum that I was moaning and groaning and was very ill. Mum pounded up the stairs and dashed into the bedroom to find me lying glassy-eyed on the floor. She examined me to see what the problem was and asked me to stick my tongue out so she could check my tonsils. As I did so a heady waft of alcoholic fumes hit her and she turned pale and said, 'Oh my God! The child is drunk!'. She was mortified and instantly banned me from draining bottles at future parties. However, I didn't need her admonishments as I hated being so ill and the thought of experiencing that again was enough to keep the BabyCham and Cherry B bottles from my lips!

II   The Life Story of Dr Dorothy Francis

Domino tournaments

A large part of my parents' social life revolved around domino tournaments, which were very popular in the 1960s and '70s. My father was a keen player and he belonged to a local league which played tournaments all over the country. The domino club would organise trips to Blackpool, Sheffield, London, Oxford and a host of other places, and the players and their partners would pile onto coaches early in the morning to be transported to these destinations. The men would play one game of dominoes after another to determine who won the league while the wives and girlfriends would explore the environs and shop. The day would always end with a dance, where it seemed that all the women competed with each other to see who could look most glamorous. We got to attend a couple of them and they were wonderful events.

We didn't usually get to see our parents when they were dressed up for the tournament dances but we always loved to see when they got ready for local dances. Dad looked smart in his suit and Mum looked like a princess and we would stare at her in admiration. This was the 1970s, so the fashion was maxi dresses, large Afro wigs and bright make-up. We though that Mum was so glamorous with her perfectly rounded Afro and maxi gowns shot through with gold thread with the look finished off with gold or silver shoes which was such a different look from her everyday apparel. We would also take in the fragrance of her perfume and inspect her make-up as Mum rarely wore make-up and only used perfume on very special occasions.

We were babysat by an older person when we were younger but once I got to around age twelve I was left in charge. We were supposed to go to bed at a certain time but we would flout the rules so that we could continue to watch television. We would listen out for the distinctive engine of my father's car and on one of us shouting 'They are here!' would turn the television off, dash upstairs, dive into bed and pretend to be asleep. I'm sure that my parents knew and doubt that they were fooled for a second!

All in all I had a fun and happy childhood and was blessed to share it with my siblings as we got on very well and had great times together playing endlessly inventive games. We spent a lot of time together and often argued like cats and dogs but always made friends again within a few minutes. It was quite tiresome. Sharon and Steadman were the worst; there is only seventeen months between them and they were very close but nonetheless fought at every opportunity. They reduced each other to tears at least five times a day but they could not bear to be away from each other. Steadman stayed with our Aunt Esme in London for a week one summer and Sharon pined and refused to eat as she missed him so much. She sat with her face to a corner of the living room and ignored her toys and books. When Steadman returned she ran to hug and kiss him and he returned her hugs whereupon she punched him and all was back to normal! Following that episode Mum always ensured that Steadman and Sharon went away together as they pined too much when they were separated.

II The Life Story of Dr Dorothy Francis

4 A new life in Coventry

Dorothy's parents migrated to Coventry in 1962, and Dorothy arrived in 1966. She describes their, and her own, experiences thus:

My parents moving to England

My parents came to England as British citizens because Jamaica was at that time a colonial country. They came because they, and thousands of other Caribbeans, were entreated to provide labour to help with the rebuilding of the country after the devastation of the Second World War. The UK had withdrawn from many colonial countries and left them stripped of resources, jobs and infrastructure and with few opportunities for advancement. My parents came to the UK because they sought new opportunities and because they wanted a better life for their children. Education played a large part in their decision because the UK education system is free, including books and other incidentals. Jamaica has a free universal system, but parents sometimes struggled to pay for books, equipment and school meals, which meant that sometimes children couldn't afford to go to school. My parents had experienced this themselves when they were growing up and didn't want their children to suffer the same. Mum is intensely intelligent but was forced to leave school at thirteen, which she has always bitterly regretted. She was determined that all her children would be educated to college level and it is a source of pride that this is the case.

My parents wanted their children to be educated so that we wouldn't have to do the jobs that they were forced to do. They were resigned to undertaking menial work so that we would not have to. As a result none of us has had to work in a car factory, or clean floors, which is what my parents did, because we are qualified to a level that enables us to obtain more professional types of employment.

My parents found it difficult to settle in England for many reasons. They arrived in winter and were shocked at how cold it was; it is never cold in Jamaica, so they had no experience of living in snow, ice or freezing fog. In common with most Jamaicans they did not own warm clothing, so for the first time in their lives they had to buy coats, boots, socks, gloves, scarves etc. and they experienced the novelty of wearing a hat designed to keep the wearer's head warm, instead of shielding them from the sun. They suffered from chilblains, coughs and colds, especially as our house was unheated. It was a big culture shock and it took them a long time to get used to the necessity of layering up. Another oddity was the fact that the climate demanded a fire in the house in order to keep it warm, which was not something that they had experienced before.

Mum recounts: 'When I came to England I looked around me for many days and I thought, "Why have they got so many factories here? Almost every building seems to be a factory"'. She explained that in Jamaica at that time most buildings were made from wood – which is a much cooler building material – with bricks being reserved for factories. She therefore assumed that the brick-built houses that surrounded her were factories! I have heard a number of elderly Jamaicans relate this same story and I often consider how odd it must have been for them to be surrounded by red brick buildings belching smoke from tall chimneys instead of the light and airy buildings that they were used to.

Another thing that puzzled Mum was that she couldn't see any means of growing food. She was used to seeing food cultivated wherever she was in Jamaica, even in the cities, but on moving to Coventry she couldn't see any farms or fruit trees and was puzzled as to how people fed themselves. Our friend, Mr Morgan, who had been in England for a few years, explained that food is grown on farms out in the countryside, unlike Jamaica where the crops are often interspersed with housing. Mum found this strict distinction between town and country very odd, and it was just yet another of the things that she had to get used to.

My parents with my brother Steadman, 1965.

Nearly every aspect of life was different from what they had known. The buildings, streets, climate and food were all strange, as were the customs, such as drinking tea and the different names for mealtimes, combined with the rules around visiting people – my parents found it all very perplexing.

The most overwhelming issue was the racism that they faced on a daily and incessant basis. The concept of racism was new to them and they had never had to deal with people taking an instant dislike to them because of the colour of their skin. Neither had they been forced to negotiate the kind of legal and institutionalised racism that barred them from jobs, banking, housing, clubs and even churches and this was a huge culture shock. Sometimes the racism was subtle but more often it was overt and it was made very plain that the services provided did not extend to black people. I have often wondered how they managed. Everything that they had formerly taken for granted was suddenly very different: food, clothes, religion, weather, shops and transportation all had to be learnt and navigated and it must have been so very difficult to learn how to do everything differently.

My father's life in Coventry

My father moved to Coventry because his sponsor was in Coventry but he could have ended up in almost any large city in England. He, and many others, came to Coventry

II   The Life Story of Dr Dorothy Francis

because it was a great industrial city famous for engineering. Coventry had been one of the cities that the Germans targeted in the Second World War as it was very productive and crucial to the war effort. [7] It remained an extremely industrious city after the war, and it was a centre of the car, watch and bicycle making industries so had many jobs to offer.

My father worked in a car factory for more than 30 years in what was Rootes, then Chrysler, and latterly Peugeot. The huge factory was sited in Ryton on the outskirts of Coventry. My father was very fit and often cycled the 14 miles there and back, even in later years when he had a car, as he enjoyed cycling for pleasure.

Most people did not have a car in the 1960s and '70s, but we did because my father worked at the car factory. It was not always feasible to cycle to work, especially in the winter, so he learned to drive and bought a car, which gave us a certain status at that time. Another aspect of my father's job that we enjoyed were trips that the factory organised twice a year: one in the summer and the other at Christmas. Hundreds of children would amass for each of the trips, which were called 'outings'.

For the summer outing we would gather at the factory early in the morning and be given a packed lunch of sandwiches, crisps, fruit, chocolate and a drink in a paper bag – we loved those packed lunches! The company would hire fleets of coaches for the day and we would be allocated to one of the coaches. Parents did not take part in the trips, so as the eldest, I would be put in charge of my brother and sisters – not always an easy task as they would sometimes be quite naughty!

The summer trips were either to Wicksteed Park in Kettering, or Drayton Manor Park in Staffordshire, which are respectively around fifty and thirty miles from Coventry. But to us it seemed as if we had travelled hundreds of miles, especially as we were all prone to motion sickness. However the collective sense of excitement at the rides and delights that were to come mitigated the travel sickness and we chattered all the way.

The winter outing was to the Coventry Theatre, [8] where we saw a pantomime each year. This outing was not by coach as the theatre was in the centre of Coventry. Our parents would take us to the entrance where we would line up excitedly to see the show and look for friends that we had made on the summer trip. During the show we enjoyed yelling 'He's behind you!' and, 'Oh no he isn't!' in true pantomime tradition. The Coventry Theatre was an old-fashioned theatre with red plush seats fitted with opera glasses. These opera glasses could be released by the insertion of a 5p coin but we soon realised that a sharp kick to the underside of the casing would release the glasses for free! The theatre seated two thousand, so you can imagine the noise of two thousand children singing and screaming at the top of their voices! We loved it and I still have a certain nostalgic attachment to pantomimes.

On leaving we would all be given a selection box of chocolates and on getting home we

II The Life Story of Dr Dorothy Francis

would barter and swap chocolates to get our favourites. My favourite was Mars bar, whereas Steadman liked Marathons (now called Snickers), Sharon preferred Twix and Lorna liked Milky Way. My mother was not really keen on chocolates but she loved Bounty bars so we always gave those to her. We loved the works outings and they were a highlight of our year.

My father enjoyed working at the car factory and never sought to move to a different job. He faced a lot of racism and people called him names, especially in the early days, but he was a strongly built man and was able to take care of himself in a fight if it came to it, so they learned to leave him alone. Working in a factory demands a great deal of teamwork so in the end they realised that they had to work together and they learned to get on with each other as colleagues. Many of the men worked together for decades, so they learned to rub along together. Those who couldn't just learned to ignore each other. My father reported that even after thirty years there were still men in the factory who referred to him as 'Sambo'[9] and other derogatory names.

The factory bosses did very little about the inherent racism within the workplace so my father and other black workers learned to ignore these people and to not be provoked into a fight. If a white and a black worker were involved in a fight invariably the black worker would be dismissed, even if the fight had been provoked by the white man, so my father was careful to keep his anger in check and to avoid confrontation, which must have been very difficult and stressful as he had a quick temper. I think he must have had to subdue a great deal of his personality to maintain a calm façade in the factory, which is perhaps why the peace and camaraderie of the allotments where he spent his free time meant so much to him. It is also, perhaps, why he took out so much of his anger on us.

The job at the car factory was basic and repetitive but it offered a number of benefits. My father worked the night shift for most of his years in the factory and complained bitterly on the occasions when he was required to work day shifts, as he didn't like working days. He made a good income because he was paid a bonus for working nights. Another reason that he preferred this work pattern was that he had two allotments, which he maintained for over 40 years. He was a natural and gifted farmer and enjoyed growing a variety of foodstuffs. Working nights gave him the opportunity to work on his allotments in the day time; he worked a 40 hour week from Monday to Thursday which meant that he was free from Friday morning until Monday evening and he enjoyed the extended weekend and freedom that this shift pattern afforded to work on his allotments or to enjoy other leisure activities.

During the week he would often come home from work at 7 am, sleep for a few hours and then go to his allotment for a while before returning home to get ready for work. The allotments took a lot of time, especially in the spring and summer months, so he would carve time out from his day to ensure that he kept on top of the planting, weeding and maintenance. He supplemented our food with organically grown and flavoursome

II The Life Story of Dr Dorothy Francis

produce that he grew on his allotments and he grew enough to sell to others. We always had people knocking our door to buy his vegetables – the kidney beans were particular favourites, and he could never satisfy the demand for these. He grew a variety of English vegetables such as carrots, potatoes, peas, turnip and beetroot, but he also grew things that reminded him of home: callaloo (a spinach-like vegetable), pumpkins, garlic, spinach and kidney beans. It was these items that were mainly sought after by Caribbean friends.

He was the only black allotment holder on that site and he grew different things from the other growers, many of whom concentrated on potatoes and other root vegetables, whereas my father grew a large amount of 'above ground' produce such as beans, peas, spinach and callaloo. Other allotment holders ringed their plots with flowers, particularly chrysanthemums and dahlias, but my father had total disdain for flowers – he couldn't imagine using prime allotment land to grow something as non-essential as flowers. As far as he saw it, the allotments were for growing food.

My father was not a great talker and did not contribute much to the lexicon of family stories but I remember one story he told of an incident that took place in the early 1980s. He had recently returned from Jamaica and brought some sweetcorn seeds back with him, which he planted to great effect on his allotment. By the middle of that summer the plants were as high as his shoulder and were beginning to form cobs and he was looking forward to a good crop. It was at this point that a deputation of allotment holders took him aside for a quiet word. Our family name is Francis, which is a surname but is also a male forename, and most people called my father 'Francis'. So the conversation went like this: 'Francis, we know that you have been in this country for some time, but perhaps you don't know all of our customs as yet. You may be able to grow that stuff in Jamaica, but you can't grow it here. We all work together well on these allotments, so we wanted to warn you before you got into trouble'.

My father was puzzled as to why his crop of sweetcorn should merit such a warning and said as much to the deputation. He asked them what they thought the crop was, to which they replied, 'Well it's that marijuana stuff that you have in your country, innit?', at which my father burst out laughing. He explained that the crop was not marijuana but sweetcorn, which, as far as he was aware, was a perfectly legitimate crop!

The allotment holders had never seen sweetcorn outside of a tin before and had no idea how it was grown. They were very shamefaced at their mistake and apologised to my father for thinking that he was growing a controlled substance! However he said that some of them still seemed very doubtful and suspicious and did not fully believe him until he harvested a huge crop of sweetcorn and invited them to eat freshly boiled and barbequed sweetcorn which he cooked outside his allotment shed. In the years to come, sweetcorn became commonplace on the allotments, but my father enjoyed making the allotment holders blush by asking them how their marijuana crop was coming on!

II   The Life Story of Dr Dorothy Francis

My mother's life in Coventry

My mother wasn't highly qualified but nonetheless she knew that she could have under-taken better jobs than those that she was offered on arrival in the UK. People of colour did not have much choice over what work they did and could not pick and choose, so she took whatever jobs were available. However she endured those jobs to ensure that we would never have to do that type of work. Her aim was to ensure that we were well educated and would have choice over our careers and working lives. This stance is com-mon to most immigrants – not just African-Caribbeans, but also Polish, Indian, Irish and many other people who undertake menial work to provide for their families and to guar-antee a better life for their children through education. Mum worked hard and her dogged determination ensured that we achieved a good education and could take up the type of roles that were never open to her.

My mother spoke often about her experiences and gave us details of what it was like to live in England during the early years. Mum's first job when she arrived in England was at the Coventry Theatre, which was a very grand large theatre which no longer exists – it was demolished in 2002. Mum worked behind the scenes in the kitchen cooking meals. She always told us stories of her time at Coventry Theatre and I know that she enjoyed working there. As children we knew the theatre quite well, as it was where we went for the annual works outing arranged by my father's workplace, and we also visited on odd occasions such as school trips.

The kitchen supplied food to the theatre restaurant which, at that time, was considered a very chic place to eat and was run by a manager called Mr Vickers. In later years, Mum would regale us with stories of what happened in the kitchen and restaurant and the famous people that she had occasionally seen dining in the restaurant after they had finished their shows. She worked a 40-hour week for less than five pounds which was a pittance and was undoubtedly below the going rate even then. It was common practice to pay black people less than their white co-workers and Mum recalls her bitterness when she realised that a colleague who did identical work to her was paid an additional ten shillings a week, which was a huge difference.

The job was very gruelling, but Mum enjoyed the work and made some lifelong friends including an older woman called Marsha, who taught Mum English expressions and customs including how to drink tea! As children we enjoyed many a visit to Marsha's bungalow, which she shared with her husband and her little white poodle – I remember that once we found the dog's chocolate buttons and ate them, not realising that they were specially made for dogs! Marsha and Mum remained friends until Marsha's death in 2001.

My mother gave birth to my brother Steadman in 1964 and returned to work at the Coventry Theatre after a short maternity break. Steadman was entrusted to the care of a white childminder called Peggy, who loved him very much and who became a firm

II The Life Story of Dr Dorothy Francis

family friend and a part of our lives for many years. My sister Sharon arrived seventeen months after Steadman, in 1965, and once more my mother returned to work after a short maternity leave. However it was not feasible to pay for childcare for two children from my mother's small wage, so the economics of the situation forced her to resign, with reluctance, from her job.

Sharon was followed by Joy, who was born in 1966, and later that year I arrived in the UK, so my mother found herself with four children under the age of six and it was impossible for her to go out to work. Mum didn't work outside the house again until Lorna started school, at which point Mum got a job at Walsgrave Hospital which was a 20-minute walk from where we lived.

This job involved cleaning the wards and Mum worked between the hours of 9 am to 3 pm, which allowed her to be home when we got back from school. She enjoyed the social aspect of the job as she was always meeting new people (which is one of my mother's favourite pastimes) and she also relished the financial stability that came with working. It was important for her to have an income of her own as it gave her independence from my father, who was tight-fisted with money and often kept her short of cash. Getting a job enabled her to start saving and she did so with a vengeance. Her heart's desire was to go back to Jamaica to see her family whom she had not seen for over ten years. In the 1960s and '70s, air travel was very expensive and people weren't as mobile as they are now when flying around the world is commonplace. Mum struggled to save, as she had bills to pay and four young children to feed and clothe. Nonetheless she yearned to see her mother, her father and sisters, and getting the job at Walsgrave Hospital was wonderful because it meant that for the first time in many years she had her own income and could save to obtain her dream.

This was important for Mum because she had lacked financial independence for many years. My father held the purse strings and he was very sparing with what he gave to Mum for housekeeping and personal needs, preferring to spend his money on socialising. He was quite uncaring of the needs of his wife and children and did not see the need for new dresses or shoes, toys or trips to the cinema. He paid the rent and the bills, gave my mother a small housekeeping allowance and kept the rest for his own spending.

The only financial element that Mum had control of was the Family Allowance which was a non-means tested benefit which is payable to all families in the UK with responsibility for children under the age of eighteen. Mum saved the allowance to buy school essentials, shoes, clothes and to pay for outings, Christmas, birthdays and other incidentals.

Even through my father worked full time in a good job we often survived in a state of near poverty because he kept the household short of cash. I firmly believe that the Family Allowance kept us away from poverty because that pot of money was eked out to pay for so much.

II   The Life Story of Dr Dorothy Francis

My mother was a good seamstress and used this skill to supplement our incomes. She would make clothes and sell them to friends and neighbours. She created beautiful dresses for other women who were happy to pay for her unique designs and this added to her small savings fund. We were always beautifully turned out as Mum made many of our clothes and ensured that we were invariably smart. She used to make us matching outfits and people would comment on how adorable we looked, although I must admit that I had tired of the matching outfits by the time I was a gangly fourteen-year-old and was still being dressed the same as my sweet little sisters!

In 1975, thirteen years after arriving in the UK, my mother had saved enough to pay for a three-week holiday to Jamaica. It was a momentous event because she did it all off her own back and she was very proud that she had earned the money to pay for the tickets. Mum took my brother Steadman and my youngest sister Lorna so that the family could meet them. She couldn't take us all because it was too expensive, so my sister Sharon and I remained behind. Sharon visited Jamaica a few years later in the care of my mother's sister Esme, who lived in London. I did not visit until I was twenty-one when I used the proceeds of my savings from my first job to buy a ticket.

My mother's experience of racism

Racism was the biggest issue that my mother faced when she came to England. Both of my parents experienced racism, but I am mostly relating Mum's history as she spoke freely about her experiences and I can therefore recount her narrative. My father was a very silent man and did not relate many stories so I do not have the same understanding of what he suffered when he came to England, although I know that he was involved in a number of racist incidents, some of them physical.

My mother found the level of racism extremely difficult to deal with when she arrived in England. She had no experience of being disliked simply because of her skin colour and had not previously experienced either the concept or reality of racism. It was a shocking revelation to realise that people called her names and spat on her in the streets simply because they objected to the colour of her skin.

The racist treatment almost wore Mum down at times and she suffered greatly. Mum started to look for a job in the first week that she arrived in England and signed up at what would now be called a Job Centre (in those days called the Labour Exchange), but she found it very difficult to find employment. The Labour Exchange would ring employers to say that they were sending a worker by the name of Miriam Francis, but many times on arriving she would find that the job had been mysteriously filled, even if she arrived within minutes of the phone call. She questioned one employer, asking how it was possible for the job to have been filled in the ten minutes since the Labour Exchange had called to say that she was on her way. The manager explained that the job had already been filled before the Labour Exchange called and that she should not have been told to come. Of course, my mother knew that this was not true and knew exactly

II   The Life Story of Dr Dorothy Francis

what he meant. He simply didn't want to employ her, but didn't want to give the real reason. Sometimes, the employers were more forthright and brutally honest. Instead of pretending that the job had just been taken they would simply say, 'Oh we didn't know that you were coloured – your name sounds English. We don't take black people', and that would be the end of that conversation.

I remember Mum telling me that one day she went to the employment office and they told her that they had a job for her in Longford, five miles away from where the Labour Exchange was based. They assured her that they had described her skills set to the employer and that he had agreed to give her the job. She had searched long and hard for a job and the thought of finally being employed excited her. Even though the bus fare from Coventry city centre to Longford was only a few pennies Mum did not have this amount and was forced to walk. It was bitterly cold but she trudged from the city centre, all the way along the Foleshill Road and onwards to Longford Road until she reached her destination, driven by the chance to get a job, and she was cold, tired and hungry by the time that she got there.

Mum presented herself at the factory reception desk saying, 'I am Miriam Francis; you are expecting me for the job'. The manager came out to see her and said, 'You are wasting your time. We don't take black people', and told her to leave. She left in tears and walked back home through the cold and the snow, crying all of the way. She cried because she was hungry, tired and desperately in need of a job. She also cried because she had left behind everything that she knew in order to come to England – her father, mother, sisters and two daughters. I was just over a year old when she left for England and she sobbed to think that she had left her baby in another country so that she could seek a new life only to be faced by ignorance, racism and prejudice. She says that day was the low point of her move to England and, even years later, she wept with humiliation as she told the story. I have tried a few times to recount this story to others but each time I find myself crying because I feel a part of her pain, despair and frustration when I imagine her walking miles through the cold and snow to be faced with such brutal rejection.

Mum said that she applied for another job, which she was told involved sitting at a bench and operating machinery, and she was sent to the factory along with a white woman. On arrival the manager took one look at Mum and put her to scrubbing the floor with cold water and a brush whilst the other woman was given a job at a bench as promised. Mum was expected to scrub the floor on her hands and knees; the company did not even provide her with a mop, and the water that they supplied was unheated. It was the middle of winter and Mum spent every working hour soaking wet and shivering with cold. She feared that the job would make her ill and she left after two weeks, as the conditions were horrendous. She says that it was the worst work she has ever done and still talks with horror about the experience.

Mum felt that a lot of people thought that black people were little more than animals and

II The Life Story of Dr Dorothy Francis

didn't have thoughts or feelings so it didn't matter if they were cold, wet or hungry, if you hit them, spat on them or called them names. In fact, some people treated their animals better than they treated black people. Indeed, she felt that many British people genuinely believed that African-Caribbean people were animals. I grew up with people saying, 'Oh you lot are monkeys. You live in the trees in your country and swing from the trees with your tails'. Some people said these things out of malicious spite but others, in their ignorance, really believed this to be the case.

I remember that Mum sent me to the shop one day when I was about eight and what should have been a simple trip to buy a loaf of bread turned into one of the most humiliating incidents of my life. It was a hot summer's day and I was in a cotton dress. As I walked along I suddenly realised that someone behind me had raised my dress above my waist and was in the process of pulling down my underwear. I whirled around and found myself facing a white woman. I screamed and demanded to know what she was doing. She responded that she wanted to see where I kept my tail, 'Because you people have tails. You are like monkeys, you swing from the trees'. She continued, 'I've seen you and your family walking around, but have never seen your tails, so you must have them coiled up in your underwear, so that's why I'm looking there'. There is so much to dissect about this incident. Firstly it is incredible that a grown woman felt able to sexually assault a child on the street in broad daylight and showed no remorse or shame. The second unbelievable element was that she really believed that African-Caribbean people comprise a separate species and have tails. Thirdly, it is shameful that her education and personal learning had been so poor that she could have been lead to believe this. However, negative propaganda about black people was promoted at all levels of the British media and social life so it is perhaps unsurprising that this woman believed something so frankly ridiculous and outrageous.

This incident took place around 1969 and at the time you would have met many people who – like that woman – genuinely believed that African-Caribbean people were akin to monkeys and swung from trees. They thought that we were animals and and – in many respects – they treated us like animals. Mum says that in Jamaica she had been a human being who was treated with dignity and pride but in England she found that dogs in kennels were often treated with more respect that she was. Mum tried to shield us from the realities of racism but often – such as the incident with the woman who tried to undress me on the street – she was unable to do so, and this made her angry and very sad.

Thankfully, we also met a lot of nice white people who became firm friends. Not everybody was racist, and some white people went out of their way to make us feel welcome and wanted. Mum developed some very good friends, Marsha and Peggy in particular, who helped her to settle in the UK. They taught her British customs and mannerisms, and educated her about the culture. They also introduced her to the British habit of 'dunking' or dipping biscuits in tea, which Mum found very peculiar! They took her under their wings, showed her how the UK works, and helped her to negotiate the maze of work, culture and social peculiarities that she faced during those early years. Both Mar-

II   The Life Story of Dr Dorothy Francis

sha and Peggy remained my mother's good friends until they died – we spent many happy occasions with them and mourned their deaths.

My first impression of England – 'Everything was grey'

The shock of moving to this country is branded on my memory. I think it was one of the most traumatic things that ever happened to me and it took me many years to recover. The contrast between Jamaica and England was stark and overwhelming. I came to England from a country where the sun shines and the sky is blue for 340 days of the year. Jamaica is lush, green and vibrant and is always hot. Christopher Columbus travelled to many places but he said that Jamaica was the most beautiful place that he had ever seen. The brightness of the sun demands bright colours and so clothing is vibrant and colourful, as are the people whose skin tones vary from light to darkest brown, including African, Chinese, Indian, Lebanese and European skin tones. There is a vibrancy about Jamaica in terms of the language, weather, culture, music and clothing, and it was this brightness and vivacity that I missed most when I moved to England.

I arrived in the UK in winter and my first impression of England was that everything was different shades of grey; it seemed that even the people were grey! I had never seen so many white people (in fact I am not sure if I had ever seen a white person). I didn't know that they were so pale and colourless and was totally disconcerted by the sight of so many pale ghostlike people. However, it wasn't just the people that were grey – their clothing was too, as were the buildings and the sky. Everywhere I looked just appeared to be a different variation on the colour grey. In Jamaica I was used to having bright colours all around me and I was shocked at the bleached-out appearance of the UK. I clearly remember standing at the top of the airplane stairs and looking out at a world that was devoid of colour and being horrified at the view in front of me.

Before I came here I had no image of England in my mind because I didn't know what England was and did not know what to expect. Perhaps my grandparents tried to tell me, but they had never left Jamaica and would have had little idea of how to describe such a very different country. How do you explain England to a five year old who has lived in Jamaica all her life? How do you convey the difference? I don't think that anything could have prepared me for the shock of arriving in the UK.

I don't remember much about leaving Jamaica. I recall that there was a big fuss, that my grandparents and other family members were crying and that I was put on an airplane with a lady whom I had not met before (she was travelling to the UK and was paid £5 to escort me across the Atlantic). I had never travelled in any vehicle except buses and the very occasional car and so it was a novelty to climb the steps of the plane. That novelty soon wore off as the journey progressed as I was violently and persistently sick for most of the passage because I suffered from motion sickness and the flight was subject to a lot of turbulence so it was not a pleasant journey.

48

II   The Life Story of Dr Dorothy Francis

English and Patois [10] – learning to move between two languages

When I came to the UK I only spoke Jamaican patois and had to learn to speak English which I found very difficult. My mother was insistent that I learned to speak English saying, 'You live in England now. You are black, female and poor. You have so many obstacles in your way and you certainly don't need another one. You will not get on in life unless you speak good English and so you will learn to do so'.

English is the official language of Jamaica but most people speak Jamaican creole or patois, which is English combined with African languages (mainly Akan) and Spanish, Chinese and Indian words as well as remnants from the language of the Tiano, who inhabited the island before the coming of the Europeans and who gifted words such as barbeque, cassava and tobacco. The language has a different grammatical structure to English, different tones and inflexions, and does not employ some of the conventions of English, so it can be difficult for non-speakers to follow.

Every time I spoke Jamaican patois Mum would discipline me, sometimes with a sharp smack to my legs, to remind me to speak English. It reached a point where I was frightened to speak because I could not understand why I was being chastised for speaking in the only way that I knew how. For many years after arriving in the UK I had to think very carefully when translating patois to English in terms of the words, inflexions, speech and grammatical patterns. Translation from patois to English is not just about the words but the tone in which they are said and the order in which the words are placed. I found it difficult to work this out, especially as my parents were not always able to help me as they were not fluent in English and were themselves unsure about placement and usage. I didn't know how to pronounce many words and I struggled with many seemingly simple terminologies and concepts. For instance, it took me years to learn the difference between 'bought' and 'brought', because neither of those words is utilised in patois and they were never employed within our home.

For my brother and sisters it was not such an issue because they were all born in the UK and grew up hearing English at their childminders', on the street and on television, even if it was not spoken in our home. The irony was that my mother would compel me to speak English whilst speaking to me in patois and that she also conversed with my father in patois, so whilst English was spoken outside, patois was the language of the home.

My mother perceived patois as an inferior form of English and did not think that we would advance in life if we spoke it. I have had discussions with Mum where I have explained that patois is not inferior to English, but is a language form in its own right. Many scholars have championed the right for patois to be recognised as a language and the Bible is now available in Jamaican patois, as are dictionaries. However Mum was brought up to perceive Jamaican patois as sub-standard to English and would not allow her children to speak it in front of her. My brother and sisters and I all speak good

49

II The Life Story of Dr Dorothy Francis

English because this is what my mother wanted as she felt that it removed obstacles from our way. She wanted us to speak the Queen's English because we were in a foreign country and life was hard enough for us as it was without speaking in a way which would bring about extra discrimination.

I am in my fifties, but even now, if I am in my mother's presence and I speak in patois, she will still chastise me. I tell her, 'Mum, I am old enough to know the difference', but she is always afraid that one day I will be in polite company and I will speak in patois. I tell her that I know how to code-switch from one language to another but she still expects me to speak English at all times. As a result, I speak English better than many English people but have lost touch with my ability to speak patois.

The upshot of this is that when I return to Jamaica on holiday I find myself unable to speak patois fluently and in the right tone as it is no longer my everyday language and because I do not have many people in England to speak patois with on an everyday basis. My husband is white and does not speak patois; meanwhile, my children have not been brought up with patois around them as a constant, and so whilst understanding it, they are not comfortable or fluent in the language. My mother spoke to us in patois but we were only allowed to respond in English. Over the years my ability to speak in patois was eroded and now when I return to Jamaica it is very obvious that I am English.

However, patois is my mother tongue and I often think in it as this comes naturally. If I am angry or telling a story that involves black people, I often revert to patois, which my children and husband find quite funny. It is the language that I still feel comfortable in because it is the language of my home.

Settling into a new life in Coventry

When I first came to this country my family was living in a house which was owned by an Asian family called Singh. The Singhs were a family of four and they lived on the ground floor. Our family and two others each had a room on the first floor. The other families were Mr and Mrs Facey, who had three children, and Mr and Mrs Morgan and their three children. My parents had four children, so in all there were sixteen people living in three bedrooms and twenty-one people in the house overall. We all shared a bathroom and kitchen and had to operate shifts to be able to use the facilities in turn.

There was only one cooker so sometimes we would have to queue to cook. The Singhs had first priority and the tenants worked out a system between them as to who would go first, second and third, once the Singhs had finished. Sometimes everyone wanted to cook at the same time, which was awkward as it was not practical for four families to cook on one cooker, so all the tenants had small one-burner stoves in their rooms and used these to prepare meals. I would watch my mother as she cooked on this small camping stove and thought that she was a genius in the way that she turned out whole meals from just one ring. She would cook the meat and then put it aside to keep warm.

II   The Life Story of Dr Dorothy Francis

This would be followed by rice or another carbohydrate, and finally she would cook the vegetables and assemble the meal from these components. She had little choice but to use a camping stove because if we waited to use the cooker in the kitchen we might not have eaten until 10 pm on some days. It was a kind of way of living that I hope does not happen today, although I am sure that some newly-arrived migrants still find themselves pushed into such poor living conditions.

I recall that the Singhs' house did not have an indoor toilet, but only a facility in an out-building in the garden. I remember walking through the snow to go to the toilet; it was horrendous. The outside toilet was not a unique feature to that house; it was how a great many people lived at that time, be they Asian, African-Caribbean or white. Hundreds of thousands of houses in the UK did not have an inside toilet and many did not have a bathroom. Most terraced houses were built without bathrooms, so people bathed in steel baths in front of the fire that were filled and emptied by hand. Other bodily functions were served by chamber pots and outside toilets and morning tasks involved emptying the chamber pots into the outside toilet.

Eventually programmes of modernisation led to bedrooms being converted to bathrooms or extensions being added to create indoor bathrooms but when I was growing up it was not unusual to visit homes that only had outside toilets. I understand that there are still houses in the UK which do not have inside toilets because the elderly owners refuse to entertain the idea, having been used to using outdoor facilities all their lives, but this now a rarity.

We lived in the Singh household for my first three or four months in this country. It was overcrowded but on the plus side we had a houseful of playmates. My parents had been friends with the Faceys and Morgans in Jamaica and they got on well together. I remember that we children were in and out of each other's rooms, and there was hardly any distinction as to which children belonged to which family. We ate together often and the adults came together to play dominoes or cards and to listen to music. My father bought the latest hits on the way home from work every Friday and had a sizeable collection of music, which he played on his beloved radiogram. The radiogram – known affectionately as the 'gram' – was one of the first things that he purchased when he arrived in England as music was very important. It was a way of keeping in touch with Jamaica and also brought a little fun into stressful lives. The tenants often pulled up the rugs and had impromptu parties to dance to the latest releases and we loved the gaiety of these sessions as we twirled around the room or tried to copy dance steps such as the 'Mash Potato' and the 'Twist'.

My brother was a great friend of the Singhs' youngest son and they could often be found playing together. My parents had lived in that house for about two years when I arrived in the UK so the two boys – one Indian and one African-Caribbean – had grown up together and were like brothers. I remember that they disappeared for a while one day and we found them happily splashing about in the – thankfully clean – water of the out-

51

II   The Life Story of Dr Dorothy Francis

side toilet!

I loved to watch Mrs Singh prepare evening meals for her family and was especially fascinated by the way that she made wafer-thin chapattis by patting them between her hands and spinning them in the air – it seemed magical to me and it was a skill that I coveted! I had never eaten curries or chapattis before coming to England and I enjoyed sharing meals with the Singhs, who took delight in introducing me to foods such as aubergine curry, dal and samosas, as well as chapattis and lassi, a yoghurt-based drink.

I had not seen a television set until I arrived in England and so watching television was another new experience. Even though we lived in cramped conditions we had a radiogram and we bought a TV when we moved to our new house. These were very important as my parents couldn't afford to take us out, so we made entertainment at home. TV wasn't very remarkable in those days because there were only three channels: ITV, BBC1 and BBC2, and sometimes transmissions didn't start until late morning, but nonetheless the world of television was exciting and interesting to me.

It's odd just how much those early days in the UK are imprinted on my mind. Sometimes I wonder if my memories are false or imbued with stories told by my parents, but I know that this is not the case. In fact, I sometimes surprise my mother by recounting stories of incidents that I had observed and noted and she often expresses surprise at my recollection of events. I was very young when I arrived in the UK but I was an observant child and I remember many things very clearly.

Moving to a Council house in Henley Green

A few months after I arrived in England our family was rehoused by the city council and we left the Singhs to move to a house in Henley Green, which was an outer suburb of Coventry. This was our first family home in England and it was blissful in comparison to where we had been living. The house had been built after the Second World War and was quite modern with three large bedrooms. My brother had his own room and my sisters and I shared a large, L-shaped space, whilst my parents occupied the third bedroom. We had a spacious living room, a large kitchen and a good size bathroom – no more outdoor trips to the toilet for us! The house was fronted by a large lawn and to the rear was a big garden with mature trees, fruits and flowers. The developers tried to incorporate as many of the existing trees as possible when the houses were built, so the gardens were very green and full of trees. My father dug up half of our garden to turn it into a vegetable plot but there was still plenty of room for us to play games. We loved that garden and spent many happy hours in it.

We had a lot of space around us, with the front and back garden at our disposal, and in addition to this our street was pedestrianised so there was no traffic to contend with. Our house faced the houses opposite and our lawns were separated by a pathway, which we used for riding our bikes, skipping and playing on our scooters. We grew up in the

II   The Life Story of Dr Dorothy Francis

1960s and '70s and we were outdoors a lot, sometimes for hours at a time. We played endless games on the lawns, including football, rounders and cricket – I remember that my brother and friends were playing football once when one of them kicked the ball straight through our living room window, leaving a perfectly round hole in the glass; my parents were not amused!

Families were bigger in those days and most households had three or four children so we had a ready stream of playmates. It was not unusual for 20 to 30 children to be out on the streets at the same time playing a variety of games. We played marbles and ball games and skipped, ran and cycled. We built and raced buggies using wheels from old prams and bits of wood and we careered around on scooters, which had a habit of pitching us off when the front wheels hit a pothole or dip. We emulated what we saw on the television with cops and robbers and Wild West games and loved to stage variety shows based on the programmes of the day, such as 'Opportunity Knocks' and 'New Faces'. Some games were seasonal and played only at certain times of the year, such as conkers in the autumn, cricket in summer and marbles in spring and summer when the ground was dry and clear. Other games, such as football, were played all year through.

We loved to play marbles, but none so much as my sister Sharon. She had an excellent eye and a great technique and could beat anyone in our school at marbles. She possessed a collection of hundreds of marbles that she had won. Although marbles was a unisex game it was predominantly played by boys and many of them retired with bruised egos at being resoundingly beaten by a 'mere' girl! One day a delegation of boys approached my brother, Steadman, in the playground and demanded that he forbade Sharon from playing marbles against them as she kept winning. Steadman responded that it was their problem if they allowed someone two years younger than them to beat them, and that he was in no position to forbid Sharon to desist from trouncing them at marbles!

We played some odd games, including one called 'kerby'. It was played with a large beach ball by players standing on opposite sides of the road. The objective was to throw the ball and make it glance off the kerb so that it bounced back to the thrower. This scored the thrower a point. I doubt that children play such games anymore – it wasn't the most interesting of games, even then!

We also used to collect car registration numbers to see who could collect the most varied numbers. We would patrol with notebooks and list all the car number plates in the area. This was a fairly easy to do as there weren't as many cars then as there are now.

We would go fishing for sticklebacks and tadpoles in the local river. It wasn't proper fishing; we would just get nets and catch tiny fish. We would spend days out and about and had a lot more freedom than modern day children do; children don't roam freely as much as they used to. We used to leave the house in the morning and spend much of the day away from home, sometimes taking a jam sandwich and a drink with us so that

II   **The Life Story of Dr Dorothy Francis**

we could have a picnic – not much of a picnic but it satisfied us! Our parents often didn't know where we were and there were no mobile phones for keeping in touch. We simply knew that we had to be home by a certain time and that we would be in trouble if we didn't get back by then – other than that we were free to roam all day especially during the holidays.

I had some good friends – even though it was an era of overt racism and some of that prevailed amongst the children that I played with. Moreover, after a while, good friends didn't identify us by colour; they just saw us as friends, although racism would often rear its ugly head in games. We were all working class and relatively poor so were pretty much in the same boat moneywise because no one else around us was well off. Oddly enough, we were probably perceived as being better off than most as we had a car and we were one of only three or four families that did because car ownership was not prevalent in the 1960s and '70s. We had a car because my father worked the night shift at a car factory on the outskirts of the city and he needed a car to get to work.

Henley Green was a nice place to grow up in, in terms of the physical environment. There was a great deal of space and far more freedom to play than where I brought my own children up in Clarendon Park, Leicester and I have often wished that they had as much space and freedom as I experienced as a child.

Going shopping

At the time that I arrived in England there was not much provision for the African-Caribbean community. Finding Caribbean food was difficult, especially for us as we lived in Henley Green on the outskirts of the city in a predominately white area where it was impossible to buy foods such as cornmeal, yam, plantain or coconut oil. Even rice was hard to come by and only featured in the local shops as the sticky type used for making puddings. We had to travel to Foleshill, which was on the other side of the city, and make a return trip of four bus rides to find the type of food that we liked to eat. My father had a car but he felt that shopping was my mother's responsibility and rarely drove us to the shops; we would have to struggle on the buses. The bus journey would take over one hour each way, so shopping took most of a day. We would leave home early on Saturday morning and not return until late Saturday afternoon. We took a bus into the city centre, which was a thirty minute journey, and then we would wait for another bus to Foleshill. That journey would take about fifteen minutes so it was not possible to get to the shops in less than an hour. We would then go from shop to shop to buy food and other items as Mum never bought everything in one shop. She would go to different shops for certain items and we would traverse the high street visiting the butcher, baker, greengrocer and hardware shops in turn.

Once we had everything we would take the bus back to the city centre and then another bus back to Henley Green and walk from the bus stop, carrying the bags. If we were lucky, we caught the bus that stopped near the end of the road, but sometimes that bus

II The Life Story of Dr Dorothy Francis

wasn't available and we would have to take one that dropped us half a mile away, which was a long walk with heavy bags. Shopping was such very hard work! I remember struggling with the bags, thinking, 'Will we ever get home?'. I would stop to put the bags down every few steps before picking them up and moving on again. Mum would cajole and encourage me saying 'Never mind, baby, come on – we are almost there', even though I knew that was not true! It was gruelling when I was so young but there was little choice, really. There should have been a choice, had my father chosen to help my mother more, but he never involved himself in that kind of thing and I hardly ever remember him going shopping. He just assumed that the house would be stocked with food, as if by magic, but he didn't do much about getting it there.

African-Caribbean people paid premium prices for food because we were a small community and the foodstuffs we ate were imported in relatively small quantities and sold by specialist distributors and therefore cost a lot more than the food that English people ate. However, when you are away from your country and are homesick food becomes a reminder of home. We craved yams, green bananas, ackee, dasheen, coco, plantain, salt fish and other things that couldn't be found in everyday shops, and we paid over the odds for them. Although African-Caribbean people tended to earn less than white people we paid higher prices for foodstuffs, so our shopping bill was always disproportionately higher, because our food was not readily available and was not mass-produced.

Nowadays, the foodstuff that we used to travel miles to buy can be found in most major supermarkets in cities such as Coventry, Leicester, Birmingham, London, Nottingham, etc. Now, it's not unusual to see yams, dasheen, green bananas, plantain, salt fish and Scotch Bonnets (Caribbean red peppers) for sale in conventional stores. The African-Caribbean community is established and the supermarkets have realised that we are here to stay and that we are a market to be serviced. They have recognised the buying power of the 'black pound'. African-Caribbean people still pay a disproportionate amount for imported foodstuffs, but at least we can now obtain what we want in supermarkets. When African-Caribbeans originally came to this country we weren't appreciated as consumers at all. Nowadays, the supermarkets have realised that they are losing a significant market if they don't cater for our community. This has made it easier to buy food, hair, skin products and make-up, although we still face difficulties in sourcing certain foods and it is still difficult to get good make-up in the UK. Nonetheless a lot has changed since those early days.

The impact of moving from Henley Green to Foleshill

We moved to Henley Green on the outskirts of Coventry when I was six and remained there for eight years. We loved our house and the surrounding fields and play areas and I have fond memories of the area. However, the house did not have central heating and was perennially damp. The city council were the landlords and my parents complained to them for many years to no avail. In the end my mother requested that we be transferred to another house that was drier and centrally heated. In the autumn of 1975 we

II The Life Story of Dr Dorothy Francis

moved from Henley Green to Foleshill, which is on the other side of the city. We later found out that the English man who moved into the house in November 1975 complained to the council about the coldness and damp and that Coventry Council immediately dug up the floors to install damp proofing and also fitted central heating, double glazing and insulation, turning the house into a cosy place to live. We were very angry when we heard this as my parents had complained about our living conditions for many years and had been ignored whereas the council provided everything for the new tenant within a few months of him moving in (and, as a result, he still lives there more than forty years later). We would probably have stayed in the house if these changes had been made as it was a large house with substantial front and back gardens in a quiet residential area and we liked living there.

Moving from Henley Green to Foleshill forced Mum to resign from her job at Walsgrave Hospital, as the new house was miles away instead of a fifteen minute walk. My mother did not drive and so relied on buses and the journey from the new house to her workplace took almost an hour each way. This was not manageable as her working day involved getting herself ready for work, the smaller children ready for school and then travelling across the city for a 9 am start. She tried it for a little while but it was too far to travel every morning; she had to get up very early and became very worn out and tired, so she had to give up the job. Mum was very upset at losing her financial independence and her social life by being forced to return to the home and she was without employment for over a year.

I didn't like Foleshill very much; it was very cramped and built-up in comparison to what I had been used to and I felt trapped and enclosed. The new house only had a small front garden with a fence round it whereas previously we had a lawn, lots of green space and no fences. On the plus side our new home was warmer, because we had central heating, which was a real luxury after the unheated house that we had left. We still had three bedrooms but they were all smaller and we felt cramped in the smaller space. A redeeming aspect of Foleshill was that it made shopping easier as the shops that we had formerly travelled miles to visit were located there. Also, it was nearer to family friends such as the Faceys and the Williams and our cousins the Ramseys which made socialising more convenient.

I didn't like living in Foleshill and only spent two years there before leaving home at sixteen. I missed the open spaces of Henley Green, the quieter streets and the sizeable house that we had moved from. However an advantage of living in Foleshill was that it was much more diverse and cosmopolitan than Henley Green, and we had neighbours from across the world – Ireland, Scotland, Barbados, Poland, Jamaica, India, Pakistan and various parts of England. There was a good community spirit and the children played in the streets and popped in and out of each other's houses. My mother was famed for feeding anyone who happened to be around when meals were put on the table and local children would turn up when they knew that it was mealtime. I still meet people who remember being fed by Mum. We, in turn, were fed by the Tanners, the Indian

II The Life Story of Dr Dorothy Francis

family next door, who introduced us to mind-bogglingly hot curries and cooked us fragrant samosas. Mrs Holder further down the road cooked us cou cou and flying fish from her native Barbados, while the Polish family at number seventy-two introduced us to stuffed cabbage and dumplings. It was a real melting pot of cuisines and we enjoyed experimenting with food from different countries and sitting at each other's tables. Eating food from other cultures has always been one of my favourite things to do. I think that you get to know a person when you get to know their food, so I was always happy to experience new and different world cultures through their cuisines.

We settled into the new area and my brother and sisters joined new schools. I remained at Woodway Park School as I was midway through my O-Levels and didn't want to move. Once we were established in the new house Mum resumed her job search and found a cleaning job at Coventry railway station which suited her especially well as she finished at 3 pm. This allowed her to get home in time for when we returned from school.

Mum enjoyed working at the railway station because she likes to talk to people and so many different people came through the station from all over the world. She made some lifetime friends amongst the regular travellers and some of them even spent Christmas Day with us. Mum saw the Queen and Diana, Princess of Wales when they came through the station on visits to Coventry, and she enjoyed the hustle and bustle of the environment.

Mum had an especially good relationship with the Transport Police who were based at the station and whom she enjoyed joking with. Mum really appreciated working at the railway station because it gave her the opportunity to be financially secure, to meet new people and to find out about other cultures.

The job did not have high status or a high salary but it suited Mum's needs and she was happy in the role. It gave her the independence to buy her own things, to treat her children and to travel. Her wages allowed her to return to Jamaica every few years and she was able to see her mother twice more before she died, although she only saw her father once, on the trip in 1975, as he died less than two years later. Mum was very sad about this as she loved her father very much and had missed him throughout her years in England. Lack of finance had meant that she had been unable to travel to Jamaica in the early days, and my grandfather died shortly after she achieved the financial means to visit Jamaica more often, which was a great sadness to her.

Mum enjoyed the job and stayed long after she could have retired. She put off retiring because she enjoyed going to work and liked the social life that was a part of it – she was quite bored when she finally gave up working, especially as she had divorced my father by this time and all her children had grown up, and she often expressed her desire to return to work. She also enjoyed the financial stability of working – this was a huge issue for my mother as she had been starved of cash by my father for many years and her independence was hard-won. She bought my father out of the house when they divorced

II   The Life Story of Dr Dorothy Francis

and was proud that she was able to pay the mortgage herself, eventually paying off the loan shortly before she retired. I am impressed by her tenacity and determination as she didn't earn a huge wage. However, she saved determinedly and doggedly and managed to pay the mortgage and find money for treats for herself and her children.

British train networks are now owned by private companies, having been de-nationalised in the 1990s. However, at the point when my mother worked at Coventry railway station the rail service was operated by British Rail as a public facility and staff were treated in a very paternalistic way. My mother gained lifetime free travel on the rail networks as a condition of her employment and this free travel extended to her spouse. As children of a British Rail employee we received free travel until we were eighteen and so were able to roam across Britain extensively by train. Having free train travel allowed our family to travel widely within England and Wales and we enjoyed family trips to places such as Bournemouth, Southsea and Brighton that we would not otherwise have been able to afford.

My mother and our clothes

I think my mother saw clothes as a form of weaponry and made sure that we were always beautifully turned out. She knew that most white people looked at us askance and needed no excuses to put us down, so she was determined that our clothes should not give them ammunition to use against us and ensured that we were impeccably dressed whenever we left the house.

Mum was a talented seamstress and made a lot of our clothes; I especially loved our church dresses, which had wide skirts buoyed up by layers of petticoats. These were worn with patent leather shoes and blindingly white socks and the outfits were set off by ribbons in our hair and little patent handbags. My mother ordered tailored suits for my brother Steadman and supplemented these with white shirts, black ties and perfectly-polished brogues. He was a good-looking little boy and always attracted attention from people on the street, especially older ladies who would give him sixpences and sometimes even half a crown (which was a lot of money in those days), because they took such pleasure in seeing him. The same applied to my sister Sharon, who was a beautiful, outgoing and gregarious child and easily charmed anyone that she met. She was dimpled and rounded and looked adorable in her ruffled dresses, so like Steadman, her pockets often jangled with money from admir-

In London 1974. Outside Aunt Esme's house in Tooting Bec. Left to right: Dad, Mr Mullings, myself, Aunt Eula, Mum, Aunt Esme, Steadman, Sharon, and Lorna. Mum made the outfits that she, my aunts, Sharon, Lorna and I are wearing.

II The Life Story of Dr Dorothy Francis

ers, and her face would be sticky with sweets that elderly ladies pressed upon her. My youngest sibling, Lorna, was delicate and exceedingly pretty and was always dressed in the most beautiful clothes so also attracted much attention. I was thin, shy and geeky, and I desperately envied the attention that my bonny siblings received!

My mother loves clothes and always dressed well. She would draw admiring comments from my school friends who thought that she dressed like a film star. She had a very small waist, even after five children, and favoured dresses and skirts that nipped in at the waist and flared outwards. These were worn with pointed court shoes and accessorised with scarfs and patent handbags. I was proud to be in her company, as she was always a lovely sight to behold. Mum still has an extensive and colourful wardrobe and loves to dress up, and she has passed this love of clothing to her children and grandchildren along with her passion for the colour purple. We all dress well and love colourful designs and patterns and take pride in being well turned-out. I enjoy going out with my siblings as everyone is always dressed to the nines and I can never be overdressed amongst them!

My mother saw clothes as power, and to some extent that is still true. She always told us that we would have barriers to overcome by virtue of being black, working class or female, and that we should not let people's perceptions of our clothes put additional barriers in our way. She felt that to dress well was to remove an obstacle from our path and so always insisted that we look our very best.

As children, we polished our shoes every night, learnt how to launder our own clothes, press pleats into skirts and iron trousers with razor sharp creases – this applied to my brother as well as the girls. This training is hard to abandon and has followed us into adulthood. One notable result of this is that I find it very hard to dress down and can sometimes appear overdressed at informal gatherings. I am used to dressing to look the part and sometimes find it difficult to dress casually. In addition, I work in the field of business advice, and people have certain expectations of how a business adviser should look, so I dress to meet these expectations. I am often the only black woman in the room, so I ensure that I am smartly and appropriately dressed so that people look at me, not my clothes. It is ridiculous that I should have to think in this way, but I know that it is a necessity.

II The Life Story of Dr Dorothy Francis

5 My school experiences and incidences of racism

Dorothy started school in Coventry in 1966 and recounts her experiences, especially of incidents of racial harassment and discrimination.

Racism at school in Coventry

I hadn't yet started school when I left Jamaica so my first experience of school was in England. I went to an infant and primary school on Wyken Croft Road called Annie Osborne. It was a fairly modern building set in acres of land, complete with a pond that contained fish and frogs. The grounds also encompassed playing fields, two large playgrounds, complete with netball and basketball hoops, and a wall for bouncing balls against – the grounds were outstanding and I doubt that many children have the opportunity to be surrounded by such acreage of land nowadays.

I joined the school mid-way through a term, and, as the new girl, initially everybody clamoured to be my friend and I was very popular. I made many friends in my first week and enjoyed my first foray into the world of education. Everybody wanted to play with me.

However, in the second week I found that I did not have any friends except Susan Williamson – who always stood by me throughout my school years – and her cousin Helen; all the others had melted away. I found out why when children stared to taunt me by making comments such as: 'My mum says I mustn't play with you because black people are heathens', or 'My ma says you are dirty', and, 'My dad says that people like you smell and carry disease', or, 'My mother said that God left you in the oven too long. That is why you are black. She said that I mustn't play with you or touch you, because the dirt will come off on me'. Other slurs included, 'My mum says that you are monkeys and you live in trees'. All I heard was, 'My mother says this', or, 'My dad says that' from children who had been my friends in the previous week but who now began to bully and harass me. They hadn't been racist when I met them but by the next week they had absorbed and internalised a range of negative concepts about black people and knew how to harm with racist words and actions. Within two weeks they learned a multitude of names to wound me with – 'blackie', 'wog', 'sambo', 'darkie', 'nigger' – and many more racist slurs that they hadn't previously known but which the adults in their lives taught them.

In Jamaica I never had to think about the colour of my skin as it was never an issue. I didn't even realise that 'colour' existed until I came to the UK; yet suddenly my colour became my outstanding definition and determined whether I was accepted or not and this was painful and confusing.

In my initial first few days at school I had many friends because the children did not know – or care – that I was a different colour; I was simply a new girl. Racism is a taught

60

II   The Life Story of Dr Dorothy Francis

concept and by my second week in the school the children had been trained to be racist and had been indoctrinated into their parents' beliefs. I can imagine that they had said to their parents something along the lines of: 'There is a new girl in my school and she's really nice. She is called Dorothy'. Then I imagine that when the parents – usually the mothers – came to collect the children, I was pointed out to them, at which point the parents said, 'Oh no, you didn't tell me she was black. You can't play with her', and then proceeded to tell their children a host of racist reasons why.

My first week at school was blissful; however, by the second week I had learned the sad reality of racism and found myself with just two friends. Susan Williamson supported me and was never influenced by what other people said, but even she found it hard sometimes to deal with being my friend because being close to me subjected her to the same barrage of abuse that I faced on a daily basis. It wore her down and sometimes affected our friendship, which was sad. However we weathered the storms and are still friends more than 50 years later. Things improved a little as time went on but I continued to be either bullied or ignored by the majority of my fellow pupils. I hated when the time came in P.E. [physical education] to choose a partner or team members, because the other children rarely picked me. They complained bitterly if I was paired with them and would hold their noses, declaiming: 'I'm going to get germs now', and they would refuse to hold my hands for the exercises. I was quite sporty and was usually an asset to their teams, but they preferred to lose rather than to have me on their side.

Many of the children refused to sit next to me in class because their parents told them I was dirty and unclean and that God didn't love black people. To be told that I was outside of God's love was painful and it hurt that this rhetoric came from adults who should have known better. Small children trust their parents explicitly and the adults in their lives are founts of all knowledge. Therefore, if their parents tell them that black people are dirty and dangerous, sadly, this is what they believe. Some of my class mates were able to use their powers of reasoning to recognise that this was not the case but others chose not to question it and opted to continue these beliefs into adulthood.

A few years ago I reconnected with one of my old school mates from junior school but after a short time I terminated the relationship as I found out that she supported right-wing organisations and believed that black people should be repatriated to their countries of origin. It is hard to understand why she sought to reconnect with me on social media and I was very happy to break off contact. I reminded her that she had been a bully in the playground and she had not changed – she had simply become an adult who was still a bully.

The bullying and pressure that I faced at school was interminable, and it came to a point when I refused to go to school because the intimidation became so bad. My mother went to the school to talk to the teacher and asked her to address the situation. My teacher was called Miss Briggs and I adored her but her words and actions dashed my adoration to pieces. Miss Briggs addressed the class, saying, 'Dorothy's mother has

II   The Life Story of Dr Dorothy Francis

been to the school to complain that she is being bullied. Now I want you to leave her alone. After all it's not her fault she is black. She can't help it, not everyone can be white'. This was a completely unacceptable way to approach the issue of bullying and only served to make the situation worse. I was seven at the time, and I always remember that incident as my introduction to institutionalised racism and to the fact that the teachers themselves were in thrall to racist ideology which they did not question and which left them unable to support me. It was a harsh lesson to learn at such a young age.

My mother found it difficult to believe that teachers were racist because in Jamaica teachers are honoured and respected and are meant to be impartial and fair, so she had no other template against which to measure UK teachers. In Jamaica most people are of black and she didn't always understand when I tried to explain my experience of racism to her. For instance, I would come home from secondary school and explain, that three of us, two white girls and I, had been talking in class, but I was the only one who was given detention. My mother would say, 'You must have been talking more', and I would say, 'No, I wasn't talking more. It's because I'm black'. I recognised that the teachers disciplined black children excessively, demeaned them in class and dished out more detentions to them, but Mum did not always appreciate this. It was a long time before Mum understood that many of my teachers were actually instrumental in holding me back because they were racist towards me.

An example of this was demonstrated in an incident with my gym teacher, who was also my track coach. I was a gifted and able sprinter and was unbeaten on the track throughout my entire time at secondary school, which brought a lot of triumph to my school. At the age of fifteen I decided to leave the track team to concentrate on my O-Levels as regular evening training and weekend meetings were taking their toll on my studies, as was the practice of pulling me out of lessons so that I could improve my sprinting. I wanted to do well in my exams and recognised that I would have to opt out of sprinting in order to do so.

My gym teacher was aghast as she derived a lot of personal glory from my success and she argued and entreated me to stay. I told her that I needed to put my energies into my exams to which she responded: 'You are an excellent sprinter. You won't need exams, you are going to be famous; you will be the next Sonia Lannerman' (a famous sprinter in the 1970s). Even at fifteen I knew this to be untrue and was surprised that my teacher was willing for me to throw my exams away for a fleeting stab at glory. I was a good athlete, but there were many who were better than me, and, besides, my heart was not in it. Also, I knew that sprinters tend to decline by the time they are thirty and that I would need to seek another career at that point – presuming I hadn't already been side-lined by injury – and that it would be essential to have some qualifications behind me to assist me into a different occupation.

I explained this to my coach but she refused to listen and grew increasingly angry at my refusal to change my mind. When she realised that she couldn't convince me she told me that I was a 'horrible, ungrateful girl', and that I would not amount to anything. I was shocked at this behaviour and found it hard to believe that an adult would speak to me in this way. She accused me of having ruined everything for her and told me that I was letting the school down too. I responded that I would be letting myself down if I failed my exams due to spending hours on the track instead of studying, but this was of little interest to her; as far as she was concerned, I was a black girl and so my place was on the track not in a science laboratory.

There was a general belief throughout my primary and secondary education that African-Caribbean children were not academic, did not understand maths and were not scientific. Other myths abounded: we were told that black people could not swim because our bones were too heavy to float and as a result I did not learn to swim until I was twenty-one.

An incident in my final year of school

I first became aware of institutionalised racism when I was seven, but an incident in my final year of school really brought home the discrepancies between the ways that black people are treated in society in comparison to white people. At age fifteen we had our one and only so-called 'careers advice' session, when we met with an adviser to discuss what career path we should take. My best friend was a white girl called Jane, and she met with the careers adviser in the slot before me. We were both in the top set of our year group and were doing the same O-Levels. On coming out of the office, she informed me that the adviser had told her to consider doing three or four A-Levels, followed by a degree and then possibly to move onto a post-graduate qualification.

It was then my turn to see the advisor, and I was very excited to hear what he would suggest for me, although I suspected that, given we were following the exact course of study, he would probably advise me along the same lines as Jane.

The advisor asked me what I was studying and I told him. He looked at me for a while, and then said, 'Have you ever considered working on the sweet counter at Woolworths? You can go a long way. If you work hard you might even become a supervisor'. Imagine the difference in aspirations that this individual outlined for me and for Jane! He told Jane, 'You can get a PhD', but to me he said, 'You can go and work in a shop'. There was little difference in our educational studies or our ambitions; in fact, I was academically ahead of Jane and was predicted to do better than her in my exams (which I did). Yet she was singled out for academic glory whilst I was consigned to the sweet counter at Woolworths. The colour of our skin determined whether we were selected to obtain a PhD or to work in a shop. This was a stark illustration of the different life expectations that were presented to black and white children.

Paradoxically, this was a positive thing to happen to me because it spurred me on to greater efforts. It made me realise that I faced many hurdles and obstacles to success

II   The Life Story of Dr Dorothy Francis

and that I would have to work much harder than my white colleagues in order to overcome them. That session with the so-called 'careers advisor' taught me to not accept other people's definition of me. I decided that I would strive to be what I wanted to be rather than what others thought I could or should be. That incident has been a strong driving force in my life and the need to disprove those negative expectations has spurred me on at times when I might otherwise have been tempted to give up.

Ironically, Jane failed to study and left school with only two O-Levels. She became pregnant within eight weeks of leaving school and dropped out of her A Level college course because she was embarrassed to attend classes, so she did not fulfil her potential at that stage, although I understand that she returned to education years later.

I was unable to go to college as my parents could not afford it, so I had to take a different route. I too had failed to reach my potential and did not achieve as many exam passes as predicted, so I enrolled for night classes and took two more O-Levels. I then completed three A-Levels via a one-year course of study; and following that went to the City of Birmingham Polytechnic to take an English Language and Literature degree. After a few years away from study I embarked on a one-year teacher-training course to learn how to teach English as a Foreign Language, and qualified near the top of my class. At the age of thirty I decided to study to qualify for the Chartered Institute of Personal Development (CIPD), and graduated 3 years later as Student of the Year. In 2005, I returned to learning, via the University of Leicester, to undertake a teacher training qualification and obtained my certificate a year later. I also have a number of other qualifications, including the ILM (Institute of Leadership and Management) certificate in Social Enterprise Development and the SFEDI (Small Firms Enterprise Development Initiative) level five qualification in Business Advice. I have eight sets of letters after my name and often wonder what that careers adviser would say if he saw me now and whether he would be surprised to know how much his words challenged me to disprove his assessment of me?

My daughters and racism

I am pleased that my daughters did not experience the same negative aspects of school that I faced. The schools that they attended had high expectations of them and I was glad of this. When Fayola was eleven, we attended a parents evening three months into the start of her first term at secondary school. Her maths teacher said, 'We predict that your daughter will get an A-grade in maths, and that is what we will be working towards'. I was astounded that they could be so confident of her success at such an early stage in her academic career at the school, and was pleased when the teacher's prediction came through and she achieved an A-grade in maths. The contrast between the expectations that my teachers had of me and those that they had of Fayola and Safiya was overwhelming, they were nurtured for success in a way that was not open to me in the 1960s and '70s.

II   The Life Story of Dr Dorothy Francis

I am aware that this level of nurture and support does not apply to all African-Caribbean children and that in many ways things have not changed. We should not believe that because a select few succeed everything is therefore fine for all. Indeed, the majority of children who are excluded from school are African-Caribbean, and the greater number of these are boys, who form a disproportionate amount of the exclusions. African-Caribbeans represent about one per cent of the population yet form about eighty per cent of school exclusions, so it is patently obvious that racism is at play here. Racism is still pervasive, and it is more pervasive in education for boys than it is for girls. African-Caribbean children are still hampered by racism in this country, which affects their ability to progress in education and later life.

Going to school in the 1960s and '70s involved facing racism in one way or another on a daily basis, including name calling, stone throwing, biting and punching. It was unrelenting and there was a lot of physical violence – I think a lot more than today. You either gave in to it or learnt how to fight back, often through physical scraps outside the school gates. I abhor violence, but by secondary school I had learned to fight and to give as good as I got. I rapidly became the best fighter in my school and the other students learned to leave me alone, as they knew that if they tormented me it would lead to a fight that they wouldn't win. I was very slight in those days but I was strong and would defend myself if attacked.

The way that fights usually developed is that another student would say something offensive to you and throw down the gauntlet by saying 'scrap', which meant that they were challenging you to a fight. If you chose to take them up on it – and you had little choice, really – the fight would take place after school outside of the school grounds. The word would spread that there was to be a fight, and crowds of children would gather and stand in big circle to urge the fighters on – it was quite barbaric. I was goaded into a number of fights in my first two years at secondary school and I won every one. The students soon learnt not to challenge me as they knew that they would be defeated, and as a result I no longer needed to engage in physical fights. This didn't mean that I didn't have to fight racism; it just meant that I didn't experience as much physical violence, although the verbal abuse continued unabated.

In some ways, the fights were easier to deal with. I have forgotten the physical blows, but still remember with clarity some of the offensive and hurtful things that were said to me. Of course I was not unhappy for every minute of every day; in the main I had a happy childhood, but it was certainly marred by racism, and so much of my schooling was affected by this as I was forced to deal with a constant undercurrent of racism all the way through school. This and other factors led to a certain level of under-achievement, because I was not pushed to succeed and lacked resources to control my learning, and that resulted in feelings of low self-esteem and dissatisfaction with myself. However, despite all this I was mostly happy because children have a great capacity for happiness and even in bad times they can find reasons to be joyful.

II   The Life Story of Dr Dorothy Francis

I am pleased that things are different for Fayola and Safiya. They experienced racism, but not in that same blatant way that I did and their schools had better ways of dealing with racist behaviour. Also, their schools and colleges had high expectations of the students and pushed them to achieve. Simply knowing that you are expected to do well encourages children to succeed and Fayola and Safiya were rarely faced with any other option except success.

6 Four generations of our family in the UK

Here, Dorothy talks about four generations of her family in the UK, about her African and African-Caribbean culture and heritage, about African heritage more generally, and about Black History Month. She also recalls some incidents from her life, including one of racial and sexual harassment at Heathrow Airport in 1987.

My parents' generation

My parents' generation came here as subjects of the British Empire and were glad to help rebuild the mother country. They had been schooled in the British system and possibly knew more about British industry, rivers, topography and tradition than many Britons. Effectively, their generation had been cultured to believe that they were simply British citizens who lived in a faraway countries. Their leanings were very much towards the UK or the 'Mother Country' as they were encouraged to call it, and they saw themselves as British as well as Jamaican.

When that cohort of people – sometimes known as the Windrush generation, after the name of the first ship that docked in 1948 – were asked to come here by a government that included Enoch Powell, to help rebuild the country after the war, they were happy to do so, because they were coming to the 'Mother Country'. The recruitment drives enticed people with the promise of high-quality jobs, but these did not always materialise and people were disappointed when they came here and found that the only opportunities available to them were in manual and low-paid labour and that sometimes even that type of labour was not open to them. My mother once applied for a cleaning job and arrived at the factory at the same time as a white woman who was also applying for the job. The foreman told my mother that she could not have the job because if faced with the choice between a black and a white applicant he wanted to offer it to the white person. They were both equally qualified to scrub a floor and polish furnishings but the other woman had the additional qualification of the colour of her skin and this won her the job.

Mum remembers lots of times when she was knocked back because she was black; she would attend interview and be told, 'I didn't know you were black; I don't employ darkies'. Or they would blame the Labour Exchange, saying, 'They should have known not to send you as they really can't expect a coloured person to work alongside decent white people'. The employers didn't even bother to give reasons; they simply decided that black people and white people could not work alongside each other. This overt segregation continued for many years until the passing of the 1976 Race Relations Act [11] which drove such unconcealed behaviour underground and challenged those who still operated openly racist practices. The Race Relations Act lessened the explicit racism in employment and services, but such discrimination still continues, albeit in a more discrete and codified way, which is damaging to black people and results in access to choice and opportunities being denied.

Myself and my mother celebrating my 50th birthday at a local restaurant.

The Windrush generation faced blatant and systematic racism in employment, education, health and housing, and until the Race Relations Act was passed there was nothing in place to prevent this happening. The Race Relations Act didn't stop the covert racism – that continued anyway – but it made overt racism an offence. For the first time, employers were unable to use race as a selection criterion and landlords were prevented from using skin colour as a reason to refuse housing. However, things did not change overnight and indeed, there is still much ground to be gained in the fight for equality.

My parents' generation faced immense racism, which they had not expected when they answered the clarion call to help the mother country. Some who arrived in the UK were teachers, doctors, accountants, nurses or lawyers in their home countries yet found that they couldn't practise here and were told that their qualifications were not valid even though they had often been acquired via the Oxford or Cambridge matriculation boards. These highly-qualified people were forced to take jobs where they could and it was not unusual to find nurses and teachers working as bus conductors or cleaners because they were unable to obtain work commensurate with their qualifications.

When I was growing up it was rare to find a black person serving in a shop in the UK, and certainly never in a bank or in any position of authority. There were a few black schoolteachers and a number of black nurses because a lot of Caribbean women had been recruited into the National Health Service although often at much lower levels of responsibility than they had occupied in their country of origin.

I believe that many of the Windrush generation failed to achieve and live their ambitions as racism left much potential unrealised. The hopes of thousands of people were frustrated and dreams remained unfulfilled and withered away. Imagine what it must feel like to be a teacher in your own country but to come to the UK only to find that the col-

II The Life Story of Dr Dorothy Francis

our of your skin restricts you to driving buses or cleaning the streets. A consequence of this was that was our parents put a lot of pressure on us to fulfil their dreams and were adamant that we should do well in education and progress in society. Sometimes this meant that we were not allowed to be outwardly African or African-Caribbean because our parents wanted us to act as 'English' as possible so that we would fit in. However, it did not matter how 'English' we were, whether we spoke perfectly enunciated 'English' or knew all the customs; in the eyes of English people we were still determinedly foreign. You might have an English-sounding name, but your skin spoke of your 'foreignness' and this potentially closed any doors that your English nomenclature may have opened. You might be highly qualified with a string of letters after your name but in essence the colour of your skin was your major qualification.

The segregation of people by colour still prevails in the UK and racial classification is yet a part of life. My daughters are second generation British but are constantly asked: 'Where are you from?' Their answer is generally 'Leicester' because that is where they were born, schooled and grew up. Yet interrogators insist on cross-examining with, 'No, where are you REALLY from?'. as they persist in their refusal to accept that my daughters are British and identify as such. In the eyes of the interrogators, Fayola and Safiya are foreigners and it is their skin colour which prevents them from being British.

Michael Howard, Helen Mirren and Stephen Fry all come from families that settled in the UK within the 20th century, as did mine. Yet Fry, Howard and Mirren are seen as quintessentially 'English' in a way that my daughters are not; why is this so? I doubt that Helen Mirren or Stephen Fry are constantly faced with inquisitive and intrusive busybodies asking, 'But where are you REALLY from?'. Essentially, they have been able to blend into society because they are white. Michael Howard was born Michael Hecht in Swansea and is the son of Bernat Hecht, who fled Romania in 1939. His parents became British subjects and changed their family name to Howard. Helen Mirren's father was Russian and she was born Helen Mironoff, in London. Her father anglicised the family name to 'Mirren' and changed his name to Basil. Stephen Fry's maternal grandparents, 'Martin' and Rosa Neumann, were Hungarian Jews, who emigrated to the UK from Slovakia. Helen Mirren, Stephen Fry and Michael Howard all have high profiles, but rarely is their ethnic background mentioned. Mohamed (Mo) Farah is a British citizen, but the fact that he was born in Somalia seems to always creep into reports and it is unusual to read a story about him that does not reference his ethnic origin. It doesn't matter how much a person of colour achieves or how well they try to fit, it seems that the colour of their skin will always be of note.

It frustrates me that my daughters – and whole generations of people who have been born in the UK and know no other country – are not perceived as being 'British' because the colour of their skin precludes this, whilst others are accepted far more readily. The Queen's husband was born in Corfu of Greek and Danish nationalities and is a naturalised British subject, having renounced his Greek and Danish royal titles to marry the Queen, but he is deemed to be British whereas whole generations of British born people

II The Life Story of Dr Dorothy Francis

of colour are still asked, 'Where do you come from?'.

I think that we will have made headway in the UK when people look at people of colour and simply see them as British rather than African-Caribbean or Black-British, or as having some other form of hyphenated existence, in the same way that Mirren, Fry, Howard and others of white extraction are simply seen as British, rather than 'white-British', or any other description.

We may feel 'British', act 'British' and speak English, but our skin colour prevents us from being deemed British. The fact that a person is of Somali, Asian, African, Chinese or African-Caribbean origin always comes first and the question of 'Britishness' follows afterwards. A lot of indigenous people don't see us as British and do not recognise that we can be both black and British, and they prefer instead to view blackness and 'Britishness' as two separate and non-related entities.

I think that my daughters' generation feels more British than my generation did, partly because they have no experience of moving to the UK; they were born in Britain and don't know anything else. Fayola and Safiya were born at the Leicester Royal Infirmary, two miles from our house and grew up in Leicester. The reality of their upbringing was formed by growing up in Leicester, the East Midlands and England and it forms a strong part of their identity, more so than Jamaica which they have only visited a few times on holiday yet it is almost impossible to convey this to the type of person who persists in asking them, 'No, where are you REALLY from?'.

My generation

I did eventually make some friends at school although it was very difficult. My friends were drawn either from

Fayola and Safiya at Fayola's BA graduation, July 2014.

among those children whose parents were non-racist or from among those children who didn't listen to their parents' rhetoric but chose to make up their own minds. I gradually gained friends and eventually they began to accept me and to invite me to their homes. I was sometimes invited to a meal called 'tea', which was an interesting but alien concept to me as in our culture tea is a drink, not a meal. However, I soon learned that 'tea' is equivalent to the late-afternoon meal that we call dinner. I have lived in the UK for over fifty years but I still cannot bring myself to describe my evening meal as 'tea'; it simply does not sit right on my tongue. I remember that my friends ate breakfast, dinner and tea as their three main meals, whereas we ate breakfast, lunch and dinner and sometimes a light snack called 'supper' in the late evening. My friends thought that made us very posh as they were not used to people talking about lunch and supper, but it was what we were used to and did not seem odd to us.

II   The Life Story of Dr Dorothy Francis

Another oddity about the meal that my friends called 'tea' was that it comprised sandwiches and cakes, eaten with one's fingers and washed down with cups of tea. This was very unusual to me as in our family all meals were eaten from plates using knives and forks and sandwiches were considered as snack food when travelling, rather than a meal. I was fascinated by the concept of tea and was always pleased to be invited to eat sandwiches and cake in the late afternoon as it was such a novel experience.

My friend Suzy (not her real name) invited me to tea a few times and eventually I plucked up the courage to invite her to my house for a meal. My mother was pleased as she knew I had been having a rough time at school and she was glad that I had a friend who was willing to come and eat with me. However the occasion turned into a horrible nightmare and I have never forgotten the repercussions of that meal.

To put this story into context it is necessary to consider what the food landscape of England was like in the 1960s in contrast to now. Today, England has a very multicultural approach to food and English people routinely eat Indian, Chinese, Thai, Jamaican, Japanese and Mexican cuisine as well as food from a host of other countries. In fact, we eat pretty much from every culture in the world and this willingness to embrace new food experiences is one of the better-known aspects of the UK.

However in the 1960s the diet was very constrained, much proscribed and quite boring. The country had been subject to rationing for many years and had been denied imports, so many people were already adults by the time when they first saw a banana or an orange, never mind what could be considered 'exotic' foods. Rationing came to an end in 1954 but even so many English people continued to eat plain and simple food and there was little variety in everyday fare. Things that we take for granted today such as avocados, rice, curry, mangoes, yoghurt, polenta, fresh coriander and most spices were almost unheard of to English families, although most of these were staples in immigrant households.

I invited Suzy home to eat and we enjoyed what was for our family a fairly normal meal of rice, meat cooked in a curry sauce and vegetables. Suzy ate her food with gusto and even had a second serving. After the meal we played and chatted and then she went home.

Ten minutes later, there was a loud knocking on the front door. Mum opened the door to find Suzy and her mother, Janice, on the doorstep. It turned out that as soon as Suzy had walked in Janice had immediately questioned her. None of them had ever eaten with a black family before, so they were curious to know what Suzy had been given to eat. On hearing Suzy's description of what she had devoured Janice instantly marched to our house to confront my mother.

Janice was enraged and began to yell and shout before we could even open our mouths, bringing our neighbours to their doorsteps to gawk with interest. She yelled, 'I've heard

II   The Life Story of Dr Dorothy Francis

about you black people. I've heard what savages you are, and how you are animals, but I decided that I wouldn't listen to what other people said but would show charity and make my own mind up. I thought I would give you the benefit of the doubt and so I sent my daughter to eat with you. And what do I find? I find it's true that you are savages after all. Everything I have heard about you is true'. We were astounded and stared uncomprehendingly at her as we could not understand what had brought on this savage onslaught of words. My mother said, 'What is the problem? What is the issue? Why are you shouting at us like this?'. Janice replied, 'How could you feed that to my daughter? It's disgusting! How could you? What kind of people are you?'. My mother had no idea what Janice was talking about and she asked her to calm down so we could ascertain the problem.

Janice continued to yell, and finally shouted, 'How could you feed my child maggots? That's disgusting! You are savages!'. Mum replied in vain that she had not served maggots to which the response was 'Suzy said you gave her a big pile of boiled maggots along with meat and vegetables'.

Mum asked Suzy to repeat her description of the food and it turned out that her response to Janice's question 'What did the black people give you to eat?' was 'They gave me meat in gravy with cabbage and maggots like what Daddy uses to bait his hook when he goes fishing but they were boiled'.

Mum finally understood that Suzy had never seen rice before and, at a loss to describe this unknown foodstuff, had likened it to the wriggling maggots that her father used when fishing! She explained to Janice that we had given Suzy rice to eat, not maggots. Janice responded, 'You must think I'm stupid. Everyone knows that you don't eat rice as part of a savoury meal; you only eat rice in rice pudding'. My mother said, 'In our tradition, we eat rice as part of our dinner'. Janice had never consumed rice except in rice pudding and had no idea that it could be served with curry or other accompaniments as part of a savoury meal. Mum took Janice to the kitchen, showed her the packet of rice and explained how rice is cooked. She showed Janice the remainder of the rice in the saucepan, and said, 'This is what we ate'. Suzy corroborated that the stuff in the pan was indeed what she had consumed. Janice finally calmed down and eventually apologised to my mother for her behaviour towards her and she left the house in a very chastened manner.

This story still saddens me and I find it difficult to understand why Janice believed so easily and implicitly that we would feed her daughter maggots. I understand that her exposure to bland English food, paired with the ongoing privations of World War Two, had limited her experience of food to the point that even as a grown woman she had no idea what rice looked like and had never eaten it as a savoury. However, what gave her the right to abuse us and call us savages without even hearing our side of the story?

Janice was our neighbour for many more years and I feel that thereafter she tried to

II The Life Story of Dr Dorothy Francis

overcompensate for her rudeness by being ultra-nice to us. She would always smile and wave if she saw us in the street and occasionally she sent cakes with Suzy when she came to tea. My mother would always tell Suzy that she was saving the cakes for later, but in reality they were thrown in the bin once Suzy had left as Mum could not bear to eat food from Janice after that incident when she had treated her so badly.

After that occasion it was a long time before I invited any of my friends to eat. Years later, I began to invite friends to my home, but I remember that these so-called friends would mock my food and refuse to eat it. I remember the mortification I felt when one of them said, 'I went to Dorothy's house yesterday and she was eating this stuff called cornmeal [polenta]. It looked and smelt disgusting and I didn't go near it'. These same people probably now serve polenta at dinner parties and hold forth on how 'absolutely marvellous' it is, yet at the time they felt that they had the right to laugh at my food and to embarrass me within my own home. This was very upsetting and I ceased to invite them to my house, although I would accept invitations to their homes if asked. I found the dishes that they ate, such as dripping on toast, grilled pork chops, rare meat and tripe and onions extremely unsavoury and couldn't understand their love of Marmite, Bovril and brown sauce – all of which I find repugnant – but I didn't mock them for eating these foods and couldn't understand why they felt that they had a right to laugh at my food. I felt that it was plain bad manners to mock someone's hospitality and no matter what negative thoughts I had about their food I would never have expressed these in front of them.

Some friends, such as Susan Williamson, enjoyed coming to my house and happily ate whatever was placed in front of them. Susan was very adventurous and open to trying new foods and she saw meal times at my house as a voyage of discovery. She often happened to drop in on Friday evenings as she knew that Mum baked on that day and Susan adored Mum's Caribbean fruit cake! I spoke with Susan in 2018 on the occasion of my mother's ninety-first birthday and she still mentioned how much she enjoyed coming to our house and that she still thought longingly of Mum's cakes!

Times have changed and nowadays, English people are likely to eat cornmeal, sweet potatoes, avocados and many of the foods that my friends used to mock me for eating. Indeed, I have been subjected to the novel experience of white people telling me how to cook a food item that they have recently discovered but which I have been eating all my life. One friend discovered avocados a short time ago and decided that she would show me how to cut one open; she was disgruntled when I demonstrated a more efficient and less dangerous way of doing so and remained annoyed even when I told her that I'd been eating avocados since I was a child. The same friend discovered mangoes in her forties and showed me her peeling method with great excitement. I was appalled at how much of the fruit she wasted, but refrained from showing her the way that I had been taught.

I must say that it is always an interesting experience when English people suddenly dis-

II The Life Story of Dr Dorothy Francis

cover a new foreign food and then try to tell me how it should be prepared and eaten, even though in all likelihood I will have eaten that foodstuff all my life! This new food knowledge can have dangerous ramifications though: I remember my university colleague Ralph discovered kidney beans during our second year and prepared a meal that included dried beans that he had only cooked for ten minutes. He was surprised when I told him that they were potentially toxic in that state and likely to cause vomiting unless boiled for much longer. This near-brush with illness did not prevent him from later criticising the way that I prepared rice whilst confessing that he had only learnt to cook it two months earlier! He insisted that I placed the cooked grain in a sieve and pour boiling water on it so that it could be served in a watery tasteless puddle and was really put out when I refused to listen to him.

Mum's 80th birthday in 2007. Fayola, Mum, Safiya, Kevin and myself.

The irony about the food escapades of my childhood is that English people thought we had savage practices but to some extent my mother and other African-Caribbeans thought the same of them! Certain of my friends used the kitchen sink for ablutions and washed babies and even dogs in it. They brushed their teeth at the kitchen sink and washed underwear and kitchen mops there, too. My friends allowed dogs and cats into the kitchen and dining room and sometimes the animals sat on their laps at meals and were fed from their fingers and allowed to lick the dining plates after the repast. My mother abhorred these practices and would not allow me to eat at these houses. If I was offered food I was expected to say that I was not hungry or that I was saving my appetite for my meal at home, but under no circumstance could I say yes to food from those homes. However, I liked English food and I would secretly eat at my friends' houses without telling my mother! I particularly liked to eat at my best friend Jane's house, and was able to get away with this as she lived a little way from our house.

Jane's family had a beautiful bathroom but her father brushed his teeth and washed his face and body at the kitchen sink and also shaved there every morning. The first time I visited Jane's house I asked her why her father's toothbrush, toothpaste, soap, and razor and shaving mirror were at the kitchen sink. She looked at me as if I were stupid and said, 'That is where he brushes his teeth and shaves his beard of course. Doesn't your father do that?'. I said, 'No, he doesn't, because we've got a bathroom'. She thought that I was being sarcastic, whereas I was merely being descriptive; but she didn't speak to me for a week, so after that I learnt to observe but not comment.

The fact that Jane's family used the kitchen sink for ablutions was a novelty to me, given that we were not even allowed to spit in the bathroom basin, never mind the kitchen sink! When we brushed our teeth we had to spit into the toilet; the washbasin was forbidden

II The Life Story of Dr Dorothy Francis

because my mother argued, 'How can you wash your face in the basin if you also spit into it?'. If my mother had known that Jane's father spat in the kitchen sink and shaved his beard there, she would not have let me eat in that house, and I would have been banned from visiting. However, I liked visiting Jane's house, so I made sure that Mum never knew!

Some incidents in my life

Everyday racism

I remember many incidents of everyday racism, and I always had to explain my culture, food and heritage, and was often forced to debunk myths, lies and misconceptions. We would be told, 'You don't have any language, you don't have any culture', not just by children but also adults, and we grew weary of explaining that we come from a rich and varied culture which stretches back over millennia.

I found the casual and ingrained racism that I experienced at school particularly difficult to deal with. If a stranger verbally attacked me in the street or elsewhere I felt able to argue and defend myself and was able to shrug it off more easily. What really hurt and was harder to bear was the behaviour of my school friends, who often attacked me but under the guise of friendship. Sometimes it proved difficult to tell my friends apart from my enemies, as they were both as hurtful. I found that my school friends did not task themselves to question perceived notions or misconceptions but simply parroted them, and they would look at me with blank faces or expressions of incredibility if I challenged them. This was very frustrating, and consequently I was always on edge, as I never felt that I was in a safe space when I was with my white classmates, even the ones that identified as my friends. I might be in a classroom, at play or at a party, when a maelstrom of racism would suddenly blow up around me without warning and I would be reminded – once again – that I was different. What's more, my friends' behaviour and comments emphasised that I was not only different, but also inferior, and they treated me as if I should be grateful to be in their company.

In secondary school, I had a friend called Esther who was from Trinidad and sometimes returned there for holidays. After one of these trips, she showed us photographs, including one of her family home, which was an elegant house with a pitched roof, beautiful wood fretwork and a long veranda dotted with chairs and tables. One of the white students looked at the photo and shouted, 'No, that's not your house – you're lying!'. Esther explained that she knew what her own house looked like, but the girl exclaimed, 'That can't be your house because you don't live in houses in your country. My mum says that you live in trees, like monkeys and swing from branch to branch'. We were too shocked to contradict this so were grateful when another white student spoke up, saying, 'That's not true! They don't live in trees!'. Esther and I were pleased to have someone on our side who could argue our case and settled down to hear the other girl put in her place. However, the second student went on to say, 'It's not true that they live in trees, but nei-

II The Life Story of Dr Dorothy Francis

ther is it true that they live in beautiful houses like that one. Everyone knows that black people live in mud huts with straw roofs and no toilets'. We had thought that she was coming to our rescue but instead she piled one stereotype on top of the other!

On another occasion my school friends and I were sitting in a circle during a lunch break trying on make-up. A lipstick was passed around and each girl outlined her lips with it. The lipstick eventually came to the girl next to me and after she had used it I reached out my hand. However, she leaned over and handed the lipstick to the girl on the other side of me. I said, 'Hey, what about me? You've missed me out!', to which she replied, 'Oh, that was deliberate; I didn't think you would be interested'. I asked 'Why not?', to which she responded 'Why on earth would you want to accentuate such fat rubbery lips? You don't want to put lipstick on those big lips, Dorothy; it would show them up even more and why would you do that?'. I was mortified, and angry and that episode stands out as one of the most humiliating incidents in my life. However, I am now in my fifties and I must admit that I have a certain feeling of justice when I observe white women of my age paying considerable amounts to have collagen and other fillers pumped into their thin lips to emulate my natural lip shape! I love my lips and their shape, and am pleased that they do not need any artificial enhancements. However it took many years to reach that state of mind as my friends made me feel so self-conscious about myself.

On another occasion, I complained to my school friends about the lack of suitable make-up for black people. It is still difficult to find suitable make up for people of colour in the UK today and was almost impossible in the 1970s. One of my friends said to me, 'What do you want to wear make up for? All black people look the same anyway with your flat noses and big lips, wearing make-up won't make a difference'. She swept my breath away with her stunning ignorance, but actually this was an everyday belief of many white people. My best friend Jackie looked nothing like me and we were very different in character, personality and outlook but teachers constantly called us by each other's names and when we remonstrated we would be told, 'Oh, you look the same', which was patently untrue. What it translated as was that the teachers could not be bothered to distinguish between us, preferring to view all African Caribbean people as an amorphous mass.

I used to enjoy Religious Education (P.E.) as I was fascinated by different religions and traditions across the world. One day we studied Buddhism and the belief in reincarnation. One of my friends turned to me and said, 'That sounds like a great religion for you Dorothy. I bet you would love that wouldn't you?'. I asked why, and she said, 'Because then you could come back higher up the ladder as a white person'. I said, 'Why would I want to come back as a white person? And why would that be a more elevated status?'. Her mouth gaped open and she said, 'Of course you would want to return as a white person! Why on earth would you come back as a black person if you didn't have to? Why would anyone choose to be black?'. She was rooted in an understanding that to be white was to exist on a higher plane and was incredulous that I did not subscribe to her belief.

75

II The Life Story of Dr Dorothy Francis

The interesting thing about these situations was that the people who sprouted this racist rhetoric were actually my friends, but they still felt able and entitled to put me down at every opportunity and seemed shocked and surprised when I remonstrated, accusing me of lacking a sense of humour or having a 'chip upon my shoulder'. I grew to hate that phrase because it was the standard response from a white racist to a black person should we ever seek to rebuke their behaviour regarding their behaviour or actions: 'Oh you're just too sensitive. You can't take a joke. You've got a chip on your shoulder'. They would wrap wounding words up as a 'joke' and use this to hide behind and absolve themselves of blame. Because the slur or taunt was hidden as a joke, if we objected they would seek to make the issue our problem for not having a sense of humour ('You black people are SO aggressive'), which disempowered us even more.

My experience of school was that some of my friends treated me with anthropomorphised interest in the same way that they would treat a pet monkey who had somehow discovered the faculty of speech. Others were more thoughtful and simply saw me as a friend and fellow student, but even they sometimes fell prey to racist attitudes; the incidents above were within my close social group. Other students treated me with outright hostility and used every opportunity to expound their racist views, and much of their behaviour was unchecked by the teachers, many of whom I felt shared these views. Very few of the students, even my so-called friends, actually treated me as just another human. It is hardly surprising that I hated my secondary school and that I left the establishment with a glad heart.

When I was growing up, English people – especially women – would often feel my hair, usually without my permission. Sometimes, I would be on the bus and would suddenly feel a hand in my hair. If confronted, the aggressor would say, 'Oh I just wanted to feel your hair to see if it is as soft as it looks or whether it is woolly and kinky'. They acted as if they had a right to put their hands in my hair and were often affronted when I told them not to abuse me by touching me without my consent. As far as they were concerned, they were showing an anthropological interest and I should submit to their ministrations. I found it infuriating and I hated the powerlessness of the situation wherein complete strangers thought that they had a right to assault me.

However, sometimes we had power in the situation as this next story illustrates. My mother's friend Edna was travelling on a bus when she overheard two women behind her talking about her hair, which she was wearing in an afro. The first one said, 'I'm going to touch her hair. It looks like candy floss and I want to see if it's as soft as it looks'. Her friend told her not to and the first woman asked, 'Why not?'. The second woman told her that it amounted to assault to touch someone's hair without permission, and reiterated that her friend should not put her hand into Edna's afro. The first speaker insisted that she was going to touch Edna's hair because it couldn't be deemed to be assault because, 'After all she's only a darkie so I'm sure that she won't mind', and with that she plunged her hand into Edna's hair and groped around, remarking on the silkiness and soft texture. Edna calmly turned around, looked the woman in the eyes and punched

II   The Life Story of Dr Dorothy Francis

her. The woman shrieked blue murder and swore that she would get Edna arrested for assault. However, various people had overheard the conversation between the woman and her friend and they all backed Edna, as did the bus driver who pointed out that the woman had initiated the assault by touching Edna's hair in the first place. The woman continued to yell and shout, so the driver asked her to leave the bus. I think that is one of the few occasions when a white person actually came out worse in such a confrontation with a black person and Edna dined off that story for many years!

What I recall about growing up in the 1960s and '70s is that we were often treated with contempt and like animals. It is almost impossible to argue with people who are in such depths of ignorance and any attempt to tell them that a variation in skin colour did not constitute a difference in species fell on deaf ears. Eventually, I gave up arguing with such people and learned to walk away from them and their ignorance.

However, it is not always possible to walk away and sometimes we have to stand our ground and argue. I remember being told, 'Well, you are not really human are you? You aren't like us so we don't have to treat you with respect'. This was said to me by a woman who had enrolled on a training programme that I was running in the 1980s, which shows that in some quarters little had changed. I had enrolled the student over the phone and she thought from my voice and name that I was white British. Her jaw dropped when we met and she refused to shake my hand. She stayed on the course but was outwardly racist and made my life a misery until I had enough and had a huge showdown with her. She spent more than an hour sprouting racist theory at me and I shot every argument down. She even maintained that I must have got my job by stealth, as everyone knew that black people are not intelligent enough to pass exams and obtain a degree!

The negative language, theories and overt racism that we faced were perpetuated on television and within popular culture in programmes such as 'Love Thy Neighbour', 'Rising Damp' and 'The Black and White Minstrel' show, all of which, along with many others, displayed racism and prejudice against women, gay people and minorities. So-called 'comedians' such as Bernard Manning made their living by lazily repeating and reinforcing racial and sexual stereotypes, and most people did not question these tropes. I particularly hated 'Love Thy Neighbour', which was a sitcom [situation comedy] about a black family and a white family who lived next door to each other. They hated each other and called each other names, with the white protagonist referring to his black neighbour as 'Nig Nog' which was a thinly veiled use of the very offensive 'Nigger'. In allowing this to be broadcast, the television company was effectively validating this abuse and this was reinforced by politicians, commentators and school-teachers, who simply shrugged it off as a 'joke' or 'banter'. I remember a teacher telling me that I was being ridiculously sensitive in objecting to being called 'Nig Nog' as it was just a term of endearment!

I hated going to school the day after 'Love Thy Neighbour' had aired and I know that other black students felt the same, because the programme gave free rein to school chil-

II   The Life Story of Dr Dorothy Francis

dren to repeat the racist rhetoric of the programme and to call us 'Nig Nog' all day. And to add insult to the injustice we were unable to argue back because if we did we were told it was just a joke and that nothing was meant by it; we just had a chip on our shoulders and lacked a sense of humour. After all, it was simply a term that was used in a sitcom, so why were we making a fuss?

In actuality, 'Nig Nog' was one of the worse terms that we were called, not just because it was highly offensive, but because the context within which it was used validated it in the eyes of society and prevented it from being recognised as the racist and offensive term that it was and removed our power to argue against it. During my childhood, I faced racist name calling on a regular basis and endured being called 'nigger', 'darkie', 'Sambo', 'blackie' and 'wog' more times than I can remember. By the time of the 1970s, it was becoming clear, even to the unenlightened in society, that it was not acceptable to call people such names. However, 'Love Thy Neighbour' validated this nomenclature by using in the name of 'comedy' and undermined much of the work in progress. Forty plus years on, I still shudder when I remember that programme and can still hear my fellow students chanting 'Nig Nog, Nig Nog' at me and other black students following the transmission of each episode.

Incidents of racism were almost every-day occurrences when I was growing up and I almost became immured to people asking to see my tail, feel my hair or touch my skin as if I was an animal in a zoo. Others would spit on their fingers and rub my skin to see if the pigment came away as they refused to understand that it was not a temporary dark tan but my skin colour.

Much has changed since I was a child, but there is still room for progress. Ten years ago, I visited a friend in Northumberland, which is a beautiful county with many splendid but isolated villages. Northumberland did not have centres of industry such as London, the Midlands, Liverpool and other metropoles, and so consequently did not attract much migration and has a very small minority ethnic population. My friend had a five-year-old daughter who sat next to me at the dinner table. After a few minutes I became aware that she was spitting on her finger and rubbing my wrist. She then exclaimed: 'Why doesn't it come off?'. I asked, 'What are you trying to rub off?'. She responded, 'The brown stuff on your skin so that you will be white like me'. I told her that my skin is naturally brown and that it was not possible to rub my colour off. She was amazed at this; I was equally amazed that she had no experience of people with different skin colours. She explained that everyone in her class at school was the same colour as her and the only time that someone was brown was if they were dirty. If they were dirty, their mum or dad washed them and they were white again. In rubbing my skin, she had been trying to rub the dirt away and make me clean. Her comments took me back to my 1960s classroom where I had encountered such reasoning and I was saddened that children still believed the same nonsense forty years on. I remember feeling that we had driven 200 miles in distance to Northumberland but had travelled back 40 years in time.

78

II   The Life Story of Dr Dorothy Francis

The incident reminded me of being at school, aged seven, sitting cross-legged on the floor for story time and being devastated by the story of *Little Black Sambo*, which my teacher read out without irony or consideration of my feelings. The story tells of a black toy that all the other toys in the playroom hate and refuse to play with because of his colour. However, one day he performs a heroic act to save one of the white toys and in the process, whilst running through the rain, his colour is washed off and he is revealed to be white underneath. Then the other toys love him, not just because of his act of heroism but because he is now white. The underlying message of the story was that black people should expect to be ostracised because of their skin colour, but that they could be 'redeemed' by becoming white. Stories like this and the prevailing attitude actually led to lots of black children washing themselves in bleach or even drinking it in an effort to become white and escape the taunts and cruelty that they endured.

I hated the story of *Little Black Sambo* and the licence that it gave for my school friends to taunt me mercilessly, not only on that day that our teacher read the tale but for years afterwards. They would tell me that I was black because I was dirty and if I washed myself it would come off. They spread the word that I was unhygienic because I never washed because, obviously, if I did wash I would become white like Sambo. The fact that I remained black meant that I was dirty and did not wash or shower. They propagated this myth for years, even beyond the time when sentient thought should have told them that it was untrue, but they enjoyed the distress that it caused me. The unwitting and innocent actions of my friend's daughter brought that experience rushing back and made me very uncomfortable.

My friend in Northumberland is a very liberal and well-travelled person but his daughter had only ever known that wholly white corner of Northumberland and therefore had grown up in a world where everyone around her was white and where darker-coloured skins were associated with dirtiness. This incident underlined once more why I am not comfortable in the British countryside and why I prefer to live in cities. I have experienced some staggering acts of racism outside of urban areas as often outdated attitudes persist and remain unchallenged, and it can be like stepping back in time.

I would like to say that these incidents have all been in the past, but I have experienced similar events throughout my life where English people have displayed startling ignorance about people of colour or have shared well-known 'facts' that have no basis in reality. I have been told that black people can't swim because our bones are too heavy – despite the fact that black swimmers have won gold medals at Olympic games – and have often been told that 'black people are not good at maths', notwithstanding that African-American women plotted the trajectories that put men on the moon and the Dogon of Mali plotted the complex movements of the heavens hundreds of years ago.

In my first year at university, I shared a house with a number of students including a woman called Suzie. I was filleting a fish one day when the knife slipped and cut my finger and Suzie exclaimed, 'Oh my goodness, Dorothy has red blood!' She honestly

II The Life Story of Dr Dorothy Francis

thought that black people had different coloured blood to white people and had never questioned that conviction. I pointed out to Suzie that the fish that I was preparing had red blood and that if she swatted a fly it would also have red blood. I asked her if she therefore placed me below a fly, given that she would expect a fly to have red blood but did not expect the same of me? She was very flustered and said that was not the case, and could only repeat that she had not expected black people to have red blood but could not explain why.

I was upset by this incident and also deeply disturbed that a university-educated young woman could believe such misguided nonsense about black people. I lived with Suzie for two years and over that time she displayed many astounding examples of ignorance in regard to black people (and life in general). Her comments made for interesting anecdotes but really made me wonder how she was able to exist in such a vacuum of obliviousness. When I was growing up, I ascribed many examples of ignorance to people being ill-educated, but I expected different when I went to university and was disappointed by the prejudice that I encountered from well-meaning students who did not recognise their racism.

Racial and sexual harassment at Heathrow Airport

On March 8th 1987 (which, ironically, was International Women's Day), I returned home to England and landed at Heathrow Airport following a visit to Florida and Jamaica. I queued at the red channel as I was carrying two additional bottles of rum and wished to pay the duty on them when, without warning, a customs official decided to wage an all-out attack on me. He questioned me aggressively, then searched my suitcases in full view of other passengers, exposing me and my belongings to the gaze of hundreds of people who passed through during his 90 minute exploration. He searched vigorously and thoroughly and was spiteful in his actions, wrenching the heels from my shoes and ripping the linings of my clothing. He used a ball-point pen to bore holes in the breadfruit, plantains and other food that I carried. Because my hands were shaking too much to operate the mechanism on my suitcase he ripped it open, sending the lock flying, and laughed at me when I protested.

One of my cousins is gifted at wood-carving and had made me some busts and wall hangings. The Customs Officer sent for a colleague and told him to drill them. I argued that he didn't need to do that as I had recently seen a television programme filmed at the same airport where an official had requested that a similar bust be x-rayed rather than drilled. He snapped at me that I should not tell him how to do his job and reiterated his order to drill the carvings to check whether or not they were solid. The carvings were brought back to me studded with holes and completely ruined. When I remonstrated the customs officer said 'Oh, you are just making a fuss. That's nothing that a bit of wood glue and paint won't fix'.

Having put his fingers into every pot of face cream, every bottle of shampoo or body lotion and even into my contact lens case, he then declared that I was to be subjected to a strip search. I became hysterical at this point but he informed me that I would have to undergo the strip search or I would not be able to leave. This, as I later learned, was untrue. I could have refused the strip search, in which case he would have had to have me arrested in order to make me comply. Had he done so I would have been able to sue for wrongful arrest, which would have strengthened my case. However, he chose to lie to me as he knew that I did not have an appreciation of my rights he and took advantage of my distressed state to force me into an illegal strip search.

My experience and 'Working together to end strip searching' 1993.

He moved me to a small room where, barely able to stand, I was subjected to a procedure over which I will draw a veil. I was so weak with crying that I couldn't even stand up. I collapsed onto the floor and the female customs officials that he had called into the room had to hold me up. Following the strip search he told me that I could pack my bags and leave. He gave me no explanation for his actions, nor did he offer an apology for subjecting me to such an ordeal.

I said to him, 'You racially and sexually abused me for over four hours. You falsely detained me and damaged my property, and yet you have not given me a single reason why you have treated me in this way'. He just shrugged and said 'What do you expect if you come off a plane from Jamaica carrying a Jamaican passport?'. The sheer callousness of his response still takes my breath away even after all these years and I find his actions and his words unforgivable.

I was too upset to talk about the strip search for some time but a few weeks later I recounted the story to a friend who was a journalist at the *Leicester Mercury* newspaper, who persuaded me that it needed to go public. The *Mercury* chose to print the story as a full front page article with a photograph and the report was taken up and syndicated by most of the national press. The story appeared in a number of women's magazines, including feminist publications such as *Spare Rib*, and also in mainstream periodicals such as *Woman* where I appeared on the front cover. The story was also covered in free supermarket publications, the *Guardian*, the *Jamaica Gleaner* and a host of other publications.

I suddenly found myself being interviewed by media from across the country, including Radio Leicester, the BBC World Service and a number of local stations, and I spoke at conferences about the injustices of strip searching. This was a particularly topical issue at that time, as strip search was being used extensively as a method of intimidation and

II The Life Story of Dr Dorothy Francis

control within Northern Irish prisons and there was a rising tide of public opinion against it.

I gave dozens of interviews and spoke at various conferences, but after a time I had to stop because each time I described what had happened it opened the wounds. It was years before I was able to speak about the events of that day without crying and I found it an exhausting and physically draining process to give interviews or stand on platforms as every time I did so I was plunged into depression. In the end, even through people were keen to hear my story, I declined all requests as I couldn't take the pain that revisiting and describing the event caused.

It was shortly after that that I took out British citizenship and applied for a British passport. I had formerly refused to swap my Jamaican passport for a UK document because I wanted to assert my right to be Jamaican, but I was too weakened by that experience to continue to fight. The experience of being unlawfully detained, watching my possessions being destroyed and stripping naked in front of strangers who stared at me with cold dispassionate eyes while prodding me was soul destroying. The search wrecked me mentally and it took a long time to recover. After that I thought, 'I don't know if I can fight this anymore', and I applied for a British passport in an attempt to escape the racist treatment meted out to me whenever I travelled on Jamaican documentation.

My children's generation

I am thankful that to a large extent my children have not had to deal with the overt racism that I have faced of people spitting on me in the street, calling me names and even resorting to violence. However, racism is still prevalent in the UK; it is just more covert and underground. It is codified and institutionalised and people find reasons to explain situations by saying that it is not racism but economics or social factors that drive their words and actions when, to be honest, it is just plain racism dressed up in a different package.

Fayola took a part-time job at a home for the elderly when she left school to earn extra pocket money whilst studying for her A-Levels. After a few days she remarked, 'Everybody who is in management at the home is white. Everybody who does the menial work and provides personal care is black, this includes the cleaners, the cooks and the carers; not a single white person undertakes that type of work'. She observed that the organisation was stratified into black and white and that the white managers had very little expectation of the black staff and remarked, 'I sometimes think they are surprised that I speak English and am capable of thought'.

Fayola received her GCSE results whilst she was working at the home, and one of the white managers said to her 'Did you get manage to pass any of your GCSEs then?'. The question that she asked betrayed her lack of expectations: she did not ask 'How did you do in your exams?' but instinctively assumed that Fayola would not have achieved any passes. Fayola said, 'Yes, I passed all my GCSEs, thank you', at which the manager was very surprised, and said, 'Really?! So what did you get?'. Fayola responded that she had passed all her exams at A or A star, and that she achieved the fifth highest marks in her school against an extremely competitive field. The manager was speechless; her jaw dropped and she literally took a step backwards in shock because she had not expected Fayola to do well. This went against her expectations of a sixteen-year-old black girl working in the kitchen of an old people's home, especially as she had never bothered to speak to Fayola previously and knew nothing of her aims and ambitions. She treated Fayola with a kind of wary suspicion thereafter, in the way that one might do on suddenly learning that a dog can speak!

Working at the home for a year taught Fayola a lot about the stratification of labour by colour, and the life opportunities of black people as opposed to white people, and it also reinforced her knowledge of the self-fulfilling prophecies that are loaded onto people of colour. She said that she never received so many negative comments about being black as she did at the care home, including from white residents who needed personal care but still screamed, 'I don't want that nigger to touch me'. Fayola would have to feed elderly, bed-ridden people who could not manage their own bodily functions or lift a spoon to their mouth yet still spewed abuse at her with every mouthful that they took. It is incredible to think that people harbour that level of racism, even towards people on whom they are wholly dependent, and I was sad that Fayola had to experience that hostility. I had hoped that my daughters would live in more enlightened times and was saddened to find that this is not necessarily the case.

The fourth generation

There is now a fourth generation within our family, who are the children of my nephew and niece. These children are of African-Caribbean descent but are British by birth, characteristics and lived experience. Their parents are themselves British born and primarily identify with the UK. This fourth generation is the first that does not have a direct contact with the Caribbean and this will no doubt shape their experience of growing up in the UK. I was born in Jamaica and experienced the challenges of moving to England, and in some ways still have an immigrant mentality to certain aspects of life. Fayola and Safiya grew up with me making regular visits to Jamaica to see family and friends and they accept this umbilical connection to the Caribbean. However, my great nieces and nephews have been born to my sister's children, who themselves were born and raised in Coventry. This fourth generation is firmly rooted in England; if they visit the Caribbean it will probably be as tourists rather than on family visits as the connections that bind us become weaker as older members of the family pass away and younger members strike out from Jamaica and make lives in different countries. To me this fourth generation is a 'British' generation and should be defined as such. However, the nature of the UK is that they will remain among the 'hyphenated people', as a famous writer described us, and will probably still be referred to as 'Black-British' rather than simply 'British' no matter how long they live here.

II The Life Story of Dr Dorothy Francis

African and African-Caribbean culture and heritage

I learnt about my heritage from my mother and taught myself additional information from books, films and talking to others. Black History Month has played a large part and books by writers such as David Olusoga, David Dabydeen, Afua Hirsch and Ivan Van Sertima have been invaluable. We were taught little of our history or culture at school. In fact the only time African heritage was mentioned was in relation to slavery and the teaching was out of context with no mention of how slavery enriched the UK and other countries or the havoc that it wrought on African countries. I remember that cringeinducing lessons about slavery were followed by merciless bullying by my fellow students, who delighted at chanting 'slave' at me and I also remember my anger and impotence at being unable to defend myself.

I don't recall anything positive ever being said about being black at school. Even the teachers perpetuated the myth that people of African descent had never achieved anything. In fact, I remember one teacher seriously considering the possibility that aliens had descended to earth and built the pyramids. It was stunning that he could more readily accept the possibility of aliens coming to earth than of Africans having the skills and ingenuity to build complex structures, but this is the kind of attitude that I faced throughout my school days.

It makes a huge difference to the confidence and esteem levels of black children and young adults when they discover the long and proud history of the African nations from which they are descended and also learn about the great achievements of people of colour in the Caribbean, USA and across the world.

I believe that black history should be taught as part of the curriculum as an ordinary aspect of history, rather than being put aside for a special month. It should simply be interwoven within history, geography, science and other lessons as a norm. So in biology children would learn that blood transfusions were perfected by African-American scientist Charles Drew. In geography they would learn that an African-American man, Matthew Henson, was the first person to reach the North Pole. In history they would hear that Nigerian and Ghanaian kings ruled over peaceful agricultural and merchandising countries and that Africans sailed to America many years before Columbus. In politics and social science they would study the works of Jamaican-born Marcus Garvey [12] and hear about the resistance of Nanny of the Maroons and her brothers. Science lessons would highlight that in 1753 Benjamin Banneker built the first working clock that was capable of striking the hour, and that his knowledge of astronomy resulted in a successful series of almanacs. In studying literature they would read Jamaica Kincaid, Toni Morrison, Kerry Young and Alice Walker, not as 'black literature', but simply as literature.

I do not feel that people of colour will be fully accepted and integrated into western societies until our experiences and culture are normalised instead of being seen as 'exotic'

II The Life Story of Dr Dorothy Francis

or outside of conventional experience. It is important that black people know of their history but it is also equally important that white people are taught this too. Much of the aggravation that I suffered as a child and young adult was from white people whose only experience of Africa and people of African descent was through the lens of Tarzan films or similar racist depictions that they believed to be 'history' and did not question. They did not know of the greatness of the African nations and their past and present contributions to the world of science, medicine, commerce, research, exploration and arts, and never for a moment questioned the factors that had brought black people to the UK.

Our African heritage

The enslaved Africans brought their culture, language, traditions and ways of cooking to the Caribbean and continued them as much as they were able. It was difficult for them to maintain African cultural traditions as the slave masters sought to stamp out such links so that they could promote disparity and keep control; as a result language, food and religion were driven underground. However some aspects continue into modern-day times and connect us to Africa.

Many African words survive in Jamaican patois, for instance Jamaicans use the Akan or Twi word 'potoo' for an owl, and the word for a ghost, 'duppy', is derived from the Akan word 'adopi'. Anansi is the Akan word for spider and has been retained in Jamaica via the very popular stories of Anansi the spider man whose tales of deviousness are woven into Jamaican folklore. Jamaicans use the Akan words 'doti' for ground or earth, 'poto-poto' for muddy, and 'Afu' for yam. The Efik language provided the word 'mbakára' which became 'backra' in Jamaica, and means 'white man'. The Fula language of Ghana supplied the much-loved word 'juk', which means to 'poke or stick', whilst Ibo contributed the words 'himba' for a yam root, 'obeah' to mean doctoring, 'soso' which means only, and 'unu' which is the plural of the word 'you'. 'Dukunu', a dessert similar to bread pudding which is steamed in banana leaves, derives from the Akan word which is spelt in the same way (and the dish is prepared in identical ways in Jamaica and Ghana). Many other words of African origin nestle within the Jamaican language and provide a direct link to Ghana, Nigeria, Benin, The Gambia and other countries from which African-Caribbeans originated.

It is comforting that so much has survived and that we are, albeit in a small way, connected to our African heritage. Many older African-Caribbean people used to be ashamed of their African heritage because they were schooled by the colonist powers to believe that Africans were dirty, shiftless people who lived pagan lives until they were blessed with the civilising presence of Europeans. Our cultural heritage was denied us, and the colonists made every effort to stamp out similarities of language, religion and culture that might bind the enslaved people together. However much of it survived via underground methods which nurtured and protected the songs, language, customs and food. Nowadays African-Caribbeans are keen to seek African connections and we are proud to make links between who we are now, as African-Caribbeans and where we have

85

II   The Life Story of Dr Dorothy Francis

come from as people of African descent. In relation to this I chose to give my children African names as a way of seeking to recognise and honour their heritage; they are both aware of the meaning and history of their names and are reminded of their heritage through the names that they carry.

The slavers had a deliberate policy of breaking families up and would send family members across an island, or disperse them to different islands. Husbands and wives, brothers and sisters would be scattered across vast distances because this fostered isolation and engendered disjointed communities. Africans who spoke the same or similar languages were separated and all enslaved people were required to speak in English and forbidden their own languages on the pain of death. These methods of control lessened the chances of rebellion and were rigorously enforced by the slave-owners, to the detriment of the language and culture of the enslaved people. This led to a fragmentation of society and certain familial values which still permeate Caribbean culture to some extent.

Many African-Caribbean people share a common heritage, even though we were dispersed across a million square miles. We were forcibly discouraged from maintaining our own languages, culture or traditions and made to adopt the customs and speech of the slave masters, and so we learned to speak English, Dutch, Spanish or French and took on Christianity and western dress. However, certain traits remained and these bind us as people of African descent. My father was born in Jamaica, as were his fore parents before him, yet his features placed him firmly in Nigeria or Ghana. I look very much like my father and this has been a source of confusion and sometimes hilarity for much of my adult life, as Ghanaians and Nigerians frequently assume that I am from their country and are puzzled as to why I do not speak a local language. I have had Nigerians vehemently argue that I am Nigerian and that I am trying to deny my culture by saying otherwise and they refuse to accept that I have never set foot in Nigeria. Then again, I have also had the same argument with Ghanaians who have frequently told me that they can even tell me what town or village I am from!

As African-Caribbean people, we don't have the certainty of knowing our origins, because we were stolen from our homelands and were not supplied with documentation. African-Caribbean people are trying to get back to their heritage and are seeking it through learning African languages, through the names that we choose for ourselves and our children, and sometimes by relocating to Africa, especially Ghana, Ethiopia and The Gambia. I would like to take a DNA test to ascertain where my family originated as I am fascinated to know where I came from originally and would love to find out whether Nigerians or Ghanaians are right when they say that I belong to their country, or whether, indeed, I come from a completely different place.

Black History Month

Black History Month was introduced to Britain in 1987, at a time when the status of black people in the UK was still being openly debated and when the National Front was demanding the deportation of all people of colour. Police harassment of black people was rife and almost standard, and had sparked massive civil unrest in many British cities. Black children were stereotyped as low achievers, subjected to a self-fulfilling prophecy of failure, and told that their problems lay with their 'bad attitudes' rather than within an institutionally racist system.

Black History Month provides an opportunity to show a history that existed but which had been hidden and suppressed. It allows black people a platform to showcase positive models of our heritage, history and achievements. It should be noted that we use 'black' as a term to describe and politically and socially unite people of African and African-Caribbean/American origins. The term is not a description of ethnicity or nationality – one is not black in terms of origin but it is a necessary device to encompass the wealth of peoples from the Caribbean, Africa, USA and elsewhere, who might be defined within this categorisation.

The intention was that the annual month-long celebration would highlight the role that Britain played in colonising other countries, but would also highlight the positive contributions black people have made, and continue to make, to the UK. Black History Month would attempt to show that black people's involvement in the UK did not start with the arrival of the Empire Windrush ship in 1948, and would allow us to tell the stories of Claudia Jones, Ricky Stennett, Phyllis Wheatley, Ira Aldridge, Mary Seacole, Bill Morris, Margaret Busby, Walter Tull, Dr Shirley Thompson, Harold Moody, Kanya King, Akhala, and many more, past and present, who have made tremendous contributions to UK society. The talks, exhibitions, plays and educational events would allow us to focus on the colour that was missing from British history and to recognise the involvement and achievement of black people in British life.

The intent of Black History Month was to provide information and raise awareness so that black history was on show because so much of our history is deeply buried, denied or lost. Black History Month seeks to mitigate this by shining a light on the achievements and contribution of people of African and Caribbean descent who have fashioned British history and along the way this has come to encompass events such as the MOBO (Music of black Origin) Awards, which celebrate the influence of black music on most other musical forms.

I am ambivalent about Black History Month and expressed this ambivalence when I was asked to write a piece for *Lost Legends*, a book produced by Serendipity Arts in 2017 to commemorate 30 years of Black History Month. The book comprises 30 articles by 30 people who live in Leicester and it contains different, and sometimes polarising, views on the effectiveness or otherwise of Black History Month. A short extract from my contribution is reproduced below.

Black History Month divides my loyalties and fosters a duality of pleasure and re-

II   The Life Story of Dr Dorothy Francis

sentment within me. I love theatre, dance, poetry, readings and debate so revel in the opportunity to satiate myself on a month long culture fest. But at the same time I feel like a binge eater greedily shoveling in as much as I can during a very short window before the treats are whisked away from me again. There is a sense of feast and famine; 11 months without and then an embarrassment of riches for 31 days.

My discontent stems from the fact that I believe that every month should be Black History Month. Why is our culture confined to a showcase of a few weeks per year? Can one single month contain the outpouring of art, culture, inventions and talent that are the contribution of people of African descent? Is it enough against a tidal wave of whiteness that threatens to sweeps away our history and culture? Examining the other side to the argument I am aware that presently the alternative would be grim should we cease to celebrate Black History Month as this would probably relegate the achievements of black people even further into the shadows.

Black History Month is a wonderful concept but its work will be done when it is no longer needed because the contribution of black people is so fully integrated.

7 My higher education and career

Dorothy's first job was at the Telephone Exchange in Coventry. She left that job to pursue a degree at Birmingham Polytechnic. Following various roles she is now the CEO of a business advice centre. She recalls her job at the General Post Office (GPO),[13] her higher education, and explains her present job and the co-operative movement in detail.

At the General Post Office

I had placements in two companies after I left school; the first was at Standard Motors in Berkswell and the second was at Clews Ivens estate agents on New Union Street in Coventry. They were both training schemes and were useful for introducing me to the world of work. I left Clews Ivens and enrolled at Henley College to obtain three A-Levels and after I had completed that course of study I decided to work for a year before starting a degree course.

I was fortunate to obtain a job at the General Post Office – usually referred to as the GPO – which was the primary telecommunications company in the UK at that time. I started work at the GPO in late 1979. At that point telecommunications essentially meant telephones because the advent of faxes, the internet, and other such communications were very much in the future. The GPO belonged to the state and was the principal telecommunications organisation in the UK. My role was a telephonist, based at the telephone exchange in Coventry city centre, and I worked on the operator service, directory enquiries and emergency service lines. I still remember the thrill of my first day; I had been issued with a pass card and felt so important as I flashed my permit to step through the gates and into the enormous and imposing building.

II   The Life Story of Dr Dorothy Francis

My friends and family were impressed when I got the job because the GPO was considered to be a high-class, quality employer and this was in the late 1970s when people of colour were still breaking into white-collar jobs and were not normally employed in such roles. There were more than 90 telephonists on the day shifts and I was the only black person. The common perception was that a job at the GPO or 'Post Office' was a job for life; it wasn't unusual for people to start work in the organisation at 16 and retire at 60. Basically if you got a job with the GPO people felt that you had made it and would never have to worry again about employment.

My mother was delighted that I was employed in a job where I wore nice clothes to work, wasn't on my feet all day and was reasonably paid. My mother and father both did jobs that were liable to leave them dirty at the end of their shifts. My father worked in a car factory and his overalls were often covered in oil and grime. My mother worked as a cleaner and sometimes had to deal with unsavoury tasks. These jobs did not command a great deal of respect and they certainly didn't get to wear suits and white shirts to work so they were pleased when I got a 'white-collar' job.

I worked on the operator service, helping people who were having difficulty connecting calls and on the directory service which people rang to obtain telephone numbers. There was no charge to the public for these services, so people rang them freely and we were busy day and night. I also did shifts on the 999 emergency line, connecting callers to police, ambulance and fire services. I worked with about 50 other people – mostly women – on each shift and we got on fairly well. They thought I and another young woman called Tina were posh because we had A-Levels; they were not a requirement of the job and most people got by without them. They also thought that I was posh because I spoke well and had clear diction – the result of endless drilling by my mother, who insisted that I spoke 'proper' English at all times. This stratagem paid off in assisting me to obtain a job where it was important that I made myself easily understood.

I think my salary was about £60 per week, which was not an enormous amount, but that went a long way in those days; my rent at that time was £10 per week. I worked hard in the job and received many commendations from customers. I enjoyed talking to people all day and liked assisting them by supplying numbers or connecting their calls and I also enjoyed the camaraderie with the other telephonists.

It was wonderful to be financially stable, but I wanted a career rather than a job and did not feel that I would achieve that aim at the GPO. The telephonist role was fairly low down in the ranks and I could not see progression routes within the organisation so I made the difficult decision to leave so that I could invest in building a career. I felt that securing a career, rather than a job, would assist me to obtain employment wherever I went, and this mattered to me, hence my decision to leave what many considered to be a 'job for life'. It was a calculated gamble, because on one hand if I stayed at the GPO I had a job and a steady income and the possibility of working my way up the hierarchy. However, by choosing to study for a degree I knew that I would have to embark on three

II   The Life Story of Dr Dorothy Francis

years of study followed by a search for a job at the end of that time. It was a risk, but one that I was prepared to take as I felt that a degree would provide a firmer foundation for a future career and generate greater earning opportunities.

I made the right decision because leaving the GPO to go to university opened a great many doors for me and exposed me to a different type of lifestyle which would not have come about if I'd remained at the telephone exchange. In addition, soon after I left the GPO was de-nationalised and became British Telecom. The organisation underwent tremendous changes within a very short period of time and thousands of redundancies were made; I think that there is a high possibility that I would have been made redundant had I stayed. I left at about the right time, whilst the GPO was still a slightly old-fashioned, paternalistic organisation with a 'jobs for life', culture and before the decidedly cut-throat practices, mass redundancies and uncertainties of the new British Telecom regime.

My manager was very angry when I left. She said, 'You are a good telephonist, you are one of our best. You could stay here and work your way up the ladder. You are a fool to throw away a well-paid job to go to university to live on a grant for three years. You don't even know if you will get a job when you leave university, but you could have a job for life here'. My last few weeks whilst I served my notice were very uncomfortable because she was angry with me for resigning.

Moving into higher education

In the 1970s it was the practice on leaving school to either go into work, learn whilst working via an apprenticeship or to follow vocational training at a further education college. Only a rare few went onto university. It wasn't necessary to go onto higher education as jobs were easily available and it was standard practice to train employees on the job so that they could rise up the ranks. There was a greater culture of on-the-job and vocational training; it was possible to start a job with no experience, be trained to a high level and achieve promotion and advancement, so university was not a norm: around ten per cent of young people attended university as opposed to approximately 50 per cent nowadays. It was even more unusual for African-Caribbeans to attend university, and choosing to do so made me unique amongst my friends, who were very surprised that I chose that route, because it wasn't something that was part of our experience.

Even though I was always in the top stream at secondary school the idea of A-Levels and a degree was not suggested to me; it was simply understood that I would leave school after my O-Levels. This was the same for most of my peers – black or white – as it was the norm at that time only to be educated to secondary school level and no one told me that university was an option.

The first person who talked to me about studying for A-Levels and a degree was a community worker called Ricky Stennett. I knew Mr Stennett well as he worked for the local

II The Life Story of Dr Dorothy Francis

Race Equality Council [14] and had assisted me in a number of ways, including finding me accommodation when I left home at sixteen. He kept a watching brief on me as he was concerned for me out in the world by myself.

I bumped into Mr Stennett by chance on the Friday that I finished my placement at Clews Ivens estate agent and I was wondering what to do with my life. Mr Stennett bought me a coffee and sat with me to discuss options. He was astounded to find that I had a clutch of O-Levels but had never considered going into higher education. He asked me why this was. I replied that people like me did not do A-Levels and degrees; they were the province of white, middle class children. Mr Stennett was shocked by this and spent two hours over rapidly cooling coffee explaining to me why people like me could, and, indeed, should undertake A-Levels and study for a degree. On that Friday afternoon in August when I met Mr Stennett I had no intention of enrolling for A-Levels, but by the end of the afternoon I had been convinced and less than a week later I was sitting in my first class.

Mr Stennett made it his job to know about educational opportunities and he was able to guide me towards a course at Henley College, a few miles from where I lived in Coventry, which offered suitable courses. I attended the enrolment day the following Monday and found that the college was piloting a programme of study that enabled students to study three A-Levels in one year instead of the usual two. This suited me because my domestic and financial situation did not allow me to study for two years and the one year option allowed me to enrol for A-Levels in English, History and Social Economics.

I often say that Mr Stennett was my 'guardian angel' as he had a habit of turning up when I was most in need and he always fashioned a response to my problems. He was a wonderful man who truly cared for the young people that he worked with and he had a seminal influence on my life. If he had not taken time out of his life on that Friday afternoon to sit with me and convince me of my abilities I would not have enrolled to study A-Levels and would probably not have achieved the other qualifications that I now hold. Mr Stennett was the first person to really show me what I could achieve and he took me beyond what my mother was able to introduce me to as she only understood the educational system to a secondary level. Mr Stennett believed in me and I owe him a great deal.

I faced a lot of adversity over the nine months that I studied for my A-Levels, and it was not always easy to concentrate on learning and sometimes became very difficult indeed. I left home at sixteen and was responsible for my own welfare so whilst studying I also had to pay rent and bills, buy food and generally manage my life. I was dependent on claiming benefits during the nine months that I studied for A-Levels. As I had no other form of income I had an agreement with the benefits office that I could claim benefit as long as my studies occupied less than eighteen hours a week and I was otherwise available for work. I stuck to this agreement, but the benefits office did not. The department that I had the agreement with was a different department to the one that paid the benefits

II The Life Story of Dr Dorothy Francis

and it seemed that they did not communicate with each other as my benefits were with-held with alarming regularity. I should have received a cheque, commonly known as a 'Giro', each Friday but many weeks it did not arrive. I was forced to trek to the benefits office – often I could not even afford the bus fare – to argue with the staff. If I was lucky I received an interim payment to tide me over the weekend, but often they told me to re-turn on Monday to pick up the Giro.

I lived from hand to mouth so was often penniless by Friday and therefore faced many weekends without a penny to my name. It was a grim time but I endured as I had my eye set on the prize of three A-Levels and knew that if I got through the nine months I would reach my goal. Had I embarked on the standard two-year course I don't think that I would have completed the programme of study, because I could not have endured that situation for so many months and would have been worn down with arguing with the so-cial security office. I believe that my life has been guided by many instances of serendip-ity, and the existence of the pilot project that allowed me to study three A-Levels in one year was one such instance. The course ran that year but was not repeated again, so thanks to Mr Stennett I was in the right place at the right time.

I faced many issues which affected my ability to study, and it was a constant battle to continue my A-Levels. I couldn't afford to eat properly and could barely meet the costs of my books. I lived in substandard accommodation and faced regular financial censure from the benefits office and was without money for long periods of time. I was twice homeless during the nine months that I studied for my A-Levels and in one of the places that I lived I was attacked by my landlady who tried to kill me and was only prevented from doing so by the quick-wittedness of Mr Stennett. He turned up by chance to visit me and entered into the middle of a farcical situation in which my landlady was chasing me with a bottle that she intended to hit me with. When that failed, she began to stran-gle me. Mr Stennett called the police, who restrained my assailant and escorted me from the premises. The police were shocked by the ferocity of her attack and I was left badly shaken. I left without many of my possessions and found myself homeless. Mr Stennett took me to his home and I lived with him and his wife for three months until I was able to find other accommodation.

All of this was a lot for a seventeen year old to deal with and there were times when I felt like giving up. However, Mr Stennett had ignited within me a desire to study and had shown me that a brave new world existed within my reach, so I persisted even when times were hard. It was gruelling to undertake three A-Levels in one year but converse-ly it was the best thing for me because I would not have been able to sustain two years of study.

Having completed my exams I decided to take a year out of studies before moving on to a degree and it was at this point that I found employment at the telephone exchange. I enjoyed the job there, but left in order to enrol onto a degree programme as described above.

II   The Life Story of Dr Dorothy Francis

I enrolled at the institution that is now called Birmingham City University, which at that time was called the City of Birmingham Polytechnic. Polytechnics offered higher diplomas, undergraduate degrees and post graduate education (Masters and PhDs) similar to universities with a focus on providing education, especially in science and technology, that was more relevant for professional working. However, most polytechnics expanded to include humanities departments, which taught courses such as English Language and Literature, which is the degree that I selected.

The Further and Higher Education Act of 1992 allowed all polytechnics to adopt the title of 'University', and Birmingham Polytechnic became Birmingham City University in 2007. In my home-town of Coventry, the Lanchester Polytechnic became Coventry University, and in Leicester the Polytechnic was renamed De Montfort University.

I enjoyed my degree, although I would have liked to have studied more literature by people of colour and women; my course was dominated by white male writers and I was frustrated by the lack of representation. In addition I also felt very lonely at times as most of my classmates and my housemates were white and I was sometimes subjected to casual or spiteful racism, which was hard to fight, especially as I did not always have the support of the university in challenging these injustices.

English literature and me

A complaint that I had about my degree was that the literature we studied was very male and Eurocentric. There are great writers from every continent, but we were not introduced to writing from across the globe. We read mainly from Chaucer up to the 1960s and I don't recall reading many black or female authors at all. We studied *The Invisible Man* by Ralph Ellison [15] and a bit of James Baldwin,[16] but we didn't read much literature by people of colour or women. When I finished my degree I sought out writings by women and authors from different cultures for my own pleasure, as I wanted to read literature that reflected my life experience and that of the diverse community around me. This thirst to introduce myself and others to diverse literature lead me to set up Radix bookshop to bring books from women and people of colour to a wider readership.

I enjoyed the experience of studying for my degree but it lacked certain crucial elements and I was driven to fill those gaps myself. However, it was a good learning experience and I made some lifelong friends at university.

I am sometimes asked why I did not study business at university, given that I have spent my entire career in the business world. However at the age of eighteen when I chose my degree I could never have envisaged a life in business. This was not presented to me as an option; the careers advisers that I encountered did not have that expectation of me and I did not consider that route. I didn't know anyone who was in business and the idea of studying for such a qualification was alien to me. I think I had a perception that business wasn't for Black people or girls or working class people, and I fitted all three of

93

II The Life Story of Dr Dorothy Francis

those categories. Even if the option had been put in front of me I would probably have rejected it due to an element of self-fulfilling prophecy as I would not have felt that this subject was right for me.

I have no regrets about studying English Language and Literature, as I love the subject and it has held me in good stead over the years. I write an awful lot of contract bids in my job, so good writing skills come in very handy! Doing an English degree was a good foundation for me in terms of the communications that I deal with in everyday life.

I chose to study English because I enjoyed the subject and always excelled in it at school despite the fact that I had had to learn how to speak Standard English when I came to the UK. English is the official language of Jamaica, but in reality I spoke Jamaican creole or patois, which is a combination of English and African languages (mainly Akan) with influences from Arawak, Spanish, Indian and other cultures. Patois is based on English but has a different grammatical structure, as well as different word placements and inflexions, which makes it far different from the language spoken in England. My introduction to formal English took place when I moved to England, and it was an eye-opening experience.

I took to the English language and loved reading, so by the time I reached secondary school I was the number one scholar in my class at English, a position that I maintained for five years, coming first each year in the annual exams. I also loved history and routinely came top of the class in that subject too. Nothing much has changed over the years. I still love researching history and losing myself in books.

I did not have much guidance regarding my early career so when it came to selecting a degree I did so based on what I enjoyed and what I was good at (which I suppose are quite good reasons). I also chose English because it was a good basic degree that wouldn't necessarily confine me to a particular area and would allow me to branch out into a variety of careers.

Midway through my English degree I decided that I wanted to be a community social worker, and so pursued this option on leaving university by enrolling onto a social work conversion course I applied for a place at the University of Warwick to study for a combined MA and social work qualification. The course was gruelling, as students were expected to obtain an MA and a social work qualification in twelve months instead of the usual two or three years allowed for such study, and this involved working 40 hours a week from October to the following September without a break for holidays. However, the interview board felt that I had the capability to undertake the study and offered me a place and a start date. I was obviously not destined for this route as three months later the university board overturned the offer as they decreed that places should only be offered to graduates with social science degrees due to the punishing nature of the course. They felt – perhaps rightly – that my in-depth knowledge of Shakespeare and metaphysical poets did not equip me for a strenuous social work course! I can joke about it now

II   The Life Story of Dr Dorothy Francis

but at the time I was devastated as I had set my heart on studying to be a social worker and particularly wanted to study at Warwick University.

I had applied for the place on the social work course in October and attended the interview in January. The place was withdrawn in late May which meant that it was too late to be considered for another place that academic year. The upshot was that I would have to wait until October of the following year to start a degree course, which left a 14 months hiatus from the end of my conversion course to the beginning of possible MA studies.

Setting up a mobile bookselling business called Radix

It was just at this point, when I was at a very low ebb, that some friends asked me to join a bookselling co-operative that they were setting up. Their aim was to sell books written by African, African-Caribbean and Asian authors. This type of literature was very difficult to obtain at this time and often had to be imported. My friends wanted these books to be readily available and had come together to form a collective to source and sell books by people of colour. Had they asked me to join two weeks previously, I would have said 'no', due to my plans to undertake an MA. However, given that my university place had been withdrawn, I was at a loose end and so agreed to join the collective for the next 14 months until I began my projected programme of study.

I was curious as to why they had asked me to join the proposed enterprise, as I knew little about business; but they explained that these skills could be taught and they felt that I would have an aptitude for business. Also they wanted someone who loved literature and books and would bring this passion to the enterprise.

I told my friends that I knew nothing of co-operatives and didn't know how they operated. They explained that this was not an issue as long as I was open to a way of working that encompassed democratic control, equal ownership and participation, and offered a fair return on labour. They explained that we would jointly own the business and would be stakeholders in the business, working for ourselves and the community rather than for the private gain of shareholders. This method of doing business was a revelation to me and was music to my ears. It made perfect sense and answered many of the questions that I had posed about different models of doing business. For a long time I had sought an area of work where I could make a difference – this was one of the reasons why I was attracted to social work. I wanted to be part of an organisation where my input made a difference – where ethics, principles and values were integral to the mission, and where I could assume ownership of my work and its output. I was delighted to find that co-operatives fitted this need and it was an enlightening experience.

I wondered how we would gain the skills to run a business effectively, whereupon my friends explained that they were in contact with an organisation called a Co-operative Development Agency, usually called a CDA, which gave free business advice and training to people setting up in business. There was a network of CDAs across the country at

95

The Life Story of Dr Dorothy Francis

that time with one in most major conurbations and about twelve in London. Our local CDA was in Coventry. A few days after the initial discussion with my friends, we went to our first meeting with the CDA and sat down with our business adviser to discuss our idea. I was impressed by the knowledgeable staff who introduced us in a calm and effective way to the vagaries and demands of running a business. They assisted us to plan the business, advised us on establishing viability, sourced a small grant that allowed us to visit similar bookshops in Leicester, Birmingham, London and Milton Keynes, and held our hands along the way as we grew in confidence and came to better understand the business world in general and our book selling business in particular.

With the assistance of the CDA we were able to set up a mobile bookselling business called Radix, which travelled to festivals, schools and events to familiarise people with books from Africa, Asia and the Caribbean. This was my introduction to business and to co-operatives and I felt that I had found my niche. I realised that I had been seeking a co-operative way of working for many years but had just not realised that it existed or that it was possible to work in a way that embraced ethics, values and sustainable business. Once I discovered the co-operative model I was hooked. I was also extremely impressed by the work of the CDA and promised myself that I would apply for a job at that or a similar agency should one arise. I worked for the bookshop for a little while, but this did not provide sufficient income so I became the area manager for an organisation that trained women in personal and business skills to equip them to set up their own enterprises or to return to the workplace. I really loved that job and enjoyed seeing the change in the women as they blossomed and grew in confidence.

Sometime later an opening became available at the Leicester and County CDA and my application for the job was successful. I was delighted to become a CDA worker and to work within the co-operative field and this delight in my work has never diminished. I consider myself lucky to have worked for so many years in a job that I love and where I have a positive impact on the lives of so many people. I came into this area of work by accident but have stayed in it through love of the co-operative movement and the great changes that it brings.

CEO of a business advice agency

I started work at the Leicester and County CDA as a business development officer and after some years I became the deputy manager. I assumed the post of Chief Executive Officer in 2000 and have remained in that role since then. Along the way the agency changed its name to the Co-operative and Social Enterprise Agency – usually known as CASE – to reflect the social enterprise structure that emerged in the late 1990s. CASE promotes co-operative working and is a co-operative business in its own right – this is an important part of our ethos, as we believe in practising what we preach. Being a co-operative gives us strength and unity as a business and also enhances our integrity amongst our clients. We offer advice, support and training to assist people to set up social businesses – these are defined as co-operatives, social enterprises and other businesses

II The Life Story of Dr Dorothy Francis

which operate to make a profit, but also have social, ethical and environmental causes at the heart of what they do.

CASE is not a funded organisation, so we bid for contracts to obtain funds to finance our operations. This involves a lot of paperwork and is perhaps my least favourite aspect of my work but it is an essential element of my job. I play a lot of roles: as well as being the Chief Executive Officer I am a business adviser and mentor and guide new and established businesses. I am a qualified teacher and I write and deliver training courses in a variety of subjects including human resources, marketing, leadership and management. I regularly deliver talks and lectures in universities and other institutions and am an Entrepreneur in Residence at the University of Leicester guiding and supporting students to establish their own businesses. My job is challenging, but every day is different and interesting. In my personal time I mentor people to achieve greater success in their personal and business lives and gain great personal satisfaction from helping people to achieve personal and professional change.

I have quite a lot of control over my work which is important to me as this is still something that women – especially black women – rarely achieve. Having power and ownership over my job is crucial to me and working in a co-operative enables this. I do a job that I enjoy and which has meaning and value and I know that I am lucky to work in such a setting. CASE is a co-operative, which means that we are all co-owners who share co-operative ethos and values of equality and democracy at work; this means that there is a great team spirit. Co-operative philosophy, principles and structure are central to what we do, and we live these values as well as promoting them to others. We are joint owners and directors of CASE and we pull together in the same direction to achieve the best for the business and our clients. The good working relationship and solid commitment to co-operative aims, coupled with the opportunity to work with clients to change their lives, is one of the reasons why I have remained at CASE for so long.

We look after our staff and try to achieve a good work-life balance for all who work with us. As an example, one of my colleagues, Cathy, asked if she could adjust her working hours so that she could take her grandchildren to school every morning to assist her daughter to get to her teaching job on time. We adjusted Cathy's working hours so that she began work at 9.30 am instead of 9 am, and this allowed her to spend time with her grandchildren and support her daughter's career whilst also fulfilling her responsibilities as a director and member of CASE. This allowed us to keep Cathy's exceptional skills within the agency so had positive outcomes for all.

CASE promotes co-operative and social ways of working that assist entrepreneurs to be successful in business whilst also addressing issues of social inequality or discrimination. All social enterprises exist to challenge a perceived social, environmental or ethical imbalance. The imbalance may be one of ethics, such as the unfair way that the that the north trades with the south, which means that people in redeveloping countries are often not paid properly for their produce or products. An example of a business that fights

II The Life Story of Dr Dorothy Francis

ethical unfairness is the Just Fairtrade shop, which seeks to work directly with local communities in India, Africa, the Philippines and many other parts of the world to ensure they are paid proper prices for their labour. This enables producers of foods and artefacts to look after their families properly and deliver better lives for themselves.

People setting up social enterprises may also perceive social imbalance in the way children or elderly people are treated. Another of my clients, Shepshed Carers, was set up in 1994 to redress the issues that they encountered when working with elderly, sick and infirm people. Shepshed Carers is a domiciliary care company, and their aim is to allow people to live independently and with dignity in their homes. They provide services for people who would otherwise have to stay in hospital or live in nursing homes. Research has demonstrated that people live longer and maintain better health if they are able to remain in their own homes with their families and pets, but all too often families are unable to look after their loved ones and so they are forced by circumstances into care homes. Shepshed Carers provide care to people in their own homes, allowing them to remain amongst their families, surrounded by familiar items and their pets, and this promotes good mental and physical health.

At the core of social enterprise is the challenge of changing a prevailing social inequality whilst also running a profitable business. Social enterprises are not charities; they do not expect donations, but instead make money from trading so that they can continue to meet their social aim. Social businesses trade to make a profit and return the profit to the stakeholders, who are the membership, rather than to shareholders. Stakeholders can be the people who work in the enterprise, its users, or its members, and these are the people who control the business, rather than shareholders.

CASE supports around 200 businesses that are at all stages of development and trading; some businesses that we assisted to establish are now celebrating their 34th year of trading; many others are in their third decade. The businesses that we assist employ between two to 150 people in a wide range of sectors and geographical settings, and we help them in all areas of growth and sustainability. Co-operatives and social enterprises are not owned by the people who run them; instead they hold the businesses in stewardship and have a responsibility to pass on the undertakings to future stewards so that the businesses might continue. A key part of CASE's role is helping social businesses to address the challenges of passing the enterprise on to future generations.

A great part of the pleasure that I take in my job is that I work with people who are trying to change the world and it is a privilege to work alongside individuals who are so passionate and committed to what they do. Everyone I work with has an ambition to make the world a better place and they reach out to wide and various communities of need including people who are young, old, have disabilities, or are homeless, recovering from mental ill health or unemployed. Social enterprises also advocate for improved conditions for farmers across the world and aim to operate businesses that have positive environmental impacts.

CASE – and many other organisations – have been promoting social business for nearly 40 years. The ethos was little understood during the 1980s and '90s, but now this form of business is now more widely understood.

Awards

The greatest reward that I get from my job is helping people to achieve their dreams and seeing the outcomes of their work. I am gratified by being involved in any community and personal development that leads to the establishment of quality and long-lasting enterprises and I never tire of helping people to set up in business. I enjoy mentoring, guiding and teaching people to run their own enterprises in the knowledge that their actions as a business will impact positively on their local communities.

I am fortunate that I have been nominated for a number of awards in recognition of what I do within my job. I was recognised as Leicester Business Woman of the Year at the Jubilee Women's Awards in 2011, and as Business Woman of the Year at the Leicestershire Asian Business Association (LABA) awards in 2014. I was the recipient of the Queens Award for Enterprise Promotion (Lifetime Achievement Award) in 2016 and I am particularly proud of that recognition, as the Award is equivalent to an OBE [17] and is only granted to one person each year. I was the first person in Leicestershire to receive it and the first African-Caribbean woman in the UK.

Presentation of the Queen's Award crystal chalice by Jennifer, Lady Gretton, Lord Lieutenant of Leicestershire.

In 2016 I was invited to become a Companion of the Chartered Management Institute, which is the highest level of membership and is by invitation only. I received an MBE (see note no.21) in 2017 for Services to Enterprise to the People of Leicester and Leicestershire. In 2018 I was presented with an Honorary Doctorate from the University of Leicester in recognition of Services to the Co-operative Movement and Promotion of Diversity.

Fayola, Kevin, myself and Safiya at my MBE Investiture, posing with my medal.

I support students, graduates and staff in my role as Entrepreneur in Residence at the University of Leicester, which gives me an insight into new entrepreneurs emerging from the university and I am also an

II The Life Story of Dr Dorothy Francis

Honorary Visiting Fellow at the university. I also appeared in a film made for secondary school children in the Netherlands to promote the concept of social enterprise. I have featured in newspapers and magazines in the UK and Caribbean, and am often asked to present at conferences and business events. I have spoken across the UK and in Rome, Florence and The Hague.

I am pleased to accept these accolades but do not consider that I accept them solely for myself. I feel that I have a responsibility to be seen as a role model and use each award, magazine article or speaking event to raise awareness of Black women in business. There are not a lot of black people in the business field, and even fewer black women. When I accept the awards I do so not just for me, but also for my daughters and for other women of colour, young and old, so that they can be inspired to succeed within their field. I use the publicity around my awards to build awareness, to promote positive images of women in general and black women in particular, and to highlight the role of women in business.

Women in Social Enterprise

There are more women in social enterprise than in other forms of business. In the UK probably 75 per cent of businesses are run by men. In social enterprise around 55 to 65 per cent are led by women. Social enterprise provides a greater level of support for women in business in terms of leadership opportunities, training, development and work-life balance, which makes it easier for women to participate and succeed. Social enterprises also tend to attract women of colour, younger people and people from different backgrounds, which makes it an interesting and diverse business sector.

Co-operatives and social enterprises are inclined to be proactive and forward-thinking in terms of human rights, workplace safety and social issues and don't wait for governments to tell them what is the right thing to do: they do what they think is right and often preempt or prompt legislation. So, for example, CASE was established in 1982 and put into place employee rights which only came into UK legislation in 2010 or later. CASE provided adoption leave in 1984, almost 20 years before this right was passed into legislation, and at the same time made other rights available, including domestic leave, paternity leave, disability-friendly policies and recognition of same-sex relationships years before these rights were put on the UK law books. CASE aims to be family friendly and has always had good work-life balance polices that allow people to work around responsibilities such as childcare and eldercare. This stance is not unique to CASE and is reflected in many social enterprises; it makes them attractive to all members, but particularly to women. Another aspect that makes social enterprise conducive to women is that the greater majority are run by women or have large female membership, which influences their policies and shapes their membership, and leadership.

II   The Life Story of Dr Dorothy Francis

The Co-operative movement[18]

A co-operative is an autonomous body of people who come together for a common aim or purpose, to provide services or goods whilst promoting autonomy, democracy and common ownership of assets. Co-operatives are a different way of doing business and are effective at meeting their financial, social and ethical aims.

The modern co-operative movement grew from the ideals of a group of 28 men and one woman who came together to open a shop in an old warehouse in Toad Lane, Rochdale, Lancashire, to realise an ambition of providing an affordable alternative to poor-quality and adulterated food and provisions. At that time it was common for shopkeepers to sell substandard food to working class people who had no other buying options, and the shopkeepers often used dishonest weights so that customers did not get the full amount of what they paid for. In 1844 a group came together to form the Rochdale Equitable Pioneers Society, which later became known as the Rochdale Pioneers. They aimed to sell good-quality food, to use honest weights and measures and to use surpluses from trading to benefit the community. Their business model was built on the idea that the enterprise should be owned by its customers and that everyone should work together for the common goal of good service over the pursuit of profit, and this is still the founding principle of all co-operative businesses. It can be argued that co-operation has always existed, but when the Rochdale Pioneers came together to fight exploitation they codified the principles and introduced a new way of doing business.

The group formed a set of working rules, which became known as the 'Rochdale Principles'. These seven Principles were radical in their time and included guidance on equality, political neutrality and trading; and variations on these rules still guide the worldwide co-operative movement today. The Pioneers offered social enterprise in action and a chance for local people to take control of their lives and become equal members in a revolution that soon spread across the world. The Principles became the foundation of a movement which now numbers approximately 1.4 million independent enterprises, with more than one billion members worldwide, who are represented by the International Co-operative Alliance (ICA) in 284 co-operative federations in ninety five countries.

In front of the Toad Lane shop.

The first two principles to be agreed were those of Open Membership and Democratic Control. These ensured that membership of the co-operative was open to everyone and all members had a vote in the running of the business. This included women,

101

II The Life Story of Dr Dorothy Francis

which was a radical departure given that women did not achieve suffrage in the UK until 74 years after the Rochdale principles were written. At the time that the Rochdale principles were codified only one in seven men had the right to vote, and these men tended to come from the landed or moneyed classes, so the idea of working-class people holding a vote was seen by many as revolutionary, and to some people even incendiary, whilst the concept of women holding a vote was inflammatory.

At this time many people were prevented from having membership of clubs, societies or business because of their political or religious beliefs. The Rochdale Pioneers disliked the inequalities that this caused and introduced the principles of Political and Religious Neutrality, which ensured that co-operative societies were open to all. The principles of Dividend on Purchase and Limited Interest on Capital dealt with the monies earned by the co-operative and ensured that any money taken by the co-operative was either ploughed back into the Society or held in reserve to help the business and local communities at a later date. This went against the established norm which was to divide profits amongst shareholders.

The co-operative also insisted on Cash Trading, so that debts and bills couldn't be run up against the limited funds of the co-operative and put it at financial risk. This principle was also introduced as an attempt to assist people to manage their finances in order to encourage them to be debt-free. The final principle to be agreed was that of a commitment to the communities that the co-operative served, in the form of Promotion of Education which saw libraries and schools established at the premises of the original Toad Lane shop and in many other co-operative stores. This was instrumental in the education of millions.

The Toad Lane shop opened four days before Christmas Day in 1844 with a very sparse stock of a few pounds of butter and sugar, six sacks of flour, one of oatmeal and twenty-four candles. Tea and tobacco were added to the shelves a few months later and although the stock was limited, the shop became a great success. More stock was added gradually, until the shop was fully stocked with all necessities.

The Rochdale Principles

Open Membership
Democratic Control
Dividend on Purchase
Limited Interest on Capital
Political and Religious Neutrality
Cash Trading
Promotion of Education

The principles were set down in 1844 and updated by the International Co-operative Alliance in 1966.

The actions of the Rochdale Pioneers were observed with interest. By 1854 the British co-operative movement had taken up the Rochdale Principles, and over a thousand co-operative stores existed across the British Isles. The model spread to other European counties and beyond.

The Rochdale Pioneers became well known and they received visitors who wanted to learn how to run co-operatives successfully. The Pioneers kept a visitors' book from 1860 on-

II The Life Story of Dr Dorothy Francis

wards, and it lists callers from across the world. In 1862 they received visitors from Germany, Russia and Spain. In 1863 Alexander Campbell paid a visit: he later originated the famous Co-operative dividend scheme, which still operates today. The first Japanese visitor was Tomizo Noguchi, in 1872.[19] There is a replica of the Toad Lane shop in Kobe,[20] Japan, which is actually larger than the original!

The Rochdale Principles and the actions of the Rochdale Pioneers brought co-operative principles of equality, democracy and participation into business. The Pioneers introduced a social conscience to enterprise, and this commitment to equality and fairness continues into the modern day.

The co-operative movement does not refer to profit, but instead deems excess money as being surplus to requirements. In conventional business the main aim is to make a profit for the shareholders, but in co-operatives the central aim is to provide a service or facility and any money remaining once the aim is achieved is returned to the stakeholder membership.

Throughout the world, millions of people operate enterprises and live lives based on the original Rochdale Principles. It's amazing to think that a small group of people came together in 1844 to change their part of the world and in doing so changed the way over one billion people trade and live. This is a considerable achievement and a testimony to the power of working for change. It is a humbling thought that the ideals of a few people formed the co-operative movement that we know today and left a legacy that ensures that co-operators across the world all have the same understanding of what it means to be in a co-operative.

John Lewis and Partners, one of the biggest businesses in the UK, runs under a co-operative format and has thrived under this structure for the past hundred years, with all staff being partners within the business and having a vote and control in how the business is managed. John Lewis has great staff loyalty and a low staff turnover and is one of the most trusted brands on the High Street.

Co-operation is a way of work which I have subscribed to for most of my working life as it brings ownership and control, which is very important for me, especially as people of colour are still not equally empowered within the working world.

II   The Life Story of Dr Dorothy Francis

8 Moving to Leicester, my marriage, my children and their education

Dorothy moved from Coventry to Leicester in 1986. She describes her marriage and her children's education in Leicester thus:

Moving to Leicester

I moved to Leicester in 1986 to take up employment at the local Co-operative Development Agency. Initially, I planned to stay for two years. However I found that I liked living in Leicester and I loved my job., and I decided to stay and have now lived in the city for more than 30 years. I chose Leicester because it is not too far from my family but was far enough away to establish my own identity, which was an important factor at that point in my life. I come from a very close-knit community in Coventry and it was sometimes difficult to express my individuality, surrounded as I was by family and friends who had known me for many years and had ideas of who they thought I was. Leicester was originally a stop-gap, but I stayed because I came to love the vibrancy of the culture, the diversity of the people and the promise of change that hung in the air.

My marriage

Myself on the way to church.

My husband is called Kevin Hudson, and we married in 1994, having been together for three years prior to that. We both knew from our first date that we wanted to be together but we took time to get to know each other before getting married. Our first date was on a Thursday evening and as we parted company on my doorstep I knew that he was the one. In fact, when I went to work the next day I announced to my astonished colleague, Geof Cox, that I had met the man that I was going to marry. Geof was extremely surprised, as he knew that I had only just met Kevin and he wanted to know how I was so sure and if Kevin and I had discussed marriage? I responded that we had not, but nonetheless I knew that we would marry!

Unbeknownst to me, Kevin went to work that same Friday morning and told his colleague Anne that he had met the woman that he was to marry and he fielded similar questions from his equally bemused workmate. We had been together about 18 months before we discovered that we had held identical conversations with our respective workmates and that we had instantly felt the same way about each other! By then we knew that we would marry but were simply waiting for the right time. I was studying for my Chartered Institute of Personnel and Development qualification and wanted to pass my exams and qualify before getting married. I sat my final exams in May 1994 and we set our wedding for the middle of September four months later.

We were married at Stoneygate Baptist Church in Leicester on the 17th of September, 1994. The officiating minister was Michael Docker who was one of Kevin's childhood friends. Kevin was a member of the Boys' Brigade [21] throughout his childhood and early adulthood and Michael had been the Captain of his division. At a Boys' Brigade reunion in Birmingham in 1992, we discovered that Michael had recently become the Minister at Stoneygate Baptist Church and was still finding his feet at the church and within the city. Stoneygate Baptist Church was about a mile from where I lived and we suggested to Michael that Kevin and I join the church so that Michael would have some familiar faces in the congregation. We found that we liked the church and quickly became part of the church family, making good friends and becoming involved in lots of activities including Junior Church, Youth Club and the Outsiders' social group. Michael left in 1999, but we stayed on as we were firmly entrenched by that time and we have continued to attend Stoneygate Baptist throughout the years.

Cutting the cake at the wedding breakfast and multitasking by stealing a kiss at the same time!

Kevin is white British and was born in Birmingham, where he grew up with his sister and parents. Birmingham is very multicultural, but there are many areas which are still very mono-cultural. The suburb of Hollywood where Kevin grew up is one such place and, even now, is predominately white. Kevin recalls that there was only one black boy in his secondary school and none in his primary school. Kevin did not meet or get to know any black people until he started his accountancy training and attended Coventry Polytechnic (later Coventry University). Until then he had lived in a world which was almost entirely white. He was aware of people of colour and of different cultures, but he did not have friends in these communities. However, he was open to new experiences and enjoyed being at Coventry Polytechnic where he met people from different backgrounds.

Kevin is the only person in his family to have married a person of colour and to have stepped outside of his culture. When we met, he knew very little about black culture, but he threw himself into learning and embraced all aspects, especially the food!

We have lived in Clarendon Park since we were married, and our two daughters have grown up in this area of Leicester. It is not a widely multicultural area and my daughters and I have usually been the only black people on our street. However, it is a socially-aware area with lots of amenities, shops, restaurants and bars, and we enjoy living here.

We moved to Clarendon Park because it is a well-connected area in terms of facilities such as bus routes, schools, libraries, shops and leisure facilities. We wanted our children to have the independence to move around by themselves rather than being driven

II   The Life Story of Dr Dorothy Francis

to all educational and social activities. Most facilities are within walking distance and regular buses run into the city centre. Our children walked to their infant, primary and secondary schools, as all are within a mile of our house. They later attended the local sixth form college, which is quarter of a mile away, and our eldest did her Masters at the University of Leicester, which is just across the park from where we live.

My children's education

One of the reasons why my parents moved to the UK was so that my siblings and I could receive a good education. The education system in Jamaica is high quality but costly, and my parents would have struggled to pay the fees and to educate us to the level that they wished. My mother was always insistent that we made the most of the educational opportunities afforded to us, because she bitterly regretted and resented the fact that she had had to leave school at an early age due to her parents' inability to pay the school fees. She loved to learn, and was disappointed that her learning was curtailed. Her ambition was that all of her children would gain a college education, and she was delighted when this dream came through.

My mother knew that education is important on many levels, as it opens doors to employment, and she also valued the contribution that education makes to enhancing the ability to question concepts rather than accepting them unthinkingly – especially concepts such as oppression. She knew that a good education would enable us to escape the restrictions that bound us in terms of ethnicity, gender and class, and we were reminded repeatedly that education is the way forward for change. Mum always stressed that education was the factor that would make a difference to our lives; and she was strict in making sure that we attended school unless too sick to leave the house and she always ensured that we did our homework. Mum never missed a parents' evening, and she listened intently to all that the teachers had to say and would work with us on any issues identified by the teachers. She had great faith in the teaching profession and rarely questioned their authority, because she trusted them to do the right thing for the children in their care.

I also wanted the best possible education for my children, and they were encouraged to aspire from an early age. Both Fayola and Safiya love learning, and found education an opportunity to be enjoyed rather than endured. They went willingly to school and loved to try new experiences. They were educated in the state system and both attended Avenue Primary School, which is the local primary school about 600 metres from our home. Their secondary education was at Sir Jonathan North Community College, where they were both selected for the gifted and talented programme, and this provided opportunities to try new areas of learning, visit institutions such as universities, museums and the International Space Centre, and meet other students from different schools.

Fayola and Safiya did well at GCSE and moved to Sixth Form College to undertake A-Levels. Fayola chose to specialise in languages, and after her A-Levels and a gap year

II   The Life Story of Dr Dorothy Francis

spent in Spain, she entered the University of Birmingham to study French, Spanish and English. Safiya was a member of The Curve young people's acting group for some years, and also acted in a number of other groups. She learnt about theatre and event management via these activities, and this enthused her to take a joint honours degree in Drama and Event Management at the University of Winchester. Safiya found that she excelled at event management, and this became her area of specialism and is the field in which she now works.

Both Fayola and Safiya graduated with First Class Honours degrees and Safiya was also designated as a Winchester Scholar. Fayola went on to take an MA in International Culture and Communication, which she passed with distinction, whilst Safiya, having considered an MA, decided to go straight into work.

Both our children have done well educationally, but it was not always plain sailing. There were times when I had to fight for their education and for them to be educated in a way that I felt was fitting and there were occasions when I argued my point with the teachers and governors because I didn't feel that they were teaching a diverse curriculum.

For instance, Fayola informed me one day that her primary school class was learning about Africa. I asked her what she had learned and she said that she had learnt about the slave trade and they were now moving on as they had covered Africa. I was horrified, and I explained to her that one brief lesson could not cover the history of earth's largest continent or do justice to Africa's 54 four nation states. I also explained that the fact that millions of its people had been taken into slavery by Europeans was not the sum total of the continent from which mankind originated. I expounded that if her teachers were truly teaching her about Africa that they would have taught her of the great and illustrious kingdoms of Benin, Nigeria and Zimbabwe. She would have learned of the superb thirteenth-century goldsmithing and bronze-casting abilities of the people from Ghana and Benin whose expert skills far surpassed those of Europeans of the same period. She would have discovered that modern numerology, as we know it, came out of Africa. The teachers would have taught about great kings and queens like Shaka and Nzinga and other wise rulers who led their countries. Further lessons could have included the great walls of Zimbabwe or the agricultural systems of Egypt or the fact that the Dogon people of Mali identified Sirius B in the night sky many decades before Western astronomers with powerful telescopes were able to see the star.

I was disgusted that my daughter's teachers saw fit to teach about Africa via the prism of the enslavement of its people for the profit of European countries. That is not the history of Africa, and is not the total of what children should be taught about this huge continent.

Following the conversation with Fayola, I visited her school and expressed my opinion that the teachers needed to promote African heritage in a better way, only to be in-

II   The Life Story of Dr Dorothy Francis

formed that they did not know how to. I was informed that they didn't have any books that spoke of the things that I described and that they didn't know where to get them. I resorted to buying books for the school library and provided a book list for future purchases so that my children and other children of colour could read books that reflected them, their experiences and their culture and that all students – black and white – could learn about the true history of Africa. It was sad and sobering that I was forced to do this in the late 1990s, because I really expected that things would have moved on from my school days but they had not. Fayola's experience of being taught African 'history' exactly mirrored mine from 30 years before in that we were only told of the negative experience of enslavement out of millennia of a history rich with arts, exploration, architecture and science.

It is important that children see themselves reflected in society, but that is not always the case. The experience of growing up black in the UK can be like looking into a mirror in which everyone else is reflected but you are not. Society holds up a mirror but it does not reflect our culture or our history, and it is as if we are rendered invisible or erased.

I know that my education gave me different and heightened expectations in comparison to my parents, neither of whom was educated beyond lower-secondary level (my father barely attended school). Education changes the way that we look at the world and our expectation of life, and can have a bearing on how we live, what we eat, whom we marry and what job we do. I absorbed my parent's educational expectations, and as a result I have a much different lifestyle from them and different aspirations. This ethos has been transmitted to my children, and they in turn have heightened expectations to those that I grew up with.

I felt very restricted growing up in England and was told, and subsequently believed, that there were many things that I could not do. My daughters did not have the same physical or mental restrictions; they were able to explore different options and choices and I am pleased with that. I think that it was beneficial that they attended an all-girls school where they were encouraged to excel at maths, science and sports, which are areas in which I was constrained within my mixed-sex school, where girls were actively discouraged from taking part in these subjects. I was often told what I could not do, rather than what I could do. In contrast, I think Fayola and Safiya have been told throughout their lives that they can do anything that they want to do and that barriers of colour and gender placed in their way by others should not hold them back. I have always emphasised to them that they can be anything they want to be and go anywhere they want to go to. I was pleased when Fayola articulated to me that, 'I am a world citizen, Mum. I can go anywhere and be anything that I want'. I am delighted that she has this view and these opportunities and aspirations.

II   The Life Story of Dr Dorothy Francis

9 My religion and faith

Dorothy discusses her religious life, as well as her mother's faith:

Religion in Jamaica

Religion is an everyday part of Jamaican life; indeed, the country is reputed to have the most churches per square mile of any country in the world. I was brought up as a Christian, and we went to church every Sunday; that was the norm within our community. In many ways, the church is an extended family and membership places an individual within their local community.

In Jamaica people don't necessarily ask if you go to church; They simply assume that you do and so are more likely to ask you what denomination you are, such as Pentecostal, Methodist, Baptist or Catholic. Most Jamaicans worship in one way or another, and the issues of faith, belief and worship are strong and play a significant role in social life, culture and music. Some people have chosen not to adopt Christianity and adhere instead to the old African religions which were transplanted to Jamaica. There is religious tolerance for other faiths, and mosques, temples and synagogues are evidenced on the island.

My mother's religion and faith in Coventry

My mother is a committed Christian and on landing in the UK sought a church to join. As Christians, we are taught that there is one God and that that God loves everybody. Unfortunately, when my mother tried to join local churches, she found that this doctrine of one love did not apply to black people who often found that they were not welcome in white churches. The church would either 'kindly' suggest that black people might feel more comfortable worshipping elsewhere or would react to black worshippers in a coldly polite and distant way, thus conveying the message that they were not welcome and ensuring that they did not return.

Mum says, 'It seemed that in their eyes God didn't love black people; he only loved white people'. My mother finally found a Black church on Old Church Road in Coventry, and she began to worship there. The congregation was mostly black and the services were very lively with tuneful singing and lots of tambourines, drums and guitars. However, we only remained in that church for a short time and left after an irrevocable falling out with the minister. In mid-1967, my one-year-old sister Joy died. My mother was engaged in discussing Joy's funeral with the minister when he told Mum – who was grieving the loss of her beloved child – that Joy had died because of a sin that my mother had committed in her life, and that her death was a punishment from God. He offered to pray for Mum so that the sin would be erased from her character. My mother was absolutely furious, and swore that she would never set foot in that church again (and never did).

109

II   The Life Story of Dr Dorothy Francis

Mum was hurt because she was in a country where she was experiencing racism on a day-to-day basis and the only place she had felt safe was in the church. For her, church was a place of safety and comfort and she had, up until then, felt cushioned and secure within Old Church Road church, worshipping amongst other black people. However, this feeling of security was pulled from underneath her feet by the outrageous words and actions of the minister and she had no choice but to leave.

We were without a church for a while until our next-door neighbour, Mrs Palmer, invited us to join Armfield Street Methodist church, where she worshipped. We joined and remained there for the next 25 years. It was a very different church to the one that we had left; our previous church was 99 per cent black whereas Armfield Street Methodist was 98 per cent white. It was a startling contrast but the church members made us welcome and we quickly became part of the church family. The style of worship was more restrained and quiet, and we missed the musical instruments, the call and response refrains and the loud music and singing. In our previous church, there was a great deal of interaction between the preacher and the congregation but this was not the case at Armfield Street where essentially the minister preached and the congregation listened. Nonetheless, we became used to Armfield Street Methodist; it was a very active church with lively and well-attended children's and youth sections, and we made good friends and took part in lots of activities.

I left home when I was 16, but I voluntarily attended the church until the age of 19 when I moved away to attend university in Birmingham. However, I still considered Armfield Street Methodist to be my home church and visited whenever I could, and it is where my eldest daughter was dedicated in 1991.

Mum remained at Armfield Street Methodist after we moved house in 1975 – even though it was difficult to reach from our new house – and she continued to worship there until around 2005, when the difficulties of travelling to the church caused her to move her membership to a church nearer home.

Rastafarianism [22]

Jamaica is deeply Christian. However, many people feel that Christianity was imposed upon us; it is a religion that was imported to the island at the same time that we were transplanted there. It may not have been our religion of choice had we remained in Africa, or if the island's indigenous population had not been eradicated. In the early-to-mid-twentieth century, many Jamaicans were seeking independence from Britain, and also liberation from the beliefs and attitudes that colonialism had foisted onto the country. People looked for an identity that reflected the Jamaican experience, and sought a religion that resonated with Jamaicans. For many, Rastafarianism, or Rastafari, fitted that bill.

Rastafari arose from an environment of poverty, racism, colonialism and class discrimination, and the Rastafari message of Black Pride, freedom from oppression and the hope of return to the African homeland was gratefully received by people keen to embrace an African-centric reality. Many people embraced this alternative, amongst them my sister Sharon, who converted to Rastafarianism in her mid-teens and has followed this philosophy ever since. People who follow Rastafarianism are called 'Rastafarians', sometimes abbreviated to 'Rastas'.

Rastafarianism derives a lot of its creed from the Bible, in particular the Old Testament, but with some variations. Christians await the return of Jesus Christ to release his people; Rastafarians believe that Haile Selassie, former emperor – or King of Kings – of Ethiopia was the second coming. Haile Selassie is revered as the returned Messiah of the Bible, and as God incarnate (or made flesh). He is seen as a messianic figure who will lead a future golden age of eternal peace, righteousness, and prosperity. Haile Selassie's full title was 'By the Conquering Lion of the Tribe of Judah, His Imperial Majesty Haile Selassie I, King of Kings of Ethiopia, Elect of God'. This title reflects Ethiopian dynastic traditions, which trace the royal lineage to Menelik I, who is understood to have been the son of King Solomon and the Queen of Sheba.

Rastafarianism is a religion which harks back to Africa and gives displaced people within the African diaspora pride in their African origin and heritage. People growing up under colonial rule in Jamaica were taught to be ashamed of their African roots and told that they should aspire to be British, not African. Rastafarism reversed this and empowered people to recognise their ethnic roots and aspire to be African. It also provided an identity in terms of being an African religion, rather than a westernised or Eurocentric creed.

Rastafari pays attention to Old Testament ways of living and to rules which are laid out within the Bible. One of these is the prohibition on cutting hair, which is why Rastas grow their hair in uncut locks. Rasta women conform to Old Testament standards, dress modestly and cover their hair, and children are brought up to be unpretentious and community-minded. Rastas are vegan and do not eat anything from animal sources or drink alcohol. Rastafarianism involves a different way of thinking which eschews ownership of possessions, and promotes sharing and minimalism. The religion is based on family and community values, and promotes practices that have a low impact on the environment. Rastafarian worship is not confined to particular buildings, but can take place wherever they chose to come together to discuss, or 'reason', the words of the Bible and their application to living this life and preparing for the next.

Stoneygate Baptist Church [23]

During my 20s, I began to I revaluate what I wanted from a church and became drawn towards Baptist theology and beliefs, and this is one of the reasons why my husband and I joined Stoneygate Baptist Church. We originally joined because Kevin's childhood friend was the minister; however, we stayed because the philosophy suits our beliefs and because it is a friendly and inclusive church and is only about fifteen minutes' walk

II The Life Story of Dr Dorothy Francis

Stoneygate Baptist Church, London Road, Leicester.

from our house.

We started attending Stoneygate Baptist Church when our oldest daughter, Fayola, was two years old. Our youngest daughter, Safiya, attended her first service one week after she was born, so both children have grown up in the church, and its members are part of our extended family. Safiya was a youth leader at the church for many years and still participates in that role whenever she can. In some ways, Stoneygate Baptist is an unusual setting for us. My daughters and I are pretty much in the minority as the church is 99 per cent white, and in some ways echoes my experience of growing up in the almost exclusively white Armfield Street Methodist church. Sometimes I feel it would be nice to go to a church where there are more black people, but we have been at Stoneygate Baptist for more than 25 years and are embedded within the church, and it would be difficult and disruptive to move; besides which, we like the people and feel part of that community.

My religion is an important aspect of my life and has played a part in the lives of my children. They were brought up in the church, but we did not indoctrinate them in our views as we felt that it was important for them to understand and appreciate religion in their own way. We encouraged them to question and to debate their faith and to make their own decisions once they were older. Our older daughter prefers not to attend church, although she will assist with events, festivals and special services. Our youngest still enjoys attending when she is at home as she likes to feel part of the church family.

I think that it's important that people are given the right to question their own beliefs and the faith systems of their parents, peers or community. Faith is a personal thing and should be open to question and debate. We always accepted that our children might not wish to stay within our religion when they grew up and we have accepted that they will make their own decisions.

My brother and sisters and I were brought up in a Methodist Pentecostal church but we took different routes once we came of age. My middle sister converted to Rastafarism almost forty years ago and has followed this doctrine ever since. My youngest sister became a Born Again Christian, my eldest sister is a Methodist, whilst I am Baptist by persuasion. We all share a broad Christian faith, but along different branches. However, the central message is the same; we all believe in one God; that we should love our neighbours, treat our parents with respect, take care of those in need and follow a moral path. Essentially, most of the world's major religions promote the same theology of love and care for community and provide a moral framework for how to live life.

II   The Life Story of Dr Dorothy Francis

I like the fact that Baptist churches are independent and are not run by a central council. They are run by their members and operate under a system of voluntary and open membership. Anyone can attend a Baptist church, and membership is open to all who choose to be baptised. All members of the congregation have opportunities to be part of the church and to take part in decision-making, although voting rights are held by the baptised members on the basis of one person, one vote.

Baptist philosophy fits well with my personal and social beliefs and resonates with the co-operative and community values that are inherent in my work life. The co-operative principles of voluntary and open membership, democratic member control, autonomy and independence, provision of education and information, co-operation among similar bodies and concern for community are all reflected within Baptist practices.

I also respect the fact that Baptist churches allow people to make their own decision to know God and to be baptised by immersion in water. Baptist churches perform blessings for new-born babies, but do not christen infants because the decision to be baptised should be a conscious decision taken once the individual is aware of the undertaking.

Events at Stoneygate Baptist Church, Leicester

Stoneygate Baptist Church is a community-based church, and we endeavour to open the church to everyone regardless of religion so that they can appreciate the love of God through the church.

We are a Fairtrade church, so only use tea, coffee, sugar etc. that are certified as Fairtrade. We promote the practices and principles of Fairtrade throughout the year, and utilise Fairtrade Fortnight each February to highlight the unfairness of trade between the West and many producer countries, and to identify ways that this trade injustice can be rebalanced.

We run Messy Church events on a regular basis for children and parents, and these are attended by dozens of local families. Each August, volunteers within the church run a free one-week Busy Bees holiday club for about 50 children. Children from across the city and from all religious backgrounds come together to play, sing and learn Bible stories. They perform a show for their parents and carers on the final day of the play scheme and also bake cakes and prepare food for a tea party. Our youngest daughter, Safiya, has acted as a play leader at the Busy Bees club for many years, and even though she has lived away from home for some years she still tries to make time – and takes holiday leave from work if necessary – to assume a leadership role at the play scheme, as she loves working with the children.

We hold a number of other events, such as the well-received Stoneygate Festivals, which allow us to open up the church to showcase the building and encourage the local community to experience the wonderful premises. The festivals allow local people to demon-

113

II   The Life Story of Dr Dorothy Francis

strate their skills by selling a variety of items such as jewellery, jams, cards and knitted goods, and the church is filled with stalls offering items for sale. The festivals also include food, programmes of lectures and talks, as well as music and performances, and the events are an effective way of highlighting Stoneygate Baptist's presence in the community.

The church has extensive meeting rooms, a large hall, a fully-serviced catering kitchen, parking to the front and rear and large gardens, and is much in demand by a number of groups. The hall and kitchen are hired for weddings, birthdays and other events. The hall has six small adjoining rooms, and until the 1970s was an independent school; some members of the church remember attending school there. Leicester Dyslexia Society has run a supplementary school in the hall and classrooms for more than 20 years, helping hundreds of local children to manage their dyslexia, and supporting parents to enable them to assist their children.

The hall is also used for yoga, exercise classes and play schemes, and the meeting rooms are used by a number of local societies. The Misfits social group meets at the church each Friday; this is an unbroken traditon stretching back to the 1950s, when the group was first formed. On Sunday afternoons the hall becomes a place of worship for a local South Asian church.

The congregation at Stoneygate Baptist has diminished considerably over the past 20 years and the demographic profile is quite elderly. This is a characteristic of indigenous churches, which are becoming smaller and losing youth members. The developmental growth in Christianity in the UK tends to be from overseas, rather than from the indigenous community and establishment of new churches is primarily within African, African-Caribbean, Chinese and South Asian communities. There are a number of Indian Christian churches in the UK, because certain places in India like Goa and Kerala have strong Christian communities and bring their Christian tradition with them when they move to the UK.

Newly arrived communities usually establish their places of worship within existing churches such as Stoneygate Baptist. Sometimes, they remain in the host church for many years, such as the long-established West African church in Brice Hall on Queens Road, but often the members club together so that they can buy a church building of their own. Examples of this in Leicester include the Chinese church on Clarendon Park Road, the Seventh Day Adventist Church on London Road, and the Apostolic Church on Saffron Lane, all of which were purchased by the combined efforts of their members. The choir of the Immanuel Apostolic Church has sung at Stoneygate Baptist on a number of occasions. The members of the church are primarily African and African-Caribbean, and they worshipped for many years at a local-authority owned leisure centre on Saffron Lane, in Leicester. However, they recently purchased a building of their own and are raising money to refurbish the premises; similarly, many other African, African-Caribbean and Asian congregations are taking the lead in establishing and building new churches.

114

II The Life Story of Dr Dorothy Francis

In effect, African, African-Caribbean and Asian churches are doing what certain dissident white church communities did 150 years ago when they created their own places of worship. Stoneygate Baptist Church was started by a breakaway group of people from churches within Clarendon Park who sought a different way of worshipping. The members saved to buy a plot of land and then – after many years of further savings – erected the church building. More than 110 years later, this beautiful building still stands as a testament to their hard work, industry and faith.

The International Women's Day celebrations at my church

We have held a number of events to celebrate International Women's Day over the years, including a large-scale festival in 2015 and a choir concert in 2018. The celebrations allow us to recognise and commemorate the contributions and achievements of women in the world and to highlight the work that must still take place to achieve equality and justice.

Alice Hawkins

The 2015 International Women's Day festival included talks from inspirational women as well as gift stalls, food and music, and was very well received. The inspirational De Montfort University Choir [24] (also known as the Emmanuel Apostolic Gospel Academy or EAGA) performed at the festival and received a standing ovation. A special event during the festival was a talk from Peter Barratt, great-grandson of the famous Leicester Suffragette Alice Hawkins [25] who spoke about her inspiring life. Peter was accompanied by his friend Dorothy Brawn, who was dressed in the type of costume that Alice Hawkins would have worn, including a suffragette sash. Dorothy Brawn read aloud extracts from the speeches of Alice Hawkins and brought Alice's words to life. [26]

10 My love of cooking, favourite writers and cultural influences

Dorothy likes cooking and reading. She describes them thus:

My love of cooking

I enjoy cooking and baking and find it a good way to relax and unwind. If I have a bad day at work, I go home and bake cakes; that always serves to soothe me and also has tasty end results!

My mother taught us all to cook, and there were no distinctions made – all of us, including my brother – were expected to know how to manage in the kitchen. We learnt to

II   The Life Story of Dr Dorothy Francis

Christmas gifts made by myself – cakes, jams and chutneys.

cook from an early age and were given a lot of responsibility in the kitchen. By the time I was ten, I could cook a full Sunday dinner. Our traditional Sabbath meal is Rice and Peas and Chicken, which is rice cooked with kidney beans and coconut served with chicken stewed in a thick sauce of tomatoes, onions, garlic and spices. My father refused to eat shop-bought chicken, so we bought a live hen from the local farm each Saturday and killed it at home. This was a part of our upbringing, so we were not squeamish about the process and at an early age we knew how to kill, pluck, joint, prepare and cook a chicken.

My childhood meals were convivial social events shared with others, and I have fond memories of the meals that we prepared and ate with friends and family. We socialised with a number of other Caribbean families and rarely ate Sunday dinner alone; either they came to our house or we went to theirs. The families included the Mullings, Faceys, Morgans, Weekes, Williams, Clarkes, and a number of others, and almost 50 years later we are still in contact with most of them. We ate Sunday dinners and shared other occasions with these families for many years, and the warm atmosphere of these meals is one of my strongest childhood memories.

We were a family of six, but my mother always cooked dinner for seven as she included a portion for 'the guest as yet uninvited'. It was not unusual for people to turn up without warning; it was not the norm to make appointments, and people would simply drop in. It is considered an honour if guests arrive at meal times and it is the height of bad manners and a great embarrassment if such a guest is not fed. My mother habitually cooked a seventh portion so that any guest who arrived could join us. On the rare occasion that a guest arrived and my mother had not cooked a seventh portion she would redistribute the food into seven servings and slice and butter bread to complement the meal. Unexpected guests were always warmly invited and were fed gladly.

My mother recounts a story of something that happened when she first arrived in England, and more than 50 years later she still tells the tale with an air of incredibility. Mum had made friends with one of the white women with whom she worked, and one day as she was passing by she decided on the spur of the moment to drop in to pay a visit. Mum's friend opened the door and looked a little surprised, but invited her into the house. Mum noticed that the table was laid with food, and realised that the family had been about to eat their dinner and – as is the norm in Caribbean culture – expected that she would be invited to join them. However, her friend cleared the table and put the meals in the oven exclaiming 'That will keep the food warm so that we can eat when you have gone'. Mum was astounded by such behaviour and felt unable to stay more than a

II The Life Story of Dr Dorothy Francis

few minutes, as her host was clearly uncomfortable with the situation and it was obvious that the food was drying out in the oven whilst they chatted. After a few minutes, she made an excuse and got up to leave, to the evident relief of her host and her family, who were hungry for their dinner. Mum said it was one of the most embarrassing experiences of her life and it made her reluctant to drop in uninvited on English people. After that, she learned to make an appointment to visit, as it seemed that this was what English people expected, and she realised that the tradition of sharing meals with unexpected guests did not necessarily translate to English culture.

Mum worked in catering at the Coventry Theatre restaurant when she first arrived in the UK, and learnt how to make many English dishes that she had not previously heard of. Many were a mystery to her, such as the dish called Yorkshire Pudding which, rather to her consternation, was a savoury cooked batter served with gravy, whereas she had expected a sweet dish served with custard, because that was her experience of puddings. She learned that minced beef or lamb was usually referred to as 'mincemeat' and could be turned into a variety of dishes such as shepherd's pie, cottage pie, meatballs and the rather exotic Bolognese. However, she was puzzled to discover that little dessert tarts produced at Christmas time were referred to as 'mince pies' even though they contained a sickly sweet concoction of mixed fruits and beef suet and no meat at all! She recalls the horror she felt when she was asked to prepare a Toad in the Hole one day until she was informed that it did not involve any amphibious creatures at all! She explains that frog's legs were a delicacy in some restaurants, so being called on to cook a dish that seemed to involve a whole toad encased in batter did not seem such an oddity. She was mightily relived to discover that Toad in the Hole is simply a dish of sausages baked in batter!

Mum enjoyed trying out the recipes that she learnt in the Coventry Theatre kitchens and from good friends such as Marsha and Peggy, two white women who took Mum under their wing. We primarily ate Jamaican food at home, so welcomed these occasional forays into English food with interest but sometimes with dubious anticipation, as my mother did not always translate the recipes faithfully. She was inclined to add spices and flavourings to the recipes, deeming them otherwise too bland, so they often tasted quite different to the dishes that we encountered via our school dinners. Nonetheless, they were very tasty; we loved all of Mum's cooking, whether it was Caribbean or British.

Mum didn't know how to bake when she came to this country, but she learnt from Marsha, Peggy and cookery programmes and became a competent baker. She baked a cake most Fridays throughout our childhood, and she sometimes baked other delicacies such as Jamaican coconut cakes and a pastry tart called gizzada. Occasionally, she baked sweet potato or cornmeal puddings, or 'pones' as they are known in Jamaica. Most Sundays she baked an apple tart, and she continued this tradition for many years. Mum's apple tarts are an enduring favourite with my eldest daughter Fayola, and Mum would bake a pie especially for Fayola when we visited. When Mum visited us she would bake a pie and pack it safely for its journey, and on arrival would say sternly: 'This is for

II The Life Story of Dr Dorothy Francis

Fayola: you have eaten enough of these in your time so this is for the child'!. Fayola loved the fact that her grandmother baked especially for her and would take great glee in informing me that I was not allowed to eat any of her apple pie!

We loved Mum's cakes and were accustomed to the fact that she made cakes every Friday. One night my brother Steadman came in hungry after a night out, and spying a delicious cake cooling on the counter he cut a big slice, ate it and went to bed. In the morning my mother said, 'Who cut a slice from the cake?'. Steadman confessed that it was he. Mum was angry, and said, 'That was your birthday cake. I filled it with special ingredients and was going to ice it today but you've spoiled it'. Steadman had forgotten that his birthday was coming up and had inadvertently ruined his birthday treat!

Teddy parcels – a birthday cake for Fayola.

I consider myself to be fortunate because as an African-Caribbean person who has grown up in the UK I am fully conversant with both Jamaican and British culture, language and food, and am able to switch between them. I might choose to cook ackee, salt fish, yam, green bananas and curried goat one day and the next I might prepare a full English roast dinner of beef, Yorkshire pudding, roast potatoes and vegetables, followed by a steamed pudding and custard. I enjoy the flexibility and diversity of being able to move between two cultures and have learnt to take pride in Jamaican cuisine instead of hiding it as I was forced to do in my childhood.

I love to bake, and all of my siblings are also competent bakers, so a family gathering usually involves a lot of cakes, and baked goods! At Christmas, I make around 50 small cakes, which I decorate and bag up as gifts for family, neighbours, friends, work colleges and church members. I also make jams, marmalades, pickles and hot sauces. I enjoy the challenge of making gluten-free cakes and finding new ways to replace wheat flour with other ingredients such as millet, ground rice, cornflower and nuts. I like to explore new ways of creating allergen-free cakes, and experiment with vegan, dairy-free and egg-free cakes, partly because I like to try new things.

My favourite writers, and my cultural influences

I have been influenced by many writers, especially women of colour. Maya Angelou[27] was a strong, confident woman who overcame a lot of difficult circumstances, but remained positive and wrote beautiful, lyrical books, which I have returned to again and again. *I Know Why the Caged Birds Sing* is a modern classic which I first read in the early 1980s and have read again and again. Alice Walker[28] is another admired author, and her book *The Color Purple* was a revelation to me when I first read it more than thirty years

II The Life Story of Dr Dorothy Francis

ago, and has remained in my top ten favourite books. *Beloved* by Toni Morrison [29] is one of the most haunting books that I have ever read, and I return to it frequently to mull over why it affects me so.

I believe that Kerry Young [30] – who is a Leicester based writer of Chinese-Jamaican origin – has written one of the defining Jamaican novels in *Pau*, which tells the story of a young Chinese man who moves to Jamaica in the early-twentieth century – it is one of the most expressive books that I have encountered, and I have bought many copies for friends and family as gifts. One cousin missed a wedding because he was so glued to the book, whilst another missed a New Year's Eve party, so I now issue a 'health warning' whenever I gift the book, so that I am not blamed for missed events!

Pau is the first book in a trilogy, and is followed by *Gloria* and *Show Me A Mountain* which tell the story of Pau's lover and wife. These books are both well-written, but nonetheless it is to Pau that I return repeatedly, as he is one of the most realistic characters I have met in fiction. His voice simply jumps from the page, and I become totally invested in his character each time I read it.

I am a member of a book club, and we read all three books in the trilogy over a period of four years. Kerry Young has attended our book club to discuss each book, and it has been fascinating to discuss the plots, characters and meanings with the author. We have been delighted to welcome Kerry to our meetings, but she is incredibly modest and has expressed her thanks each time that we have read and enjoyed her books and have invited her to speak to us. The film rights to Pau have been optioned, and I look forward to seeing if Pau's voice and energy can be replicated on screen.

A book that affected me similarly is *Small Island* by Andrea Levy. [31] This is the novel which for me most eloquently depicts the experience of the Windrush generation and their experiences in England during the 1940s and 50s. The voices of Hortense and Gilbert, the two main characters, reach out from the book and speak directly to the reader. I have given at least a dozen copies of this book as gifts, and I re-read it annually and find myself moved to laughter and tears each time.

Oprah Winfrey [32] is an inspiration for millions of people around the world, as a woman who came from a poor background filled with adversity but overcame her circumstances to rise to the top of the ladder. Above all, she has never forgotten where she came from, and has sought to grow and develop thousands of women, girls and men to achieve their potential. She is an icon and a role model across the world.

Another of my inspirations is Civil Rights activist Rosa Parks, [33] whose refusal to surrender her seat to a white passenger on a segregated bus in Montgomery, Alabama generated the 381-day Montgomery Bus Boycott that helped launch nationwide efforts to end segregation of public facilities and brought Dr Martin Luther King [34] to prominence. The upshot of the boycott was that the city of Montgomery was forced to lift the law requir-

II The Life Story of Dr Dorothy Francis

ing segregation on public buses. Rosa Park's small act of defiance led to a huge change in policy, and she received many accolades and awards during her lifetime in recognition of this. Fayola's middle name is Rosa in remembrance of the way that Rosa Park's actions changed history.

Rosa Parks and American Civil Rights Movement

On December 1, 1955, after a long day's work as a seamstress, Rosa Parks boarded the bus for home. The Montgomery City Code demanded that all public transportation be segregated into white and 'colored' areas, and Rosa Parks took a seat in the first of several rows designated for 'colored' passengers. The designation between white and black passengers was defined by a line roughly in the middle of the bus, which separated white passagers in the front of the bus from black passagers in the back. Additionally, black people were not allowed to walk through the 'white' part of the bus. They had to get on at the front to pay their fare and then get off and re-board the bus at the back door. Frequently, malicious drivers would accelerate away before black passengers could re-enter the bus, leaving passengers stranded and having paid their fare for nothing. The City Code required drivers to provide separate but equal accommodations for white and black passengers, and it was partly the violation of this code that lead to Rosa Park's refusal to give up her seat. As the bus continued on its journey it became full and the driver noticed that several white passengers were standing in the aisle. He stopped the bus and moved the sign separating the two sections back one row, telling four black passengers to give up their seats. Because a black person couldn't sit next to or adjacent to a white person, it often meant that a whole row of four black people would have to get up so that one white person could sit down. On the day in question three black passengers got up but Rosa Parks did not, on the basis that she had sat in a seat designated for black people that the driver had now unfairly reclassified as white. The bus driver had the authority to refuse service, so he called the police and had Mrs. Parks arrested. In later years, Rosa recalled that her refusal to give up her seat was not because she was physically tired, but because she was tired of giving in to racism, inquality and injustice, and the time had come to make a stand. Rosa Park's actions paved the path for many people including former President Obama, and she is a true hero to me.
(written by Dr Dorothy Francis)

Of course if we are talking about people of influence, I have to mention Martin Luther King [34] and Malcolm X [35] as people who fought for our rights and laid their lives on the line. Martin Luther King's 'I Have a Dream' speech is easily one of the most impressive examples of oratory and captivates me every time that I hear it.

I also highly admire Tommie Smith [36] and John Carlos, [37] who conducted a protest during their medal ceremony at the 1968 Summer Olympics in Mexico City. Tommie Smith won gold and John Carlos bronze in the 200-metre event and used the opportunity on the podium to highlight the injustices that black people faced in the USA. They received their medals shoeless but in black socks, to represent the enforced poverty of African Americans, and as they turned to face their flags and to hear the American national anthem they each raised a black-gloved fist, which they kept in the air until the anthem had finished. Carlos later said that it was a human-rights salute, rather than a Black Power salute, and that they were driven by the need to bring to the world's attention the inequality suffered by African Americans. It was a brave action, and one which saw them resoundingly ostracised by the US sporting establishment whilst being simultaneously supported and lauded by people of colour across the globe.

I also remember the Australian silver medalist in that race, Peter Norman, [38] who supported the protest by wearing an Olympic Project for Human Rights (OPHR) badge on his jacket, and staring straight ahead during the podium ceremony. This act stalled his Olympic career, and the selectors failed to choose him for the 1972 games despite his having qualified 13 times over. It took a lot of courage and quiet dignity to do what these men did in front of millions of people and all three knew that they would suffer personally, but did not shy away from taking action.

Other people whose actions and words have affected me include Mahatma Gandhi, [39] Nelson Mandela, [40] Mahalia Jackson, [41] Kanya King, [42] Claudia Jones (who established the first African-Caribbean newspaper in England), [43] Angela Davies, [44] Venus and Serena Williams, [45] Michelle Obama [46] and Ellen Johnson-Sirleaf, [47] the world's first elected Black female President and Africa's first female Head of State. I could write a much longer list, as there are many African, Caribbean, Indian and Asian people of influence who showed us the way, restored our pride and forged a path for us, and we are beholden to them. They stood up for what is right and in doing so changed their lives and ours.

11 The notion of 'home'

Growing up in England, Dorothy harboured a desire to return to Jamaica before the age of 30. However, by the time she reached that age she had decided, for a number of reasons, to make the UK her home. She explains why, and recalls the decision-making process that led to this. She also talks of her experience of visiting other Caribbean countries, and of her desire to build a house in Jamaica.

My ambition to return to Jamaica

I came to the UK at the age of six, but it was more than 20 years before I felt that I belonged here. I didn't enjoy growing up in England, and indeed one of my motivators for doing well at school and in higher education was to gain qualifications to enable me to return to Jamaica and get a good job. I saw Jamaica as home, and my ambition was to return to live there as I felt it was where I belonged.

II   The Life Story of Dr Dorothy Francis

However, by the time I reached my late 20s I recognised that this ambition was destined to remain unfulfilled, as I had lived the majority of my life in the UK and in effect was pining for a dream. I had sustained myself through bad times with fantasies of home, but came to appreciate that home is more than a physical location. Yes, I could return 'home' to Jamaica, but to what would I return and to whom? My mother was in England, as were my three sisters, brother, nieces and nephews and many good friends. I had a job that I loved and which offered good prospects, and I knew that it would be very hard to walk away from family and friends as well as the social and cultural lifestyle that I had become accustomed to.

My years of pining to return to Jamaica left me with a sense of dislocation, as I did not feel rooted within England, but after an absence of 20 years I was not truly at home in Jamaica either. I recognised that the time had come to locate myself in one location or the other, both physically and mentally. For years I had bodily lived in England, but my mind and heart were in Jamaica, and it was time to root myself in the UK so that I could devote myself to living instead of wishing. I had to accept the fact that England was now my home and to learn how to make the best of this.

It was at this point, and shortly after a harrowing experience at Heathrow airport, that I applied for British citizenship; I had never felt the need to do so before because I had not intended to remain in the UK. I am part of the Windrush generation, and I came to this country as a British subject with right to remain. However, the government changed the law and required people such as me to apply for British citizenship. I took out citizenship as a safeguard, as I realised that I was in an unstable position without it. I liked to travel, but without citizenship I ran the risk of arriving at a UK port to find that I was arbitrarily denied entrance to the country where I had lived for much of my life. I could not afford for this to happen, and so applied for citizenship.

I primarily took on British citizenship so that I could travel on a British passport, as I was tired of the way that I was treated whenever I travelled on my Jamaican passport. I was constantly stopped and questioned at airports, and had been subjected to false imprisonment in Yugoslavia and a harrowing and abusive strip search at Heathrow airport. Being strip searched at Heathrow is truly one of the worst experiences of my life, and had a direct bearing on my decision to obtain UK citizenship. I had had enough of the regular and repetitive questioning and overt racism at border points, and although I am proud of my Jamaican passport it has been relegated to the back of a drawer.

The decision to adopt a British passport is even more pertinent in the light of the Windrush scandal, where so many people of my generation who had lived here for 50 or more years were told that they did not have a right to live in the UK. Many were deported back to the Caribbean and Africa, even though they had worked here all their lives, paid tax and contributed to British society.

So now I am in my 50s, and the UK is home. I have given up on dreams of returning to

II The Life Story of Dr Dorothy Francis

settle in Jamaica even in retirement, and am likely to remain living in the UK. If I was to move anywhere it would be to Ireland, as I really love that country, but I doubt that I would move any further than that. My children are in the UK as are my siblings and mother, and whilst I could return from Ireland relatively quickly and inexpensively, the five thousand-mile journey from Jamaica would require different considerations.

I have to acknowledge that I am very British now; I have lived here for so long that I am used to the British way of life and would find it difficult to live permanently in Jamaica. I have grown to like, or at least appreciate, many of the things that I hated when I first came here, and can even tolerate the winter! I love to watch the seasons play out and am filled with a sense of wonder, awe and joy each year as I watch spring unfold; I don't think I will ever tire of spring and it is a renewed pleasure each year to welcome winter turning into spring. I would miss the seasons if I returned to Jamaica, as tropical countries have less demarcation in the weather and really only have gradients of summer; it is either hot and sunny or hot and rainy, with little in between. If I left I would also miss the British sense of humour and the easy and wide access to books, magazines, films and theatre. I would especially yearn for the variety of theatrical experiences that are on offer – from plays, to dance, to spoken word and comedy – as going to the theatre is one of my favourite pastimes.

I have made my peace now and recognise that England is where I belong; whether the British think the same is another thing, but that's a whole other story!

I have not ruled out having access to a small place in Jamaica where I could spend a few weeks at a time to escape the cold, wet UK winter. Even after all these years I find it incredibly difficult to deal with the overcast grey skies which are still my least favourite manifestation of winter weather, and I still find the lack of blue skies very depressing.

I am seeking to buy a plot of land with my cousin, to build a small house which will be his retirement home and within which he will maintain a room for me for whenever I wish to visit. This is an ideal option, as I have no desire to own a property in Jamaica which is used for only two or three months of the year, as I consider that to be selfish and wasteful. This alternative would allow me the flexibility of always having a place of my own to stay when visiting Jamaica.

Property in Jamaica is generally cheaper than in the UK, and sterling goes a long way. Many people who have normal sized houses in England find that they are able to build or buy much larger properties when they return to Jamaica, and many returners, as they are called, build huge, and frankly, ugly, piles with as many as eight bedrooms with corresponding en suite bathrooms, a host of reception rooms and triple or quadruple garages. Quite often these ostentatious houses are occupied by only two people, which is a tremendous waste of resources. A huge house such as these does not appeal to me, and I would be quite happy to co-own a small three bedroomed house which allowed me, Kevin and other family members to visit when we wish. If there was a need to en-

II   The Life Story of Dr Dorothy Francis

large the house at a later date we would do so; this is common practice in Jamaica, where house owners gradually expand their homes as circumstances require and finances permit.

It is common in Jamaica to build one's own house rather than buying a standard dwelling. Some people, especially those returning from the USA, Canada or the UK, construct a house entirely from architect's plans, and the house is built in one stage. Others build a house over a period of time, and completion may take up to 15 years. They buy a piece of land that is big enough for their eventual needs and build a small house which they expand as finance allows. Instead of saddling themselves with a mortgage for 20 to 40 years, they put money aside to purchase lumber, timber, bricks, concrete and other building materials. These are stored until there are enough supplies to embark upon the next stage of building, and then a builder is employed to erect a new room or verandah or to extend existing spaces. In that way, the house is enlarged to meet the needs of the owners but without incurring loans.

Houses in Jamaica are built of different materials from the UK because they don't have to contend with snow and cold. Floors tend to be tiled for coolness, and carpet is not widely used. Most houses have verandas for catching cool breezes, especially in the heat of the night, and they are important social places.

Until a few years ago my family lived high in the hills on a beautiful plot which commanded panoramic views, and this is where I lived as a child. In the 1980s they relocated to a plot lower down in the valley, as this offers better access to facilities. My aunt and cousins bought a piece of land and have gradually built a good-sized property which brings four generations of the family under one roof. I return to Jamaica every two years on average, and each time I arrive I am met with changes to the house. I have watched it grow from two bedrooms, one bathroom, a living room and small kitchen to six bedrooms, two bathrooms, and a large kitchen. A spacious living room leads to a light and airy verandah overlooking landscaped gardens. All of the current accommodation is on the ground floor; however plans are afoot to add two self-contained flats to the upstairs of the property, which can be rented or used by returning members of the family. A large water tank and solar panels are to be added to enable water and energy self-sufficiency. The proposals are ambitious but achievable over a period of time, and by working on the improvements on a gradual basis, the house will eventually be finished without outstanding mortgage or loans.

Reflections on some other Caribbean countries

It is now easier to plan independent travel, and sites such as Airbnb aid flexibility of booking, enabling us to explore places that would have otherwise been difficult to access. I enjoy returning to the Caribbean to visit family, but I also want to see as many other Caribbean islands and adjacent places as possible, so I try to combine a journey to Jamaica with a visit to another Caribbean island or destination. I usually stop en route to

II The Life Story of Dr Dorothy Francis

Jamaica and in this way have visited Florida, Grenada, Trinidad, Tobago and Antigua, and in addition to my solo travels I have also visited Cuba on a family holiday. I intend to visit Barbados and St Vincent and to make a return trip to Tobago in the next few years, and hope one day to have visited most of the Caribbean islands as well as Guyana and Surinam.

The Caribbean islands share similarities but are also very different in topography, language, culture, music and food, and it is educational and fun to explore these differences whilst also identifying and embracing similarities.

I thought that Grenada was similar to Jamaica in terms of the mountains and valleys, and I enjoyed the national 'pepperpot' dish, which is similar to a dish prepared in Jamaica. A highlight was a tour of the island that took in beautiful mountain views, thundering waterfalls and a simmering lake in the caldera of an extinct volcano. The fish in the lake have protected status and number in the thousands. It is a popular tourist activity to feed the fish with bread, and it is quite a sight to see hundreds of fish tumbling over each other and jostling for scraps of food.

Trinidad was vibrant and lively with a great deal to see and do, including a boat journey through the Caroni mangrove swamps to a lagoon to watch the scarlet ibis, Trinidad's national bird, return to their roosting spots. It was magical to see thousands of bright red birds glide back from their feeding spots in southern Trinidad and Venezuela and watch them cover the small green islands in the lagoon, filling them with colour until the vegetation looked like Christmas trees decorated in red. Another highlight of the visit was the incredible food. I love to eat street food wherever I go, and enjoyed the Trinidadian snack of doubles – small pancakes filled with spicy chick pea curry – which are served at roadside stands and are dangerously addictive!

Tobago was idyllically beautiful with pure white sands, bright blue sea and some of the friendliest people I have ever met. It is easily accessible from Trinidad via a twenty-minute flight so we took a day trip to explore the island. However, a day was not enough, so I look forward to a return visit to get to know the island better.

Antigua is another beautiful island, which I have visited twice. It is calm, peaceful and stunningly beautiful, and reputedly has 365 beaches, so visitors could attempt to visit one for every day of the year should they choose. The beaches range from pure white through to almost black, encompassing yellow and pink along the way, and no two beaches seem to be the same. Antigua also has many lagoons and beautiful natural harbours, which makes it one of the sailing capitals of the world. Leicester has one of the largest concentrations of people from Antigua, so it is not unusual to bump into people who formerly lived in Leicester and have now retired to Antigua, or indeed people from Leicester who are also on holiday in Antigua – it is very odd to meet someone on an Antiguan beach who one last saw in the local supermarket in Leicester!

II   The Life Story of Dr Dorothy Francis

I would like to spend more time in Cuba; I visited with my husband and children for two weeks, but it is a huge island filled with diversity and I am sure that we could spend a lifetime exploring it. Cuba is of such a size that all the other Caribbean islands could fit into it, so it demands more than a short trip. We visited in 2005, as we wanted our children to experience Cuba whilst Fidel Castro (1926–2016) [48] was still alive; we were concerned that once Castro died the country would be changed and probably not for the better. There were many noticeable differences from other countries that we have visited; the lack of advertising was conspicuous and welcome, as was the lack of the usual ubiquitous fast food outlets.

We stayed in a beach resort and spent a few days in Havana, renting rooms in the beautiful home of a physics professor. The stay in Havana was the favourite part of my visit to Cuba, as I felt that I was walking amongst history and was able to see places where Castro had given talks, where Che Guevara had strolled and where local people had rallied in support of the revolution. The housekeeper in Cuba cooked lovely food, which was wonderful, since overall, dishes in Cuba were poorly executed and lacked flavour and imagination.

Hurricane Katrina struck New Orleans whilst we were in Cuba and we experienced some of the effects as we were on the tail end of the storm and Havana was deluged by rain. However, we were obviously so much more fortunate than the people in New Orleans, who suffered so greatly. We had limited time in Havana, so continued to sightsee through the torrential rain as the weather was still hot, and we spent a day with our clothes plastered to our bodies, which was an unusual sightseeing experience!

I was interested to observe the differences in skin graduation and colour in Cuba, and the obvious class distinctions that this seemed to entail. Despite the revolution it seems that darker-skinned people of African origin have less status in society than lighter-skinned people of Spanish extraction, and I was dismayed to observe this. However, I was only in Cuba for a short while and did not speak extensively with local people, so perhaps this is only an impression gained from brief contact and casual observation.

There are at least twenty-eight island nations and more than 7,000 individual islands in the million square-mile region in the Caribbean. This includes islands off the coasts of South and Central America, as well as those in the Leeward and Windward Islands and the major islands of Cuba, Jamaica, Hispaniola (home to Haiti and the Dominican Republic) and Puerto Rico. However, most British people have difficulty in naming more than four or five Caribbean islands. Most people know Jamaica and Barbados; Antigua is usually mentioned, as is Tobago, but after that the answers tend to dry up. People are often surprised when I describe the diversity of the Caribbean islands and explain that they are not all English speaking (this is a popular misconception). Languages widely spoken within the Caribbean include Dutch, Spanish, French, Hindi and English, as well as local languages and creoles, yet I have spoken to well-educated people who express their surprise that the whole Caribbean does not converse in English. I have also had amusing, if somewhat worrying, conversations when I have been amazed and a little disconcerted to realise that British people confuse the location of Jamaica with that of Cape Verde, Tenerife or even Ghana (which is a country in Africa not an island!).

I have spent many hours correcting assumptions and misconceptions about Jamaica and other Caribbean islands, and it becomes a little tiresome; I am constantly surprised by how little even well-educated and well-read British people know about other countries, yet how much we are expected to know about theirs. It is necessary to have an extensive and almost encyclopaedic knowledge of UK culture, economy, government, food, topography and social life, to gain citizenship, yet many British natives do not know this information. A few years ago I took the British citizenship test along with a group of English friends and I was the only one who passed; most failed miserably. They were surprised by my knowledge of English culture, traditions, politics and customs, while I was surprised by their lack of knowledge of their own country. African-Caribbean people and other immigrants to the UK operate in a duality of experiences and tend to know facts about the UK but also about their countries of origin. However, British people are not required to know about other cultures in such depth, as they usually gain entry to other countries with ease. It has been my experience that many British people display a startling ignorance of UK history and culture, so I suppose that it should be no surprise that they know so little about a collection of small islands scattered across a sea 5,000 miles away from the UK.

Changes in Leicester

There is a difference between being tolerated and being accepted, and that difference has evolved in Leicester. Nowadays, people in Leicester are very proud of the fact that they live in a multicultural city. However, it was not always so; in 1972, as Asians were being expelled from Uganda by Idi Amin, [49] Leicester City Council placed an advert in the *Ugandan Argus* telling Asian people not to come to Leicester as it was full. This was an incredibly racist act and one which Leicester is now, quite rightly, deeply ashamed of. However this tactic backfired on the city council and had the opposite effect, because Asian people fleeing Idi Amin's Uganda thought that Leicester must be a wonderful place if it had already attracted so many Ugandan Asians, and so many changed their travel plans and came to Leicester instead!

Leicester is a good place to live and is, in my opinion, safer than many other UK cities. However, in the 1970s Leicester was a stronghold of the National Front [NF] [45] and when I moved to Leicester in the mid-1980s it was still recovering from this extreme reputation. The NF was a nationalist organisation, which believed that the British Isles should only belong to people that the NF defined as being British, and that all foreigners should be made to leave via deportation. They tried to follow this policy through by attempting to gain seats in government and by intimidating black people to make them leave the UK. My mother wept when I announced my decision to move to Leicester, as she feared for my safety. She knew that it was a racist city and it was many years before

II The Life Story of Dr Dorothy Francis

she ceased to worry about me.

Leicester has fought against its past and strives to be multicultural. The city has achieved a level of success to the point where it is held up as a beacon for other places. This attitude of multiculturalism has been spearheaded to some extent by the City Council, which realised that they had to change their way of thinking and lead the way to build a more inclusive city, and therefore developed policies to support festivals and events to bridge racial divides and join fragmented communities. The Council strives to promote diversity throughout all its offerings.

I believe that Leicester is multicultural in that it contains many different cultural or ethnic groups, but it is still working towards being intercultural. People live alongside one another in Leicester, but different cultural groups do not necessarily engage or interact with each other and there is little two way traffic between cultures. Communities live in demarcated groups and areas, but do not always communicate with each other. The difference between interculturalism and multiculturalism is that intercultural communities have a deep understanding and respect for all cultures, and communication focuses on the mutual exchange of ideas and cultural norms and on developing deep relationships so that everyone learns from one another and grows together. This might seem an ideal, but hopefully it is an achievable model towards which Leicester, and other cities, can aspire.

However, I feel that the way that Leicester has done things has much to offer to other cities. Teenagers and young people have friends of different colours and from varied cultures, and intermarriage is slowing becoming acceptable or even a norm. Young people are leading the way towards being intercultural, and do not necessarily view cultural background as being a major issue.

The Queen's visit to Leicester

The Queen visited Leicester on 8th March 2012, [50] as the first stop in her Diamond Jubilee Tour. The decision to start the Diamond Jubilee tour in Leicester was seen as recognition of the fact that the UK has a very different complexion and composition from when the Queen first ascended the throne. Leicester is the most diverse city in the UK, and was chosen because it showcases positive aspects of diversity. When Queen Elizabeth came to the throne more than 60 years ago, she was Queen of a mostly white UK and an emerging Commonwealth. The Commonwealth and the UK are now very different from 1953, and communities have changed; Leicester was chosen because the city shows this change in a positive and inclusive light.

The Leicester Caribbean Carnival [51]

One of the features of Leicester is the Caribbean Carnival, which started in 1985 and is an annual fixture on the city's calendar. The Caribbean Carnival is the second biggest

128

carnival in Europe after Notting Hill, and is a great cultural tradition, which really puts Leicester on the map. The event is very inclusive and all are made to feel welcome, with people from many different communities taking part. It brings people to Leicester from around the UK and further afield; a friend of mine is a travel agent and he flies people from Antigua, New York, Jamaica and other locations each year to attend Leicester Carnival. Carnival is a great opportunity to catch up with people you might not have seen for a long time and to eat good food whilst relaxing in Victoria Park. It often seems to rain on Carnival day, but that doesn't stop people from coming out in force!

I have held a party on the evening of the Carnival for the past 22 years, and this has become such a fixture that I don't even need to issue invitations anymore, as people just turn up. Two friends travelled 100 miles to attend one year without checking that I was holding the party, because they simply assumed that I would be. Given that guests are so dedicated to attending I hardly dare cancel it! We invite family, neighbours, work colleagues and friends from church and various social groups, and our biggest party was 85 people. The party is a norm in our household and we don't travel in the first week of August, so that we are available to prepare and host the event.

12 Awards

Dorothy received the Queen's Award in 2016, followed by an MBE in 2017. She recalls both events:

Queen's Award – Lifetime Achievement for Promotion of Enterprise

The Queen's Award for Enterprise Promotion is recognition for people who support others to achieve business outcomes or develop business skills, and it is awarded annually to people who play an outstanding role in promoting the growth of business enterprise and/or develop entrepreneurial skills in other people. Winners of the Award are announced on the Queen's birthday, April 21st, as part of the Queen's Birthday Honours list. Entry is by nomination only, and individuals cannot put themselves forward. Nominators are required to keep the nomination a secret from the nominee, and the first indication of the award is usually a letter from Buckingham Palace. Between five to ten people are selected for the Queen's Award for Enterprise Promotion each year, and of that number one person is selected to receive the annual Lifetime Achievement Award. I was fortunate to be chosen as the recipient of the Lifetime Achievement Award in 2016. It is perhaps the greatest honour that I have received in my career, and is the award of which I am proudest, even more so than my MBE.

The award is bestowed by the Queen on the advice of the Prime Minister, following a rigorous selection process, and recipients receive an engraved crystal goblet or similar commemorative item. They are also bestowed a Grant of Appointment from the Queen, which entitles them to use the Queen's Award title after their name, and recipients are

II The Life Story of Dr Dorothy Francis

invited to a reception at Buckingham Palace, where they are usually presented to the Queen.

I received notification of my award in February 2016, and was tasked with keeping it a secret until April 21st, when it was announced in the press. I told my husband but not my children, and they were annoyed that I kept it secret from them for such a long time!

The Queen's Award is presented by the Lord Lieutenant of the county that the recipient lives in, so I received mine from Jennifer, Lady Gretton [52] JP, the Lord Lieutenant of Leicestershire at that time. The presentation was at Leicester Town Hall on Monday 20th June 2016, and was attended by around 60 guests including family members, friends and clients, as well as various dignitaries including Leicestershire's Vice Lieutenant, Colonel Murray Colville, the Lord Mayor of Leicester at that time, Stephen Corrall, and the City Mayor, Sir Peter Soulsby. Also in attendance was Ed Mayo, the chief executive of Co-operatives UK, the federation body for co-operatives.

This was a very special day for me, even more so than my later visit to Buckingham Palace, because I was able to share it with friends and family. Also, the Queen's Award ceremony at the Town Hall was a ceremony just for me, which was lovely. I think I posed for photographs for a full hour after the ceremony, and smiled until my face hurt! Lady Gretton presented me with a crystal chalice as my award, whilst Vice-Lieutenant Colville read the declaration from the Queen in ringing tones, before presenting it to me. It was an impressive and awe inspiring occasion, and one which I shall always remember.

The fact that I had won the Queen's Award Lifetime Achievement Award received a great deal of publicity for a number of reasons. Firstly, only one award is presented each year and it had never been won by someone in Leicestershire before, so although Lady Gretton had been the Lord Lieutenant for 13 years, it was the first time that she and her deputy had made a Queen's Award Lifetime Achievement Award presentation, and she was excited to be presented with the opportunity. Also, it was the first time that the Award had been won by an African-Caribbean woman, which attracted attention as well. In addition, the award was made in recognition of services to the co-operative movement, which helped to put co-ops on the map. All too often, the co-operative movement seems to be a forgotten sector, and the award drew attention to the work that is undertaken in this area. The story was covered in the co-operative press, in the *Leicester Mercury* and on local radio, and was also picked up in the *Jamaica Gleaner*, to the great delight of my family.

Four weeks after the Town Hall presentation, Kevin and I attended a reception at Buckingham Palace, where we mingled with other award winners and I was presented to Prince Philip. It was interesting to see behind the scenes at Buckingham Palace, and it felt special to walk through the gates and to crunch over the gravel towards the main reception building with its grand staircase, beautiful state rooms, oil paintings, antique furniture and what seemed like acres of gilding on every possible surface. The rooms were

II The Life Story of Dr Dorothy Francis

ornamental and magnificent, and we were also able to admire the beautifully-landscaped gardens. Waiters passed through the rooms bearing trays of canapés and magnums of champagne, and we chatted with other award winners and their partners, and shared our experiences of being in business.

I was approached by the senior assessor, who plays a large part in deciding who receives the Queen's Award. He recognised me by my name badge and told me how particularly delighted he was to meet me. When I enquired why this was, he informed me that I had been the forerunner in the process from stage one, and that five independent assessors had each chosen me as their number-one choice for the Lifetime Achievement honour, which he said was unprecedented during the ten years that he had been involved in the Awards process.

He explained how the awards are decided, and described the six assessment stages to be surmounted before the winners are agreed. Firstly, the person is nominated in secret and the nominator obtains up to six testimonials to support the application. The nomination and supporting documentation are sent to the senior assessor, who reviews them and then mails copies of the documents to five independent assessors. These assessors score the nominations, and a number of nominees are eliminated at this point. The five assessors each nominate the person that they think should receive the overall Lifetime Achievement Award, and it was at this point that they all independently chose me for the award. The Queen's Award for Enterprise promotion is an MBE equivalent award, whereas the overall Lifetime Achievement Award is an OBE equivalent.

The documents are returned to the senior assessor, who moderates the applications before sending them to a further panel where the nominees are vetted, police checked and assessed for suitability. After this, the nominations are delivered to the Prime Minister for his or her approval. The Prime Minister has a veto and can decide, without supplying a reason, whether or not to accept applicants; the senior assessor told me that seven were submitted to the prime minister in the year that I won, but he rejected two of them, so only five went forward to the sixth stage. The final stage is that the nominations are sent to Buckingham Palace for the approval of the Queen, and it is only after this has taken place that the awards are agreed and winners notified.

I was happy to receive the Queen's Award and accepted it gladly, as I did not feel that it compromised my principles. I had always hoped that I would not be nominated for an OBE or MBE, as I felt that there is an inherent contradiction in people of colour, from former colonies, accepting an award that proudly proclaims the Empire (OBE is an acronym for Officer of the Most Excellent Order of the British Empire whilst MBE stands for Member of the Most Excellent Order of the British Empire). The British Empire was instrumental in devastating the countries that it colonised, and there is nothing about colonialism or the Empire to celebrate. The Queen's Award was a perfect honour for me as it allowed my work to be recognised by providing me with an OBE-level award, but without the colonial overtones of an OBE, and I was able to accept it with a clear con-

II   The Life Story of Dr Dorothy Francis

science. It also allowed me to visit Buckingham Palace as a guest of the Queen, which was a wonderful experience, and in accepting the award I ruminated that this was probably likely to be the first and only time that I would be invited to Buckingham Place by Her Majesty; little did I know!

My MBE

In October 2016, five months after my Award ceremony at Leicester Town Hall and four months after my visit to Buckingham Palace, I received a letter with a royal crest on the envelope. On opening it, I was shocked and stunned to read that I had been nominated for an MBE for 'Services to Enterprise and the Communities of Leicester and Leicestershire'. This was a complete surprise to me, especially as I had assumed that winning the Queen's Award, which is the equivalent to an OBE, had put me out of the running for an OBE or MBE. The nomination also put me on the horns of a dilemma, as I had always vocalised my strong opposition to the OBE/MBE awards system because it references the British Empire. I was angry and upset that I was now being forced to make a decision that I had not anticipated, and I was at a loss regarding how to respond; it took lot of soul searching before I finally accepted.

I shared the news of the award with Kevin, Fayola and Safiya, but swore them to secrecy, especially as I was not decided whether or not I should accept it. I carried the letter around with me for weeks while I mulled it over. I also canvased the opinions of friends and family, by posing the question to them in the guise of collecting information for a debate that I was due to chair at a conference. I asked whether or not people of colour should accept MBE or OBE, given the colonial implication of the awards? I sent the message to most of my African, Asian and African-Caribbean friends, and the responses that I received contributed in great part to my decision to accept the award.

The general text of the responses was that people of colour should accept such awards, as doing so recognises our contribution to UK society and allows the recipient to be seen as a role model for younger people or others who are striving to achieve. Most commented that the inclusion of the words 'British Empire' within the awards is unfortunate, but pointed out that the awards are usually known by their acronyms anyway, and this distances them from the original meaning. The majority argued that the awards should be accepted in the spirt of modern-day perspective rather than with reference to the Empire. All responses commented that black people have a responsibility to accept awards, as they raise our profile, and that this is perhaps more important than the name of the award.

These responses were invaluable to me in terms of helping to make my mind up, and I felt fortunate to have such insightful friends and family who were able, albeit unwittingly, to guide me toward making my decision. Another contributory facter was that I read that the government was aware of the reluctance of proposed recipients to accept awards that referenced the British Empire, and were responding to this by considering

II The Life Story of Dr Dorothy Francis

a change of name to the Order of British Excellence. This would retain the acronyms of OBE and MBE, but would change and defuse the negative connation. This commitment to changing the name of the awards was a deciding factor in accepting the MBE. However, I later read that the Most Excellent Order of the British Empire was instituted by the Queen's grandfather, King George V, and that the Queen has said that she doesn't want to see any changes to her grandfather's Order during her reign, so it is unlikely that there will be any changes for some time. Perhaps a new order will be established instead, and all future nominees can be appointed to that order? Only time will tell.

However, the ultimate deciding factor in my deliberations was my mother. I considered how hard she had worked to ensure that her children received a good education and status in life. To achieve this she relocated herself 5,000 miles from home to a hostile and unwelcoming country, and left behind family and friends. She had high hopes of us, and I knew that she would be thrilled to know that I had been nominated for an MBE, and would see this as a great reward for my hard work and also all that she had worked for. I also knew that my siblings, cousins, aunties and uncles would be filled with pride to know that I had been honoured in this way. In the end, I accepted the award because I did not feel it was within my gift to refuse it. What right did I have to refuse something that represented so much to my mother, my brother and sisters, wider family and friends?

My MBE offers validation not just for me, but also for other women and men of African-Caribbean origin who have dealt with society's negative expectations for generations and have been told that they are without worth. I also took it in thanks for the efforts of those who had nominated me (I discovered that I had been nominated separately by two people, one of whom is a person of colour).

On reflection, I also accepted the MBE in remembrance of the stories that my mother told me of her early days in the UK, and in particular the story of when she walked five miles in the snow to apply for a job only to be rejected because of the colour of her skin. I know that she was only able to endure such humiliation because of her firm determination that her presence in England meant that her children would gain a good education and would use that learning to fight such oppression. It was my mother's determination and commitment that put me on the path to receive the nomination, and in the end she was my reason for accepting the award.

I had a great sense of pride when notification of my MBE was printed in *The Times* and the *Leicester Mercury* on the 31st December 2016, in the New Year's Honours list. This was my second notification in eight months, having appeared in the Birthday Honours list in April 2016, and I received some good-humoured teasing to the effect that if I kept visiting Buckingham Palace on such a regular basis I would soon be on first-name terms with the Queen!

The invitation to Buckingham Palace to attend the Queen's Award reception had only

133

II The Life Story of Dr Dorothy Francis

been extended to me and Kevin, so we had been unable to take our daughters with us. However, the MBE invitation included three guests, so I was able to invite Kevin, Fayola and Safiya to accompany me, which made the investiture into a lovely family event.

We stayed overnight in London to ensure that we would be early for our 10 am arrival at Buckingham Palace, and we enjoyed sweeping up to the Palace gates in a London cab and being ushered onto the pink gravel of the forecourt. This was the second visit for me and Kevin, but the first for Fayola and Safiya, and they took in every moment of the visit and enjoyed turning to wave to the crowd of tourists who were observing from the other side of the railings.

I was presented with my MBE by Prince William, The Duke of Cambridge, and had a pleasant sixty-second conversation with him until it was time for him to move on to the next recipient. However, I can't remember a single word that was spoken, as the ceremony was nerve-wracking, as I tried to remember the protocol of curtsying, shaking hands, walking backwards from his presence and so much more. I was so busy concentrating on these details that what we spoke about went straight out of my head. However, I managed to get through the ceremony without fuss, unlike the woman who followed me, who went the wrong way and had to be rescued by the stewards! After my presentation I was able to join the audience and watch as others received their honours.

We queued to have our photographs taken by professional photographers and we took dozens of photographs of our own and have great memories of the day.

Account of Honorary Doctorate of Laws, Graduation Day

In late 2017 I received a letter from the University of Leicester informing me that the University wished to confer an Honorary Doctorate of Laws on me in recognition of my service to diversity and the co-operative movement. An honorary doctorate is the highest honour that the University can bestow and it was of special significance to receive the degree in 2018 as that year marked the 100th anniversary of women receiving the vote in the UK. The University wished to commemorate this by awarding a number of degrees to women who play a significant role in UK society and I was delighted and honoured to be chosen for this distinction.

I believe I was chosen because I have worked with the University of Leicester for some years to promote entrepreneurism to students, delivering projects that develop business skills and an understanding of the world of work and which allow students to gain valuable skills through a variety of routes including placements in local social enterprises.

In addition I am an Honorary Visiting Fellow at the University of Leicester and also volunteer my skills and expertise as an Entrepreneur in Residence. This support service offers students, alumni and staff the opportunity to discuss entrepreneurial plans, explore skills needed to become an entrepreneur and to deliberate on business planning,

II   The Life Story of Dr Dorothy Francis

market research, raising finance and other aspects of setting up in business. The provision is also available to students or alumni who already run existing businesses and are seeking to grow, diversify or develop. I meet with local students on a face-to-face basis; however the University of Leicester operates on a worldwide basis and I have held telephone or Skype meetings with students in Canada, Kuwait, Oman, UAE, Kenya, Malawi, Ghana and many other countries. I consider it a privilege to speak to people from across the world and to share my knowledge with diverse individuals and I have spoken with a host of inspiring people. I usually have a waiting list of people wishing to meet with me because I specialise in social enterprise legal structures and additionally I am the only female, and person of African descent, operating as an Entrepreneur in Residence which attracts interest from women, African and African-Caribbean students and staff.

My history of working with the University, combined with publicity regarding the Queen's Award for Enterprise Promotion, the award of my MBE and recognition as a Companionship of the Chartered Management Institute also contributed to the decision to honour me with a doctorate.

I had no hesitation in accepting the nomination as it is a wonderful accolade and I knew that it would make my family, friends, church members and work colleagues very proud and happy to see me recognised in such a way. Also I was conscious, as always, that in accepting such awards I act as a role model and assist to raise the profile of people of colour. A great deal of work is needed to achieve equality in the conferring of doctorates, as in many other areas of life: the University of Leicester has conferred 193 Honorary Doctorates of Laws since 1958 yet only 44 women have been recognised – almost 80 per cent of awards have been to men which is a situation that the University is keen to redress. I was the ninth woman of colour to receive an Honorary Doctorate of Law and the second African-Caribbean woman to be recognised in 60 years so I appreciated the significance of the award and why it was important to accept it to acknowledge the contribution that I and other African-Caribbean women make to British society.

The ceremony took place on a beautiful summer's day at De Montfort Hall, Leicester on Friday 20th July 2018 and I joined a large gathering of students as they prepared to celebrate their success. I was accompanied by my brother, sisters, cousin, close friends and church members and I had managed to stretch my guest list from three people to twelve but unfortunately was still unable to invite everyone that I wished and my work colleagues and some family were not at the ceremony although they were able to watch via online streaming.

The event began with a VIP lunch at which I was seated next to Mr Mike Kapoor, the newly appointed Lord Lieutenant of Leicestershire and we had a lively conversation throughout the meal including fond reminiscences of his predecessor, Jennifer, Lady Gretton, who presented my Queen's Award in 2016. However I was far too nervous to eat much so unfortunately the delicious food was somewhat lost on me although my guests enjoyed the meal!

II   The Life Story of Dr Dorothy Francis

Following the meal my guests were led to their seats whilst I was taken through my paces on the stage regarding where I would sit, stand and speak during the event. This run-through was useful as it was ascertained that I was too small to be seen properly over the lectern, and would require a step to raise me to the appropriate height – so it was fortunate that we discovered this at that point rather than when I went to the lectern to speak!

Following the rehearsal I was taken to the robing room where I donned beautiful cherry red robes and a black cap all of which looked very grand and imposing. With a few minutes to go all members of the degree congregation lined up in order of precedence and awaited the signal to enter the auditorium The procession into the hall was nerve-wracking but exciting as I concentrated on keeping my place in the line, walking carefully and not tripping over my feet as I climbed the stairs! As I sat in my chair facing the assembled gathering of more than 1,000 people I had an opportunity to appreciate the gravity of the event and experienced a few palpitations as I gazed upon the sea of faces in front of me!

I watched as hundreds of proud students came on stage to receive their awards from the Chancellor of the University. It was wonderful to see the pride on their faces and that of their families and to hear the whoops, cheers and wild clapping from family, friends and colleagues as students received their degrees.

The awarding of my doctorate came towards the end of the graduation ceremony and after a short introduction I was asked to stand whilst Mr Nigel Siesage, the University of Leicester Public Orator, gave an oration covering aspects of my life, work and achievements which culminated in a recommendation that the University of Leicester confer upon me the Honorary Degree of Doctor of Laws. After the Chancellor of the University presented me with the award I ascended the lectern (making use of the previously mentioned step!) to give a short address to the degree congregation. I was aware that one of the criteria for choosing the honorary graduate for any given ceremony is that 'the recipient provides a role model to graduating students or is otherwise likely to add value to a degree congregation, engage the interest of the students and enhance the graduation experience' so I was conscious of the need to fulfil this requirement and had given my speech much thought. It was exciting to speak to such a large assembly and I enjoyed the opportunity to highlight aspects of my business career and to use the occasion to impart encouraging words to graduates starting out on their journey into work.

On the conclusion of the degree ceremony we filed from the auditorium to the sound of a trumpet playing and I breathed a sigh of relief at having negotiated the event successfully. My guests and I were ushered into a champagne and cupcakes reception which I am told that they enjoyed but I did not manage any refreshments as I was whisked away to be interviewed on video and to take photographs. It was a bit of a whirl! I posed for photographs with various University of Leicester dignitaries including the Chancellor and Vice-Chancellor and was also photographed signing the University Honorary Grad-

II   The Life Story of Dr Dorothy Francis

uates Register.

In signing the register I was awed to realise that my name joined national and international figures such as Betty Boothroyd, first female speaker of the House of Commons; Sir Herman Ouseley who has been at the forefront of challenging institutional racism for many years; Indarjit Singh, inspirational journalist and broadcaster; The Rt Hon. The Baroness Amos, politician and diplomat; popular broadcaster Sir Michael Terence (Terry) Wogan who hosted the popular Radio Two breakfast show for more than 30 years; and much loved owner of Leicester City Football Club, Vichai Srivaddhanaprabha who received his degree in 2016 two years before his untimely death.

The register also includes many local figures that I have been honoured to work with over my years in Leicester such as Rita Patel, founder of the Belgrave Baheno Women's Centre and the Peepul Centre social enterprise; Freda Hussain, a dedicated educator and first Asian female High Sheriff of Leicestershire; Vijay Sharma, who pioneered and led the development of the national digital radio station BBC Asian Network; and Manjula Sood, an educator of many years and the first Asian female Lord Mayor in the UK. These are people who I admire greatly and I have cheered their many successes and applauded when they were awarded Honorary Doctorates of Laws but never imagined that I would one day join them in receiving the same honour. Another person in the register is a close personal friend, Jean "Binta" Breeze, who received an Honorary Doctorate of Letters in 2017 and was delighted to see me join her as a Doctor!

The day concluded with many photographs taken with family and friends followed by cocktails at the Grand Hotel and a meal at my favourite restaurant. It was an occasion to remember. I was so pleased to share it with my guests and was glad that digital streaming allowed family and friends in Jamaica, England and the USA to view the ceremony too.

Below is the address by the Public Orator, Mr Nigel Siesage, given on 20 July 2018.

> **Dorothy Francis**
> To quote Charles Darwin, "It is the long history of humankind ... that those who learned to collaborate and improvise most effectively have prevailed." Dorothy Francis's purpose in life has been to help people to collaborate with others to achieve the goals of their communities.
>
> To many of us, "the co-op" may make us think of a local supermarket, or possibly a funeral directors. But the co-operative movement is very much more than that, and Dorothy, as chief executive of CASE, the Co-operative and Social Enterprise Development Agency in Leicestershire, has made an outstanding contribution to the movement - a movement so diverse it extends from retail to community energy, from farming to

II The Life Story of Dr Dorothy Francis

football, from social care to no-landlord student housing. There are over 7,000 independent co-operatives in the UK, providing employment for 235,000 people, with a combined turnover of £36 billion. The defining characteristic of them all, whether they are called co-operatives or social enterprises, is that they are owned and run by their members.

Dorothy recognises two particularly important influences in her life. The first is her mother, whom she describes as "a brave woman" who made the 5,000 mile journey from the Caribbean to follow her husband to England, leaving behind her children (who later joined her) and friends and family, in search of a better life; and who believed that the key to a better life was education. The thought of her mother has been a constant inspiration to Dorothy when things have been tough.

Thanks to her mother's support and encouragement, Dorothy had a successful school career. With a decent set of O levels, the possibility of training as a nurse beckoned. This was the 1970s. What could be a more suitable career for a young black woman? Here the second important influence – and a lot of chance – came into play. Though only 16, Dorothy had left home with very little idea of what she would do or where she would live. She went for advice to the Coventry Race Relations Council, and it was the adviser on the desk that day, a Mr Enrico Stennett, who took her under his wing, helped her find somewhere to stay, and, with immense persistence, overcame her assumption that "working class black girls don't do A levels".

Dorothy's path from then on was certainly not smooth, but this was a turning point, and 3 A levels, a degree in English, two teaching qualifications and membership of the Chartered Institute of Personnel and Development (achieved through part time study as a single parent) have followed.

Chance also played a part in Dorothy's discovery of the co-operative movement. Plans to train as a social worker had received a setback, when some friends asked her to join a co-operative they were setting up to sell books by African, African-Caribbean and Asian authors. Having nothing better to do, she said yes, and was introduced to this way of working that encompassed democratic control, shared ownership and participation and a fair return on labour.

This brought Dorothy into contact with the Coventry Co-operative Development Agency. She was impressed, and a few years later she applied for a job with the Leicester equivalent – the organisation which she now runs.

Many of the hundreds of social businesses whose establishment Dorothy has personally assisted have now been operating successfully for over 30 years and have themselves gone on to win awards. Dorothy's passion for her work, and the pleasure she takes in the success of the people she advises, shine out. As Mr Stennett did with her years ago, she will not let people assume that they are not capable of achieving. She is

II   The Life Story of Dr Dorothy Francis

clearly devoted to her own family, and she brings the same commitment to her extended family of co-ops. This is reciprocated. "It's been a huge difference, to have someone who can give you impartial advice and to know they've been there"; "There was always someone there I could talk to" are typical of the many testimonials her work has received.

Dorothy does not do things by halves. Her favourite book is *Pau*, by the Leicester-based writer, Kerry Young. But Dorothy doesn't just recommend it. She buys copies for friends and family as gifts, so that they can share her pleasure. She would like to be remembered as someone who liked to party, laughed a lot, tried her best and helped others – and that surely is a description which she has fully earned.

Her recognition extends far beyond the Leicestershire area. Having worked part-time for her original Chartered Institute of Personnel and Development professional qualification, she is now also a Companion of the Chartered Management Institute – the highest level, awarded by invitation only. In 2016 she received the Queen's Award for Enterprise Promotion, Lifetime Achievement Award – something which is given to only one person a year; and in the 2017 New Year's honours list she was appointed MBE for services to enterprise and the community.

It is high time the University matched these many awards with one of its own highest honours. Mr Chancellor, on the recommendation of the Senate and the Council, I present Dorothy Elaine Francis, that you may confer upon her the honorary degree of Doctor of Laws.

13 The EU Referendum and Brexit

Dorothy talks about the EU Referendum and 'Brexit' thus:

Over the years most people in the UK gave little thought to EU membership – it was simply seen as a fact of life. However, certain factions began to agitate for an exit from Europe, citing 'sovereignty' and 'control (especially immigration control) as reasons why the UK should rule itself, rather than be ruled from Europe (as they saw it). I believe that the Brexit (British Exit) demands caught most people, especially David Cameron, by surprise, and they did not take them seriously or prepare effective counter arguments as to why the UK should stay in the EU, which was the downfall of the Remain campaign.

David Cameron had promised an EU referendum as an inducement to hard liners in his party as a part of his re-election campaign, and was held to ransom to make good on this promise. He felt that it was safe to call a referendum, because he did not believe that people would vote to leave and clearly did not gauge the mood of the people nor antici-

139

II   The Life Story of Dr Dorothy Francis

pate the underhand methods of the Leave faction. It is said that he was advised to set super-majority conditions, such as 70 per cent of votes being required to trigger a decision to leave, if so, he failed to heed this advice. The UK went to the polls on Thursday 23rd June 2016, and the result was extremely narrow, with 51.9 per cent of UK voters voting to leave. The leave vote was strongest in England, at 53 per cent, followed by Wales at 52 per cent. However, Scotland and Northern Ireland voted to remain by 62 and 55 per cent respectively, and were bitterly disappointed by the result.

The UK government and Labour – the main UK opposition party – both say Brexit will happen. There are some groups campaigning for Brexit to be halted, but this is unlikely to happen so, as it stands, it seems that the UK will indeed leave Europe in 2019. This will be the end of an era, and no-one really knows what to expect when the UK leaves the union, nor what life will be like for its citizens thereafter.

The European Union

The European Union – often known as the EU – is an economic and political partnership involving 28 European countries, which began after World War Two to foster economic co-operation based on a philosophy that countries which trade together are more likely to avoid going to war with each other.

It has since grown to become a 'single market' allowing goods and people to move around as if in effect the member states were one country. The European Union has its own currency, the euro, which is used by nineteen of the member countries. It also has its own parliament and sets rules in a wide range of areas including consumer rights, transport and the environment.

The United Kingdom joined the European Economic Community, as it was called at that time, on the 1st January 1973, as it feared political isolation from the rest of Europe if it remained outside of the partnership. The Labour Party initially sought renegotiation of membership, but this was toned down to a referendum on whether the United Kingdom should remain part of the Community. This referendum was held in 1975, and 67 per cent of those who voted were in favour of continued membership.
(written by Dr Dorothy Francis)

The Brexiteers had no plan except to pull the UK out of Europe, and the Remain camp failed to put together strong arguments as to why the UK should stay in the Union. In my opinion, the country should not have been required to vote on this matter; I see it as a squabble between David Cameron and a few disruptive individuals which got out of hand but now affects the entire nation and Europe. David Cameron caved in to the idea of a referendum so that he could secure another five years in power, and in his weakness, he did not seriously consider that a leave vote would happen or what it might mean. He sought to secure his personal future by throwing the concession of a referendum, and the future of the UK, to Nigel Farage, Boris Johnson and Jacob Rees-Mogg, who had been baying at his heels. However, the manoeuvre failed, and the results of the referendum forced him to resign, so it was all for naught. I believe that Cameron gambled with the future of the country and lost, and in my

140

opinion he acted in a weak and uncalculated way by putting his personal ambition above the safety and security of the United Kingdom.

I think that the results of the referendum have polarised the UK. The campaign was fought on blatant racism and xenophobia and exposed a dark underside of the UK, which is worrying for people of colour and immigrants. It has been a very negative process, was not necessary and has changed the face of the UK. It has increased racism and given bigots, xenophobes and racists a free hand to chant racist rhetoric, and has officially sanctioned racism, especially towards Muslims and people from Eastern Europe. The situation resonates with the state of affairs when Hitler incited hatred by using the same kinds of words about Jews that Donald Trump, Boris Johnson and Nigel Farage now use about Muslims. They employ the same inflammatory and derogatory language, and seek to apportion blame on Muslims and foreigners, blaming them for all of society's ills in the same way that Hitler used Jewish people as scapegoats in 1930s Germany to facilitate his rise to power.

In many ways, Brexit has put race relations back to the 1970s, as it has given racists a free hand to say things that they previously suppressed, because they now they feel that their views have the backing of the majority of the electorate. I feel that Brexit has destabilised our communities and made life more difficult for people of colour and migrants, and has set into motion matters which will not be sorted for many years. I doubt that we will appreciate the full effects for maybe another 15 to 20 years, and I am fearful for the outcome.

I am aware that this opinion is not shared by all, and that many others feel differently. Those who voted 'Out' have a spirit of optimism that 'sovereignty' will bring back power to the UK and that throwing off the yoke of European control will make Britain 'great' again. However, many people who voted 'Out' feel that they were misled and that they voted without realising the ramifications, especially as less than ten hours after the vote, a number of promises were exposed as lies and processes began to unravel. The Leave camp sold the campaign by promising an additional £350 million pounds each week for the National Health Service (NHS) if the UK left the EU. The NHS means a lot to the people of the UK, and many voted 'Leave' because they wanted to protect it. The day after the vote they were told that it was untrue that £350 million would be pumped into the service, and the Leave Campaign denied that they had promised this, even when faced with pictures of double-decker buses on which they had plastered this statement.

Many people feel unsettled by Brexit, and thousands of people who have the right of citizenship in other countries have been applying for passports and citizenship. Ireland was overwhelmed, as thousands of people evoked Irish ancestry so that they could obtain Irish passports and stay in the EU.

Significant numbers of people who have dual Caribbean-UK nationality have now re-applied for their passports, or are applying for their British-born children. Though I have

II   The Life Story of Dr Dorothy Francis

dual nationality and hold British and Jamaican passports I have never applied for Jamaican citizenship for my children, but am now considering doing so.

Theresa May consistently repeats that 'Brexit means Brexit', but we will have to wait to know what this means once Brexit is truly achieved. I see a bleaker future for the UK, but desperately hope to be proved wrong.

14 Reflections on Japan and Japanese culture

Dorothy discusses her reflections on Japan and Japanese culture:

I have never been to Japan, so my knowledge of the country and its culture has been gained from films, books and people that I have met. My impression of Japan is that it is a fairly closed and homogenous society that in previous generations chose to cut itself off from other societies in order to maintain the Japanese way of life and is now seeking to reverse this policy. Having been brought to its knees by World War Two, Japan reinvented itself within a rapid timeframe and has worked to become a more outward-looking country that encourages people from across the world to experience its culture.

I feel a number of negatives are perpetuated about Japan and would like to explore the truth of these. We hear that Japanese people are overworked and under social pressure which makes it difficult for them to relax, and we read that Japanese workers have a strong adherence to their employers to the detriment of family and social life which leads to a breakdown of society. However, we also know that Japan has led the way in many innovations and has a dedication to change, which is envied across the world. Japan is strikingly modern but retains a rich and enviable cultural heritage with beautiful ceremonies and festivals which are an important and vibrant aspect of society, and I think it is wonderful to have such an enriching tradition whereby age-old practices flourish within contemporary society. I hear that in ancient cities like Kyoto it is still easy to find establishments, shops and restaurants with hundreds of years of history where traditional crafts and dishes have been steadily improved and perfected for generations, and I would like the opportunity to visit these places.

Japan's contemporary art and culture, including architecture, design, film, dance and crafts, as well as pop culture such as *anime, manga*, and video games, are cutting edge and yet appear to sit side-by-side with traditional culture, which is a great balancing act.

I am an admirer of a number of contemporary Japanese, including Yayoi Kusama, 'the artist who produces sculpture and installations but also paintings, film, clothing, fiction and poetry. She has used polka dots in art and installations for many years, because to her they are the form of the sun and represent the energy of life and the entire world. I marvel at the way that she has produced an ongoing body of work around this theme, and that it has been a constant in her work for many years. Conversely, the polka dots

II The Life Story of Dr Dorothy Francis

also stand for the calm roundness of the moon, as well as representing infinity and movement, so she moulds the shapes to fit almost any form of expression. I would love to experience one of her Mirror/Infinity rooms, where hundreds of neon coloured balls hang in mirrored-glass spaces. The balls are hung at different heights and are endlessly repeated in the reflections of the mirrored walls, floors and ceilings, to play upon the idea of the perfection of infinity.

It is fascinating to view Yayoi Kusama's art and to interpret the many ways that she uses polka dots in her work. Her work is timeless and never grows stale, and she is not afraid to challenge conventions in her art, in the way that she dresses or in her very avant-garde and slightly eccentric life, and in doing so has become one of Japan's greatest living artists.

I also greatly respect Kazuo Inamori,[53] a highly successful Japanese entrepreneur who brings compassion and empathy to business. His style resonates with my idea of how business should be done, and I am particularly impressed that he attributes his success to 'doing what is right as a human being' whenever he is faced with making difficult business decisions. I believe that many CEOs and high ranking business people forget about the human cost of their decisions, but Kazuo Inamori brings his Zen Buddhist faith to his work and puts people at the heart of all processes.

Kazuo Inamori is an example of compassion in decision-making, and his contribution has resulted in great recognition, including business schools named in his honour. I am impressed that he established the Inamori Foundation over 30 years ago, to award the annual Kyoto Prize to those who have exhibited 'extraordinary contributions to science, civilisation, and the spirituality of humankind'. He has also endowed the Inamori Ethics Prize for people who demonstrate examples of ethical leadership and make contributions to improve global society.

Kazuo Inamori's style of working is to create a single philosophy that everyone in a company, from top to bottom, believes in, and once this is established he then manages the company along this principle. His major goal is to pursue the physical and mental happiness of all employees, which is where he believes shareholder value lies; if the employees are happy, the company will do well. This adherence to a single overall philosophy ensures that all employees have the same mind-set as the executives, and run the company together rather than in conflicting directions.

I am rooted within the co-operative tradition of business, so this management style resonates with me as it is similar to the co-operative principles of creating a culture of ownership and control within workers so that they have common aims and objectives and run their enterprises along commonly-agreed lines. It is a paramount objective of co-operatives to make the mental and physical happiness of their members a central interest, because happy, engaged and informed workers deliver better results. Co-operatives are concerned with delivering social good, aligned with good ethics, values and principles,

II   **The Life Story of Dr Dorothy Francis**

and these ideologies are core to the successful operation of any co-operative business. This resonance with co-operative culture is one of the reasons why I subscribe to Kazuo Inamori's style and admire his work.

I would like to visit Japan so that I can see the country for myself and make my own assessment of its culture and people. I feel that if I were to visit Japan I would be treated as an oddity, but I hope that this would be out of curiosity rather than hostility. I have experienced being pointed at when visiting market towns within a fifteen-mile radius of Leicester and faced uncomfortable situations in Shropshire and Devon, so I'm sure that I will be able to withstand any novelty interest in Japan!

15 Reflections on the 'Memory and Narrative Series' [54] (No.1 & No.6)

Dorothy read the 'Memory and Narrative Series' No.1 and No.6, and she comments on the books thus:

Memory and Narrative Series 1:
   Life Story of Mrs Elvy Morton: First Chair of the Leicester Caribbean Carnival

I was very interested to read the life story of Mrs Elvy Morton, who is one of the great influencers of Caribbean culture in Leicester and is a person to whom we owe a great deal. Her journey from the Caribbean to the UK and her struggles are well documented in the book, as are her eventual triumphs. She was active for many years in community work, and really changed the face of Leicester. Mrs Morton's legacy is her involvement in establishing Leicester Caribbean Carnival, which has now run for over 30 years. It is the second biggest Caribbean Carnival in Europe, and much of its success is down to Mrs Morton's dogged determination. She is a force of nature, and someone to be deeply respected.

Memory and Narrative Series 6:
   Life Story of Mr Terry Harrison, MBE: His Identity as a Person of Mixed Heritage

Terry Harrison's life is fascinating, and in many parts reads like a novel. He and his twin sister Susan were born to a white-British mother and an African-American serviceman father in 1944 in a small Leicestershire village called Gaddesby. Gaddesby is still around 98 per cent white, and in 1944 Terry and his sister were the only children of colour in the village. Terry and Susan were doubly conspicuous within the village, as they were born to their mother whilst her white husband was away serving in the war. On his return, their mother's husband adopted them and took on the responsibility of bringing them up even though it was clear that they were not his children. Perhaps circumstances would have been different if Terry and Susan's birth father had not been killed during the war.

II   The Life Story of Dr Dorothy Francis

Terry grew up in a completely white community where no-one except his twin sister looked like him; he acted white whilst at the same time knowing that he was dual-heritage, but he had little contact with black people and no role models so found it very difficult to root himself within black culture. When he became older, he researched his background and found that what he had been told about his father's death was a heartbreaking lie. I won't say much more as I don't wish to spoil the narrative, because it is an intriguing read and the story unfolds almost like a novel.

Notes

1   For Jamaica, see Dorothy's explanation in her text; Paul Clammer, *Lonely Planet Jamaica*, Lonely Planet Travel Guide, 2017; Alicia Z. Klepeis, *Exploring World Cultures*, Jamaica, New York: Cavendish, 2018; Appendix 13: Select bibliography and websites, African-Caribbeans, mainly in the Caribbean Islands [including Jamaica], pp. 284–294.

2   For the independence of Jamaica from the United Kingdom in 1962 and the post-colonial era, Rex Nettleford (ed.), *Jamaica in Independence: Essays on the Early Years*, Kingston: Heinemann Publishers Caribbean, 1989; Birte Timm, *Nationalists Abroad: The Jamaica Progressive League and the Foundations of Jamaican Independence*, Kingston: Ian Randle Publishers, 2016; Jermel Shim, *The Long Road to Progress for Jamaica: The Achievements and Failures in the Post-colonial Era*, Parker, Colorado: Outskirts Press, 2018.

3   John Enoch Powell (1912–1998), MBE, British Conservative, Unionist politician and classical scholar. He served as a member of Parliament from 1950 to 1974, and was Minister of Health from 1960 to 1963. He is famous for his controversial 'Rivers of Blood' speech against continued immigration in Birmingham in 1968. See Rex Collings (selected), *Reflections of a Statesman: The Writings and Speeches of Enoch Powell*, London: Bellow Publishing, 1991; Simon Heffer, *Like the Roman, Enoch at 100: A Re-evaluation of the Life, Politics and Philosophy of Enoch Powell*, London: Biteback Publishing, 2012.

4   For Coventry in detail, see Joan C. Lancaster, *Godiva of Coventry*, Coventry: Coventry Corporation, 1967; Bill Lancaster & Tony Mason (eds), *Life and Labour in a 20th Century City: The Experience of Coventry*, Coventry: Cryfield Press, 1986; Albert Smith & David Fry, *The Coventry We Have Lost*, Vol.1, Berkwell: Simanda Press, 1991; Albert Smith & David Fry, *The Coventry We Have Lost*, Vol.2, Berkwell: Simanda Press, 1993; Adrian Smith, *The City of Coventry: A Twentieth Century Icon*, London: I. B. Tauris, 2006; Pippa Virdee, *Coming to Coventry: Stories from the South Asian Pioneers*, Coventry: Coventry Teaching PCT & The Herbert, 2006; Jordan Well, *Coventry at Work: A Collection of Memories*, Coventry: The Herbert Art Gallery & Museum, 2014; Jeremy and Caroline Gould, *Coventry: The Making of a Modern City 1939–73*, Coventry: Historic England, 2016.

5   The International Slavery Museum, located within Liverpool's Albert Dock opened in 2007. It focuses on the history and legacy of the transatlantic slave trade. Also, it

II The Life Story of Dr Dorothy Francis

discusses slavery in the modern day and racial discrimination (International Slavery Museum – Liverpool [https://www.visitliverpool.com/things-to-do/...]; About 'the International Slavery Museum – National Museums Liverpool' [https:www.liverpoolmuseums.org.uk/ism/about/].

6 According to a news article in the *Leicester Mercury*, 'What is the Windrush scandal?' (Friday, August 10, 2018): 'The Windrush generation arrived in the UK between 1948 and 1971 from Caribbean countries. After the ship Windrush brought the first group in 1948, about 500,000 people had moved to the UK from a Caribbean country by 1971. The Home Office did not keep a record of those granted leave to remain, meaning it is hard for Windrush arrivals to prove they are here legally. Landing cards belonging to Windrush migrants were destroyed in 2010. Those without documents are now being told they need them to continue working, get National Heath Service (NHS) treatment, or remain in the United Kingdom'.

The Empire Windrush arrived at Tilbury in 1948, carrying 493 passengers from Jamaica wishing to start a new life in the United Kingdom. They (including one stowaway) were the first large group of West Indian immigrants to the UK after World War II. For the Empire Windrush and the Windrush children, see Onyekachi Wambu (ed.), *Empire Windrush: Fifty Years of Writing about Black Britain*, London: Phoenix, 1999; Mike Phillips & Trevor Phillips, *Windrush: The Irresistible Rise of Multi-Racial Britain*, London: HarperCollins Publishers, 1998; Charlie Brinkhurst-Cuff (ed.), *Mother Country: Real Stories of the Windrush Children*, London: Headline Publishing Group, 2018.

7 One of the most devastating dates in Coventry's history was 14 November 1940 when St Peter's (Coventry) Cathedral was destroyed in the German air raid. 'For eleven long hours over 500 bombers unloaded 500 tons of high explosives and 30,000 incendiaries on the city's heart'. The human cost was about 550 dead and 870 injured, with about 45,000 homes and 75 per cent of Coventry's industry lost or severely damaged. See David McGrory, *Coventry: History and Guide*, Stroud: Alan Sutton, 1993; McGrory, David, *Coventry at War*, Stroud: The History Press, 1997; Smith, Adrian, *The City of Coventry: A Twentieth Century Icon*, London: I. B. Tauris, 2006; David McGrory, *Coventry's Blitz*, Stroud: Amberley, 2015.

8 For the Coventry Theatre (former Coventry Hippodrome Theatre), see 'Coventry Theatre in Coventry, GB – Cinema Treasures' (http://cinematreasures.org/theaters/25418); Coventry theatre [images] (bing.com/images).

9 *The Story of Little Black Sambo*, a children's book by Helen Bannerman, a Scot who lived for about 30 years in Madras in India, was first published in London in 1899. The original illustrations showed a caricatured southern Indian or Tamil child. The story was a children's favourite over a half a century, but it became controversial due to the use of the word, 'sambo', a racial slur in some countries, and the illustrations, which are reminiscent of 'darky iconography'. For the story in detail, see Robin Bernstein, *Racial Innocence: Performing American Childhood from Slavery to Civil Rights*, New York: New York University Press, 2011; Dashini Jeyathural, *The Complicated Racial Politics of Little Black Sambo'*, 'South Asian American Digital Archive (SAADA)' [https://www.saada.org], 2011; Helen Bannerman, *The Story of Lit-*

tle Black Sambo: Color Facsimile of First American Illustrated Edition, Eastford: Martino Fine Books, 2017.

10 See Dorothy's explanation in her text. For Patois in detail, see L. Emilie Adams, *Understanding Jamaican Patois: An Introduction to Afro-Jamaican Grammar, with a Childhood Tale,* by Llewelyn 'Dada' Adams, Kingston: LMH Publishing Ltd, 1991; Teresa P. Blair, *A-Z of Jamaican Patois (Patwah): Words, Phrases and How We Use Them*, Bloomington: AuthorHouse, 2013; Krissey Headley, *Jamaican Patois: Story Come to Bump*, Independently published, 2017.

11 For the Commonwealth Immigrants Act in 1962 and the Race Relations Acts in 1965, '68 and '76, see Ian R.G. Spencer, *British Immigration Policy Since 1939: The Making of Multi-Racial Britain*, London and New York: Routledge, 1997, pp.129–151; Panikos Panayi, *The Impact of Immigration: A Documentary History of the Effects and Experiences of Immigrants in Britain Since 1945*, Manchester: Manchester University Press, 1999, pp.47–49; Christina Julios, *Contemporary British Identity: English Language, Migrants and Public Discourse*, Aldershot: Ashgate, 2008, pp.97–100.

12 Marcus Garvey (1887-1940), a Jamaican-born political leader who organized the first important American black nationalist movement in New York City's Harlem. See Amy Jacques Garvey and E.U. Essien-Udom (eds.), *The Philosophy and Opinions of Marcus Garvey*, London: Cass, 1977; Blaisdell, Bobb (ed.), *Selected Writings and Speeches of Marcus Garvey*, New York: Dover Publications, Inc, 2004; Adam Ewing, *The Age of Garvey, How a Jamaican Activist Created a Mass Movement and Changed Global Black Politics*, Princeton: Princeton University Press, 2016; Encyclopaedia Britannica [https://www.britanica. com/biography/Marcus-Garvey].

13 The General Post Office (GPO) was established in England in 1660 by Charles II. Since then it grew to combine the functions of state postal system and telecommunications carrier. In 1969 the GPO was abolished and the assets transferred to the Post Office. In 1980 the telecommunications and postal sides (Royal Mail and Post Office Ltd) were split prior to the British Telecommunications Act 1983. See Dorothy's explanation in her text; Stephen Ferguson, *The GPO: 200 Years of History*, Blakrock, Co. Cork, Ireland: Mercier Press, 2014.

14   The race relations legislation of the 1960s and 1970s (see no.11) had provided for the establishment of local Community Relations Councils, which, after 1976, became Racial Equality Councils, of which 91 were established in 1991. In that year they received £4.5 million, from both the Community Relations Commission (following the 1968 Race Relations Act) and local councils, to employ Racial Equality Officers (Panikos Panayi, *op.cit.*, p.28)

15 Ralph Ellison, a twentieth century African-American writer and scholar. He is best known for his novel, *Invisible Man* (1952) on the African-American experience. There are other books including *Shadow and Act* (1964), *Going to the Territory* (1986), and *Juneteenth* (1999). See 'Ralph Ellison biography – Biography' (https://www.biography.com/people/ralph-ellion-9286702) 'Ralph Ellison/Biography, Books and Facts' [https://www.famousauthors.org/ralph-ellion]; 'Ralph Ellison/Biography, Books, & Facts/ Britannica.com' [https://www.britanica.com/biography/Ralph

II The Life Story of Dr Dorothy Francis

Ellison].

16 James Baldwin (1924–1987; born in New York), American author. 'He left home at 17 and eventually settled in Paris in 1948. His first novel, *Go Tell It on the Mountain* (1953), the story of one day in the lives of the members of a Harlem church, established him as a leading novelist of Black American life'. A lot of his other works explore racial, national, sexual and personal identity. During the American civil rights movement, he wrote *Nobody Knows My Name* (1962). See Melanie Parry (ed.), *Chambers Biographical Dictionary of Women*, Edinburgh: Chambers, 1996, p.68; 'James Baldwin (1924–1987) geboren.am' [https://geboren.am/person/james-baldwin].

17 The Most Excellent Order of the British Empire is an order of chivalry established on 4 June 1917 by George V of the United Kingdom. The Order comprises five classes in civil and military divisions. In descending order of seniority, these are: (1) Knight and Dame Grand Cross of the Order of the British Empire (GBE), (2) Knight and Dame Commander (KBE and DBE respectively) Grand Cross of the Order of the British Empire (GBE) or Dame Commander of the Order of the British Empire (DBE), (3) Commander of the Order of the British Empire (CBE), (4) Officer of the Order of the British Empire (OBE), (5) Member of the Order of the British Empire (MBE). The Order's motto is 'For God and the Empire'. It is the most junior of the British orders of chivalry, and the largest, with over 100,000 living members worldwide (A. Winton Thorpe (ed.), *Handbook to the Most Excellent Order of the British Empire*, Milton Keynes: Lightning Source UK Ltd, pp.9–18; 'The Most Excellent Order of the British Empire' [https://www.centralchancery.org.uk/Content/documents/OBE...].

18 See Dorothy's explanations in her text. Also, for a history of the co-operative movement in detail, see Appendix 13: Select bibliography and websites (section on British Co-operative movement), pp. 293–294.

19 For Tomizo Noguchi in 1872, see 'About The Pioneers – Rochdale Pioneers Museum' [http://www.rochdalepioneersmuseum.coop/about-us/about].

20 For a replica of the Toad Lane shop in Kobe, Japan, see Appendix 7: 'Day trip awards in business', pp. 251–252.

21 The Boys' Brigade (BB) is the largest Christian uniformed youth organisation in the UK and Republic of Ireland. The object since its formation has been 'the advancement of Christ's Kingdom among boys and the promotion of habits of obedience, reverence, discipline, self-respect and all that tends towards a true Christian manliness'. The BB was founded in Glasgow in 1883 by Sir William Alexander Smith (1854–1914). From this one company formed in Scotland the BB has grown into a world-wide movement, having worked with millions of children and young people for well over a century [http://boys-brigade.org.uk/history.htm].

22 See Dorothy's explanation in her text. Also, for Rastafarianism and Haile Selassie, see Horace Campbell, *Rasta and Resistance: From Marcus Garvey to Walter Rodney*, Hertford: Hansib Publications Limited, 1985, London: Macmillan, 1997; Peter B. Clark, *Black Paradise: The Rastafarian Movement*, Wellingborough: The Aquarian Press, 1993; A. Robert Hill, *Dread History: Leonard P. Howell and Millenarian Vi-*

sions in the Early Rastafarian Religion, Chicago/London/ Republic of Trinidad and Tobago, Caribbean, 2001; R.A. Douglas Mack, *From Babylon to Rastafari: Origin and History of the Rastafarian Movement*, Associates School Times Publications Frontline Distribution Int'Inc., 1999.

23 Stoneygate Baptist Church has a history of about 115 years. The church is part of the Bible reading fellowship and a fairtrade church. For the church, see https://www.stoneygatebaptist. org.uk.

24 For the inspirational De Montfort University Choir, see Appendix 4, p. 218; *Leicester Mercury*, December 24, 2015.

25 For Alice Hawkins, see Appendix 4: A Celebration of International Women's Day at Stoneygate Baptist Church, 2015, pp. 211–218.

26 The 2018 International Women's Day event was a celebration of voices and included two choirs – the Glenfield Co-operative Ladies Choir and the Emmanuu-el Apostolic Church, as well as performances from local musicians Fiona Hossack and Anthony Meads. The event was held to raise money for Jasmine House, otherwise known as the Leicester Rape Crisis Centre.

27 Maya Angelou (1928–), American writer, poet, singer, dancer, performer and black activist. She was raped by her mother's boyfriend when she was eight years old, and for the next five years was mute. As a teenager she moved to California to live with her mother, and at 16 gave birth to her son, Guy. During the 1960s she was involved in black struggles and then spent several years in Ghana as editor of the *African Review*. Her multi-volume autobiography, commencing with *I Know Why the Caged Bird Sings* (1970), was a critical and popular success, 'imbued with optimism, humour and homespun philosophy'. In 1981 she became the Reynolds Professor of American Studies at Wake Forest University in North Carolina. Also, in 1993 she read one of her poems at President Clinton's inauguration. See Melanie Parry (ed.), *Chambers Biographical Dictionary of Women*, Edinburgh: Chambers, 1996, p.23; M. Elliot Jeffrey (ed.), *Conversations with Maya Angelou*, Jackson: University Press of Mississippi, 1989.

28 Alice Walker (1944–), American novelist. Her writing talent was already recognized by the late 1960s. She is the author of three volumes of poetry and two collections of stories, *In Love and Trouble* (1973) and *You Can't Keep a Good Woman Down*. Her first novel, *The Third Life of Grange Copeland* (1970), and her second, *Meridian* (1976), were widely acclaimed, and built on her own experiences during the civil rights movement. In 1992 she wrote *Possessing the Secret of Joy*, an impassioned novel on the subject of female genital mutilation. See Melanie Parry (ed.), *Chambers Biographical Dictionary of Women*, Edinburgh: Chambers, 1996, p.561; 'Alice Walker /Biography, Books & Facts/Britannia.com'. [http://www.britania.com/biography/Alice-Walker].

29 Toni Morrison (1931–), a Nobel and Pulitzer Prize-winning American novelist. She was the first African-American woman to receive the Nobel Prize for Literature (1993). She also became a professor at Princeton University in 1989. Her novels include *The Bluest Eye* (1970), *Sula* (1973), *Song of Solomon* (1977), *Pulitzer for 'Beloved'* (1987), *Playing in the Dark: Whiteness and the Literary Imagination* (1992) and

II The Life Story of Dr Dorothy Francis

Paradise (1998). She has also published children's literature with her artist son Slade, including *The Big Box* (1999), *The Book of Mean People* (2002), *Little Cloud and Lady Wind* (2010). In her works, she focuses on the experience of Black Americans, particularly emphasizing black women's experience in an unjust society and the search for cultural identity. See 'Toni Morrison Biography – Biography' [https://www.biography.com/people/toni-morrison-9415590]; 'biography/Toni-Morrison' [https://www.birtannica.com/]; 'Toni Morrison Biography: Nobel Prize Winning Novelist' [https://www.thoughtco.com/toni-morrison-biography-3530577].

30   Kerry Young was born in Kingston, Jamaica. She has a Chinese father and mother of mixed Chinese-African heritage. She came to England when she was ten years old. Her publications include *Pao* (2011), *Gloria* (2013) and *Show Me A Mountain* (2016). She was writer-in-residence at the University of Sheffield (2014–2016). She is also Honorary Assistant Professor in the School of English at the University of Nottingham and Honorary Creative Writing Fellow at the University of Leicester. See 'Kerry Young: Writer' [https://www.kerryyoung.co.uk].

31   Andrea Levy (1956–; born in London), an English novelist. Her father sailed from Jamaica to England on the Empire Windrush in 1948. She is of primarily African-Jamaican descent. Her novels frequently explore topics related to Jamaican diaspora peoples in England and the ways in which they negotiate racial, cultural, and national identities. Her main novels include the semi-autobiographical *Every Light in the House Burnin'* (1994), *Never Far from Nowhere* (1996), *Fruit of the Lemon* (1999), *Small Island* (2004) and *The Long Song* (2010). See 'Andrea Levy (Author of *Small Island*) – Goodreads' [https://www.goodreads. com/author/show/24732.Andrea_ Levy].

32   Oprah Winfrey (1954–), billionaire media giant and philanthropist. She is best known for hosting her own internationally popular talk show (called *The Oprah Winfrey Show*) from 1986 to 2011. See 'Oprah Winfrey's Official Biography' [http://www.oprah.com/pressroom/oprah-winfrey-offcial]; 'Operah Winfrey Biography – Biography' [https:// biography.com/people/operah-winfrey-9534419].

33   Rosa Parks (1913–2005), an African-American activist in the civil rights movement. For Rosa Parks, see Dorothy's explanation in her text; Rosa Parks with James Haskins, *Rosa Parks: My Story*, New York: Scholastic Inc., 1992; Jim Haskins, *Rosa Parks: My Story*, 1999; Douglas Brinkley, *Rosa Parks: A Life*, Penguin Books, 2005; Jeanne Theoharis, *The Rebellious Life of Mrs. Rosa Parks*, Beacon Press, 2015. Hourly History, *Rosa Parks: The Woman Who Ignited a Movement (Biographies of Women in History)*, 2017; Philip Steele, *Rosa Parks and her Protest for Civil Rights, 1 December 1955 (Dates with History)*, 2019; 'Rosa Parks – Life, Bus Boycott & Death – Biography' [http://www.biography.com/people/rosa-parks-9433715].

34   Martin Luther King, Jr (1929–1968), a social activist and Baptist minister. He played a key role in the American civil rights movement from the mid-1950s until his assassination in 1968. He was awarded the Nobel Prize in 1964. See Martin Luther King, Jr, *Stride Toward Freedom: The Montgomery Story*, 1958 (2011); Dr Martin Luther King Jr, *A Testament of Hope: The Essential Writings and Speeches of Martin Luther*

King Jr, 1986 (1991); Clayborne Carson (ed.), *The Autobiography of Martin Luther King Jr*, 1998; 'Martin Luther King, Jr – History' [https://www.history.com/.../martin-luther-king-jr].

35 Malcolm X (1925–1965), African-American leader and prominent figure in the Nation of Islam in the early 1960s. See 'Biography/Malcolm X' [Malcolm.com/biography]; Alex Haley and Malcolm X, *The Autobiography of Malcolm X*, New York: Ballantine Books, 1973.

36 Tommie Smith (1944–) is an African-American former track and field athlete and wide receiver in the American Football League. At the 1968 Summer Olympics, Smith won the 200-metres dash finals in 19.83 seconds – the first time the 20 second barrier was broken. His Black Power salute with John Carlos on the medal podium caused controversy at the time as it was seen as politicising the Olympic Games. It remains a symbolic moment in the history of the African-American Black Power Movement. See Tommie Smith, *Silent Gesture: The Autobiography of Tommie Smith*, Philadelphia: Temple University Press, 2008; Richard Hoffer, *Something in the Air: American Passion and Defiance in the 1968*, new ed., Lincoln, NE: University of Nebraska Press, 2018; 'Tommie Smith: Track and Field Athlete' (1944–), [http://www.biograaphy.com/people/tommie-smith-9487382].

37 John Wesley Carlos (born in 1945 in Harlem, New York, of Cuban descent) is a former track and field athlete and professional football player. He was the bronze-medal winner in the 200 metres at the 1968 Summer Olympics and his Black Power salute on the podium with Tommie Smith caused much political controversy. He is the author, with sportswriter Dave Zirin, *The John Carlos Story: The Sports Moment That Changed the World*, Chicago: Haymarket Books, 2011.

38 Peter Norman (1942–), an Australian track athlete. He won the sliver medal in the 200 metres at the 1968 Summer Olympics in Mexico City. He is known for his support of John Carlos and Tommie Smith when they made their famous raised-fist salute at the 1968 Olympics medal ceremony.

39 Mohandas Karamchand Gandhi (1869–1948), the leader of the Indian independence movement against British rule. Born in a Hindu merchant caste family in Gujarat, western India, he trained in Law at the Inner Temple in London. His doctrine of civil disobedience and non-violent protest greatly influenced movements for civil rights and freedom across the world. See Clifford Manshardt (ed.), *The Mahatma and the Missionary: Selected Writings of Mohandas K. Gandhi*, Chicago: Henry Regnery Company, 1949; B.R. Nanda, *Mahatma Gandhi: A Biography*, Oxford: Oxford University Press, 1958; Ved Mehta, *Mahatma Gandhi and His Apostles*, New Haven & London: Yale University Press, 1977; Henry Scholberg (ed.), op. cit., pp.202–206; Judith Brown (ed.), *The Essential Works of Mahatma Gandhi*, Oxford: Oxford University Press, 2007; Mahatma Gandhi & Mahadev Desai, *An Autobiography: The Story of My Experiments with Truth*, Mumbai: Om Publications, 2009; Sujit Mansingh, *Historical Dictionary of India*, New Delhi: Vision Books, 2000, pp.145–150.

40 Nelson Rolihlahla Mandela (1918–2013), South African anti-apartheid and civil rights activist and President of South Africa from 1994 to 1999. He struggled to dismantle the legacy of apartheid. He was born into the Thembu tribe. See Nelson

II The Life Story of Dr Dorothy Francis

Mandela, *Long Walk to Freedom: The Autobiography of Nelson Mandela*, New York: Back Bay Books, 1995; Carl W. Hart, *Nelson Mandela*, Oxford: Macmillan, 2009; 'Nelson Mandela – History' [http://www.history.co.uk/biographies/nelson-mandela].

41 Mahalia Jackson (1911–1972), American gospel singer. She sang for President Eisenhower on his birthday in 1959, and at President Kennedy's inauguration in 1961. During the 1960s she became associated with the Civil Rights Movement. See Melanie Parry (ed.), *Chambers Biographical Dictionary of Women*, Edinburgh: Chambers, 1996, p.479.

42 Kanya King was born to an Irish mother and a Ghanaian father. She gave birth to her son, causing her to drop out of school. The first MOBO Awards took place in 1996 at London's Connaught Rooms, broadcast on Carlton Television. In 1999, she was appointed a Member of the Order of the British Empire (MBE). See 'Kanya King MBE: Executive Profile & Biography' [https://www.bloomberg.com/research/stocks/private/person...].

43 Claudia Jones (1915–1964), a Trinidad-born journalist, activist and communist. She is well known as a founder of Britain's first black weekly newspaper *The West Indian Gazette*; also as the 'mother' of the Nottingham Hill Carnival. ('Claudia Jones: Communist, Black Activist and Mother of...' [https://the culturetrip.com/Europe/united-kingdom/England/]).

44 Angela Davies (Yvonne), [1944–], American Black radical. She spent a year in Paris where she met many Algerian student radicals, and on her return to the USA her sense of political commitment was cemented by the deaths of the Sunday-school children in the Birmingham church bombing of 1963. She became a civil rights activist and after the death of Martin Luther King in 1968 she moved to Los Angeles and joined the Communist Party, completing her Master's degree under Herbert Marcuse. She teaches ethnic studies at San Francisco University. Her book *Women, Race and Class* appeared in 1980. (Jennifer Uglow, Francis Hinton and Maggy Hendry (eds.), *The Macmillan Dictionary of Women's Biography*, London: Macmillan, 1982 (1998), p.151.)

45 Williams sisters (Venus Williams [1980–] and Serena Williams [1981–]. They are two of the best women tennis players in the world., See James Buckley Jr., *Who Are Venus and Serena Williams?*, New York: Penguin Workshop, 2017; Jeanette Winter, *Sisters: Venus & Serena Williams*, San Diego: Beach Lane Books, 2019.

46 Michelle Obama(1964–), the wife of former U.S President Barack Obama. Before then she was a lawyer, Chicago City administrator and community-outreach worker. see Peter Slevin, *Michelle Obama: A Life*, New York: Vintage, 2016; Michelle Obama, *Becoming*, New York: Vintage, 2018; 'Michelle Obama Biography – Biography' [https://www.biography.com/people/michelle-obama-307592].

47 Ellen Johnson Sirleaf (1938–), Liberian politician and economist. She was president of Liberia (2006–2018). She was the first woman to be elected head of state of an African country. Johnson Sirleaf was one of three recipients, along with Levmah Gbowee and Tawakkol Karman, of the 2011 Nobel Prize for Peace for their efforts to further women's rights. See 'Ellen Johnson Sirleaf – President (non-U.S.) – Biography' [https://www.biography.com/people/ellen-Johnson-sirleaf...]; 'Ellen John-

II The Life Story of Dr Dorothy Francis

son Sirleaf/Biography, Nobel Peace Prize, &...' [https://www.biritanica.com/biography/Ellen-Johnson-Sirleaf].

48   Fidel Castro (c.1926–2016), political leader of Cuba (1959–2008). He transformed his country into the first Communist state in the Western Hemisphere. He became a symbol of Communist revolution in Latin America. See 'Fidel Castro', Encyclopaedia Britannica. Encyclopaedia Britannica Online [https://www.britanica.com/biography/Fidel-Castro]; Fidel Castro Biography – Biography – Famous...[https://biography.com/people/fidel-castro-924187].

49   The President of Uganda, Idi Amin Dada, announced on 4th August 1972 that his country's Asian population would be expelled, giving them 90 days to leave. He declared that non-African Ugandans were no longer needed in Uganda. As a result, residents of Asian origin left Uganda for India, Pakistan, Canada, the United States, Australia and Europe. A number of them held British passports, and over 27,000 migrated to Britain, around 7,000 of them to Leicester. See W.G. Kuepper, G.L. Lackey and E.N. Swinerton, *Ugandan Asians in Great Britain: Forced Migration and Social Absorption*, London: Croom Helm, 1975; Valerie Marett, *Immigrants Settling in the City*, Leicester: Leicester University Press, 1989; do., 'Resettlement of Ugandan Asians in Leicester', *Journal of Refugee Studies*, Vo.6, No, 1993; Z. Lalani (compiled), *Ugandan Asian Expulsion: 90 Days and Beyond Through the Eyes of the International Press*, 25th Anniversary Edition, USA: Expulsion Publications, 1997; 'From Kampala to Leicester' (http://leicester.gov.uk/your-council-services/Lc/leiceste...), permanent exhibition display at Newarke Houses Museum; Kiyotaka Sato (ed.), *Life Story of Mr Jaffer Kapasi, OBE: Muslim Businessman in Leicester, and the Ugandan Expulsion in 1972*, Tokyo: Research Centre for the History of Religious and Cultural Diversity (Meiji University), 2012.

50   Leicester was the first stop on the Queen's Diamond Jubilee tour. Her Majesty the Queen, accompanied by their Royal Highnesses the Duke of Edinburgh and the Duchess of Cambridge, visited the city on Thursday 8th March 2012. For the Queen's visit to Leicester on 1st August 2002 as part of her Golden Jubilee celebration, see the *Leicester Mercury* (3rd August, 2002).

51   The Leicester Caribbean Carnival started in 1985 as a commemoration of the emancipation of slaves in the British West Indies on 1st August 1834. In fact, the start of the festival is not related to the hard reality faced by those who came to Britain and their children in this 'Mother Country'. The riots which swept through Britain in 1981 greatly influenced the motivation for the start of the festival. See Kiyotaka Sato (edited and written), *Life Story of Mrs Elvy Morton: First Chair of the Leicester Caribbean Carnival*, Tokyo: Research Centre for the History of Religious and Cultural Diversity (Meiji University), 2010.

52   Jennifer, Baroness Gretton, DCVD, DStJ, JP, DL (born in 1943). She is a former Lord Lieutenant, serving for over 15 years between 24 February 2003 and 14 June 2018. Lord Lieutenants are the Queen's representatives, acting on Her Majesty's behalf. Their duties are now all ceremonial. The office's creation dates from the time of the Tudor dynasty. The present Lord Lieutenant of Leicestershire (14 June 2018–) is Michael Kapur OBE, a leading Leicestershire businessman. See Juliet

153

II   The Life Story of Dr Dorothy Francis

Gardiner & Neil Wenborn (eds.), *The History Today Companion to British History*, London: Collins & Brown, 1995, p.483; http:// www.yevolvy.com/topic/Jennifer Gretton.

53   Kazuo Inamori (1932–), Japanese philanthropist, entrepreneur and the founder of Kyocera and KDDI Corporation. He was the chairman of Japan Airlines. In 2011, he received the Othmer Gold Medal for outstanding contributions to progress in science and chemistry.

54   I established the 'Research Centre for the History of Religious and Cultural Diversity' at Meiji University in October 2010, and I have recorded many of the findings I have gathered from interviews and other types of research in a collection of booklets entitled the 'Memory and Narrative Series'. So far I have published ten booklets, each of which illustrates a unique individual life story. See 'Introduction', p.15 (note.1).

III
Kevin's contribution to Dorothy's story

III Kevin's contribution to Dorothy's story

Me, aged, 5 years.

Me, aged, 9 years.

When people ask where I'm from I always say Birmingham, but my first home was in Redditch, about 15 miles from there. In mid-1960s my family bought a grocery shop in Yardley Wood in Birmingham. In 1967, retaining the shop, we moved about 3 miles, to Hollywood, into a newly-built house that my mother still lives in today.

I attended Silvermead County Primary School, about a half-mile walk from home; the school was almost exclusively white, although I remember one of my friends, called Jarwar Sarwar, who lived on a local farm with his family. I have no idea where his family was originally from, I don't think I ever asked; it didn't seem important to know. As far as I can recall, there was one African-Caribbean boy at my school, in the year below me. I don't remember any racism from any of my friends, but I do remember that this boy, David, used to regularly be in fights. My sister, who was in his year group, met him many years later and he explained that he was constantly challenged by school bullies who felt it necessary to fight him just because he was black and that they had made his life a misery. They never beat him in a fight, but that just seemed to increase the other boys' desire to try. I was unaware of this and I only saw an African-Caribbean lad who was always fighting and I did not appreciate the reasons why he got into such scraps.

In 1971, I moved to a much larger school in Redditch which, again, was almost entirely white, so I had very little experience of meeting children from other cultures. This was also a feature of my social life; I was a member of the Boys' Brigade from the ages of 11 to 18 and most of the boys were white, with probably only two or three African-Caribbean boys out of a total of about 20. Although I met and played with all the boys at Boys' Brigade every week and was friendly with everyone within the unit outside of that setting all of my friends were white.

I did well at school up to the age of 16, achieving academic success in a wide range of subjects including Latin. I then relaxed for the next two years and struggled to achieve two A levels in Maths and Economics. These were enough to obtain a place at Lanchester Polytechnic (now Coventry University) to study on a foundation course in accountancy, which was followed by a training contract with a small Birmingham-based accountancy practice, where I completed my Chartered Accountancy training in 1983.

Some years later, I tracked down an old school friend who had moved to Leicester. He

III Kevin's contribution to Dorothy's story

invited me to his friend's birthday party which was held in a Leicester night-club called Vamos, run on a voluntary basis by five friends: Sally, Bev, Clive, Paul and Dorothy. I soon became a regular at the club, where I met four of the five organisers, including Bev, who also ran the café next to the club, and Paul, who was the DJ. However, despite numerous visits I had yet to meet the fifth member, Dorothy. One night in early April, whilst I was helping to clear up after the club had closed, Sally explained that she had loaned her house to her friend Dorothy to host her birthday party. She asked me if I wanted to come to the party as her guest. I said yes and this was the first time that I met Dorothy.

As the hours passed and guests gradually left, I moved through to the kitchen where I found Dorothy and her eight-month-old baby, Fayola the only other people awake in the house. As I was staying at Sally's house that night, I sat down at the table, and Dorothy, who was busy tidying up, placed the baby on my lap. I was unused to babies and I asked Dorothy what I was supposed to do to keep her entertained. I was wary of being in charge of the baby; however Dorothy said that she did not intend to leave all the washing up for Sally and her house-mates to do after they had so kindly loaned their house. She suggested that, as we were the last two people there, that either I would have to do the washing-up, or she would do the washing-up while I looked after the baby. I'm not keen on washing up, so, given that choice, I looked after the baby. Once the washing-up was completed, Dorothy gathered her things together, kissed me on the cheek, thanked me for looking after the baby, and left.

Our first photo as a couple, 1991.

On subsequent Saturdays, I continued my visits to Leicester, occasionally seeing Dorothy at the club, and I was aware that I was falling in love with her. One Saturday in August, she told me that she was organising a children's party for her daughter Fayola's first birthday the next day. I asked whether there would be trifle, and when Dorothy confirmed that there would be, I enthused about my absolute love for trifle and how nice it would be if I could come to the party and eat some trifle the next day. Dorothy politely acquiesced to my hints, and the next day I joined Dorothy, her family and friends for a children's tea party (with trifle). For the rest of the next week I was determined not to seem too keen by calling Dorothy too soon, but on the Thursday I gave in and rang her, and discovered that she had a spare ticket to a gospel concert that evening. I jumped into my car and drove quickly to Leicester, arriving just in time for the concert. We had a lovely night out and I even forgot that I don't really like gospel music. To be honest, I'm not that keen on trifle either.

It's difficult to describe what happened between us, but I immediately felt that this was the woman with whom I would spend the rest of my life. I later found out that Dorothy

157

III   Kevin's contribution to Dorothy's story

instantly felt the same way about me. The day after our first date Dorothy told a close friend that she'd met the man she would marry. This was the same day that I told one of my work colleagues the same about Dorothy – I was positive that I had met the woman that I was intended to marry.

My general philosophy in life has been 'everything will be alright in the end' and it usually is, but as a result of this I can sometimes be a bit unaware of the scale of any potential problems, and in hindsight I think I was completely naïve about any reaction our relationship might potentially cause. I simply saw a woman that I loved and did not think about other people's racism or potential opposition. In the eventuality, there was very little opposition to our relationship; friends and family were delighted that we had found each other. A few work colleagues made negative comments but I did not let these affect me.

We married in September 1994; our wedding took only eight weeks to organise, helped by family, friends and friends of friends who took photographs, decorated the church, wrote and performed music, provided and drove the wedding car, catered, and made dresses. Amongst the friends who helped our wedding to go so well was Michael Docker, with whom I had been in the Boys' Brigade in Birmingham during the 1970s. During the intervening years Michael had become Reverend Docker and coincidentally was the minister of the Baptist church less than a mile from Dorothy's house. Our wedding gave him the opportunity to say that little did he think, during those Boys' Brigade years, that he would end up marrying Kevin!

Nine months after our wedding our second daughter, Safiya, was born, and our family was complete.

Kevin Hudson
March 2016

IV
Appendices

Appendix 1: Photo memories of Dorothy and her family

My first ever photograph! This photo is of my mother and my elder sister Hortense in Bog Walk, St Catherine, Jamaica. My mother is approximately five to six months pregnant with me. So the photo would have been taken in late 1960 or in early 1961.

My mother, circa 1962. This was the photograph taken for her passport as she prepared to leave for England.

Unusually informal photo of Velma (left wearing bonnet) and myself (right). Taken outside my grandparents' house, St Mary, Jamaica, in approximately late 1963. Velma is my neice, the daughter of Hortense, my elder sister.

My mother and father, taken in late 1963.

My parents with my brother Steadman, 1965.

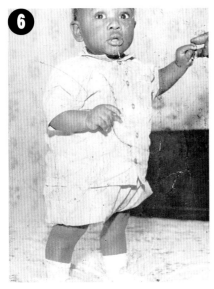

An early photograph of my brother, Steadman, taken in 1966.

Left to right: myself, Sharon, Joy and Steadman. Photo taken in early 1967. Joy died in late June 1967.

Left to right: Sharon, Steadman and myself at our house 12, Ashburton Road, Coventry, in approximately 1967/8. Also in the photo is my father's beloved radiogram, one of his first purchases in the UK.

Mum with Lorna outside our house in Ashburton Road, Coventry, circa 1968.

Lorna (my youngest sister), 1969.

In London, 1974. Outside Aunt Esme's house in Tooting Bec. Left to right: Dad, Mr Mullings, myself, Aunt Eula, Mum, Aunt Esme, Steadman, Sharon, and Lorna. Mum made the outfits that she, my aunts, Sharon, Lorna and I are wearing.

My youngest sister Lorna around 1973 or 1974. She had recently been released from hospital. She spent much time in hospital due to sickle cell anaemia.

Left to right: Rudy, myself and Milo. Rudy and Milo are my cousins. This photo was taken to send to my parents in England. I was living in Jamaica with my grandparents and cousins.

Myself, April 1978 (17 years old).

Myself, 17 years old.

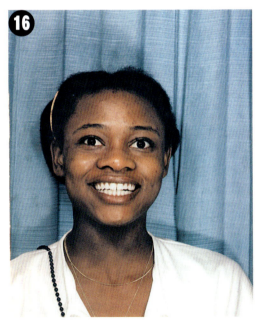

Myself, college dance, April 1979 (18 years old).

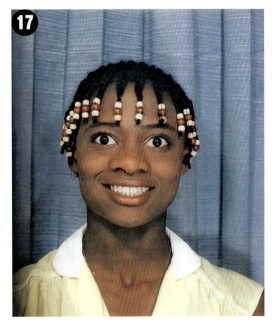

Myself, 1980 (19 years old).

Myself and Lorna on holiday, circa 1978.

Dad, myself, Sharon, Mum (partially hidden), Lorna. At front: Steadman, 1978.

Sharing a joke in my university bedroom, 1981.

Looking pensive. Birmingham, 1982.

At the International Black Book Fair, 1984.

164

With my great-aunt, my grandmother's sister in 1982.

On holiday circa 1978. Left to right: Lorna, myself, Steadman, Mum and Dad.

Lorna and myself, circa 1979.

A family Christmas 1980. Left to right: Steadman, Sharon, myself, my father and my mother. In front is Lorna.

165

Mum and myself on a day trip, 1980.

Mum and Dad at the seaside, 1978.

In the grounds of university student house, December 1980.

Left to right: Lorna, Mum and Dad, 1978.

Celebrating my 21st birthday on 6th April 1982. My best friend ran into the room and told us that we were at war with Argentina over the Falklands. I was the only person in the room who knew where the Falklands was!

With Alice Walker, author of 'The Color Purple' in London, 1984.

This is me and my brother Steadman in 1984 on the day that I graduated in English Language and Literature in Birmingham.

'ICOM Women's Link-up' conference in Sheffield, 1985. I am 2nd from left. I was area coordinator of ICOM Women Link-up Coventry, a training and development programme to encourage women into business.

This is a photo of me in Italy on my first solo foreign holiday – I subsequently undertook a number of holidays by myself. On this trip I travelled to Venice, Verona and Lake Garda.

In Egypt in January 1987 with friends that I met on my visit.

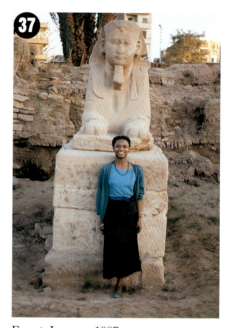

Egypt, January 1987.

At Hatshepsut's tomb in the Valley of the Kings, Egypt, January 1987.

Egypt with friends Nabil and Jay at the Pyramids, August 1987.

This photo was taken in 1989 by photographer Roshim Kempadoo for an exhibition called WOMANESS about Black women. It toured nationally throughout the UK.

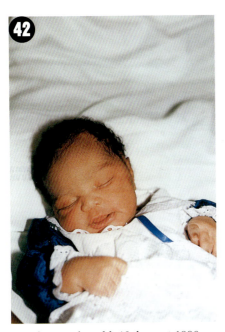

Fayola, one day old, 19 August 1990.

Fayola on the day she was born, 18 August 1990.

My brother Steadman with Fayola the day she was born, 18 August 1990.

Myself and Fayola outside my mother's house, 8 September 1990.

Fayola and my mother, early 1991.

Fayola seven months old, March 1991.

Fayola's dedication with her paternal birth grandmother and sister, Patience, June 1991.

Myself and Fayola, September 1991. This photograph was taken on the day that we attended the christening of a friend's child.

Fayola (approximately 14 months old).

Myself and Fayola in the garden at Wordsworth Road, Leicester, September 1991.

Myself and Fayola, 8 September 1990.

Dorothy and Kevin, summer 1993.

Fayola with my mother in 1991.

Kevin, myself, Marcia, Mum, Hortense and Trevor at a friend's wedding, summer 1993.

Myself and Fayola in the garden at Wordsworth Road, Leicester in 1994.

Safiya, a few days after her birth, surrounded by flowers from family and friends.

Fayola and Safiya, 1995.

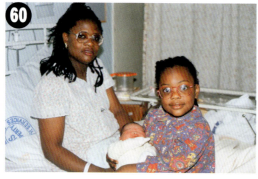

Myself, Safiya and Fayola at the Leicester Royal Infirmary Hospital, 11 June 1995. Fayola was delighted to meet her new sister Safiya for the first time.

Myself, Safiya and Fayola, July 1995.

A birthday cake for Safiya.

Myself, Safiya and Kevin, October 1995.

With my certificate for being voted Institute of Personnel Development (IPD) Student of the year.

Receiving my award as 'Student of the Year' on completion of my IPD course in 1994. I graduated top of my class and received a certificate and a cheque.

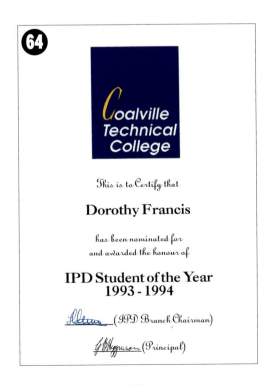

This photo was taken by 'Woman' magazine in July 1993 to accompany a magazine article in September 1993.

Photograph taken by France Winddance Twine for a book on mixed heritage marriages, April 1997.

The wedding of my sister Hortense to Azariah Mullings. I was a bridesmaid and my niece Naomi was a flower girl.

Fayola, 3 years old.

Myself with afro, 1997.

Myself and Safiya reclining on sofa – around 1998.

Myself, May 1999.

Safiya and Fayola, 2000.

Kevin at his father's house, summer 2001.

Stoneygate Baptist Church 100th Anniversary, dressed in Victorian style clothing to celebrate that occasion, 2001.

Three generations of Francis women. Left to right: Fayola, my mother and me. We all have the same smile!

Myself, 2002.

This photo was taken on the occasion of my nephew Samuel's dedication ceremony in August 2004. Left to right: Fayola, Kevin and myself with Safiya at front.

Myself, Fayola, Kevin and Safiya, September 2005.

Kevin and myself at my mother's house. Christmas day, 2006.

On holiday in Torquay with Mum and Lorna, October 2007.

On holiday in Torquay, October 2007.

Mum's 80th birthday photo session, 2007. Myself, Hortense, Sharon, Lorna, Talitha, Mum, Naomi, Fayola and Safiya.

Mum's 80th birthday in 2007. Fayola, Mum, Safiya, Kevin and myself.

Mum's 80th birthday photo. Left to right: Kevin, Joseph, Trevor, Steadman, Mark, Talitha, Safiya, Naomi, Sharon, Lorna, Fayola, Hortense, Mum, myself and Samuel.

Fayola at her 18th birthday party with godparents, Nelista Cuffy and Kate Gordon.

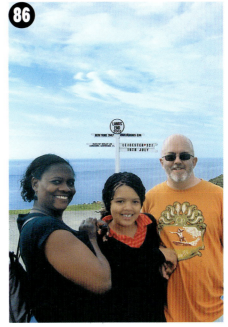

Myself, Safiya and Kevin at Land's End, Cornwall, 2007.

Myself and Safiya, 2007.

On holiday in Cornwall, 2007.

Myself, Kevin, Safiya and Fayola in Tunisia, 2009.

90 Dorothy is 50!

We'd love you to join us
at Dorothy's 50th party

When: from 8pm on 16th April

Where: Midas Bar, 17 Yeoman Street, Leicester

If possible, please bring along your favourite photo of you and Dorothy for a secret birthday surprise

The invitation to my 50th birthday party as designed by my daughters.

Myself and Mum celebrating my 50th birthday at a local restaurant.

Safiya and my niece, Grace at my 50th birthday party.

At my 50th birthday party with friends and family, April 2011.

Birthday portrait, May 2011.

Family portrait, 2011.

Lorna and myself at my 50th birthday party, April 2011.

Family portrait, 2011.

Fayola, 2011.

Safiya, 2011.

Myself and my daughters, 2011.

Myself and Kevin, 2011.

Family portrait, 2011.

With strings of ackees in Jamaica, March 2012.

In Jamaica, March 2012.

Ackees prepared for me by my family, with mangoes in background, March 2012.

My aunt and cousins preparing ackee for me to take back to UK, March 2012.

Safiya, summer 2012.

A house in my neighbourhood, St Mary, Jamaica.

A house similar to my grandparents' house. My grandparents' house was destroyed in a hurricane. This house is nearby. I spent my early years in a setting similar to this.

The view from the family home, St Mary, Jamaica, March 2012.

My friend Jean 'Binta' Breeze, MBE (right) and her mother, Mrs Holness-Muir on their veranda in Sandy Bay, Jamaica March 2012. Jean Breeze is a dub poet and author. I usually visit Jean and her family when I am in Jamaica.

My local school, Richmond Hill, St Mary, Jamaica. This is where I would have attended the school had I not moved to England.

My daughter, Fayola's birthday dinner at an Indian restaurant

My mother-in-law, Linda and my sister, Hortense.

My sister-in-law, Ros and mother-in-law, Linda, August 2014.

Fayola at her birthday meal, August 2014.

Kevin and myself.

Safiya and Fayola, January 2014.

Fayola and Samuel.

My brother, Steadman and sister, Sharon, 2015.

With my sister Sharon on the occasion of her birthday 2015.

Kate, myself and Heather, friends since university, at the christening of Kate's grandson, August 2015.

Fayola on her 25th birthday with godparents, Kate and Neville Gordon.

Mrs Esmie Small, one of my aunts and younger sister to my mother.

With Mr Glenton Morgan, an old family friend who acted as a loving surragate father to me and my siblings.

Visiting Joy's grave with Mum. Joy was my sister who died in 1967.

My niece, Talitha in New York, 2015.

The family plot in St Mary's Jamaica. The graves shown are those of my maternal grandmother and grandfather and of two of their daughters – my aunts. Spaces remain for other members of the family.

Fayola and Safiya at Fayola's BA graduation, July 2014.

Myself and Fayola at her BA graduation.

Fayola at her MA graduation, January 2016.

Fayola, myself and Kevin at Fayola's MA graduation.

Safiya at her graduation, from the University of Winchester, 22 October, 2016.

Safiya, Fayola, Kevin and myself at Safiya's graduation, 22 October, 2016.

With Safiya at her graduation, 22 October, 2016.

Safiya, Kevin and myself at Safiya's graduation, 22 October, 2016.

I love to bake and to entertain. I design and bake birthday cakes for my daughters each year. I also bake cakes for friends, work colleagues, family and neighbours.

Teddy parcels – a birthday cake for Fayola.

A Christmas cake for a friend.

Preparing for Christmas dinner. I host Christmas dinner for family and friends each year.

A cake for a neighbour.

Christmas gifts made by myself – cakes, jams and chutneys.

Receiving flowers from Nilima Devi of the Centre for Indian Classical Dance (CICD) in thanks for support given to the centre over many years.

Leicestershire County Council Chairman's Dinner 2015.

With the Lord Mayor of Leicester, Cllr Ted Cassidy, the High Sheriff of Leicestershire, Gordon Arthur and local businessman Mr Patel, July 2015.

(Reproduced with the permission of Dr Dorothy Francis)

Appendix 2: Dorothy and Kevin's wedding, 17th September 1994

Section 1: Dorothy and Kevin's wedding, 17th September 1994

Myself in my garden shortly before leaving for church.

Myself on the way to church.

My sister Lorna was Matron of Honour at our wedding. My niece, Talitha, was a bridesmaid and Fayola was a flower girl.

My brother Steadman walked me down the aisle on my wedding day.

Myself signing the register after our marriage.

Kevin signing the register.

Wedding of myself and Kevin at Stoneygate Baptist Church, Leicester.

Outside the church after our marriage ceremony.

Our wedding guests in front of Stoneygate Baptist Church.

My side of the family on our wedding day.

Kevin's sister, mother, father and nephew at the reception venue.

Myself, Fayola and Kevin, at Grace Road Cricket Club which was the venue for the wedding breakfast and evening reception.

Myself.

With my sister Hortense, and our mother Miriam.

Kate and her son Ahira. Kate and I met at university in 1981 and have been friends since. Kate and her husband Neville are Fayola and Safiya's godparents.

Myself and Fayola at Grace Road Cricket Club.

With my cousin Trevor.

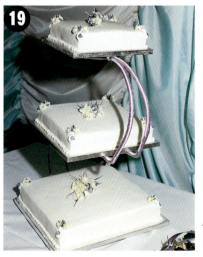

Steadman, Dorothy and Fayola at the reception.

The wedding cake which was made by my brother Steadman and his partner.

Cutting the cake at the wedding breakfast and multitasking by stealing a kiss at the same time!

My mother, Miviam Walker, and Kevin's mother, Linda Hudson, were presented with flowers by us at our wedding breakfast.

The evening wedding reception at Grace Road Cricket Club.

Our first dance at our wedding reception.

Leading a wedding conga at our wedding reception.

196

Section 2: Photos from married life

On holiday in Devon, 2005.

At home, 2007.

On holiday in Tunisia, 2008.

Ready for a night out, 2010.

August 2012.

At a family wedding, Easter 2014.

June 2015.

20th anniversary breakfast table setting prepared by Fayola.

A favourite photo from 2003.

(Reproduced with the permission of Dr Dorothy Francis)

Appendix 3: Gathering Dorothy's extended family in Jamaica, 2015

A view of the Caribbean sea from Jamaica.

Kevin, Lorna and Patrick – Jamaica, April 2015.

Visiting Jean Breeze in Sandy Bay, Jamaica. Jean is a writer and performer of poetry and plays and lives between Jamaica and England. We met in 1984 and have been friends ever since.

My cousin, Trevor Johnson.

Patrick, Trevor's brother.

Playing cards with my good friend Sally Norman in Jamaica, April 2015.

My cousin Milo celebrating his birthday during the family reunion weekend.

Sharon and Fayola, Jamaica, 2015.

Lorna and Samuel, Jamaica, 2015.

Sally, Dorothy, Kevin and Milo.

Kevin on the beach in Sandy Bay enjoying the local specialty, Dragon Stout.

Dragon Stout and Dragon Stout ice cream from Devon House ice cream parlour in Sandy Bay. They were both enjoyed on the beach!

Having fun at my birthday breakfast celebrated whilst in Jamaica.

Having fun at the resort. From left Fayola, Safiya, Gina, Sharon, Lorna, Sally and myself.

My uncle Mr Emmeard Johnson.

Fayola.

Sharon.

My mother catching up with Mr Glenton Morgan in Jamaica at the family reunions. Mr Morgan is a family friend of many years standing who formerly lived in Coventry but returned to Jamaica some years ago.

Fayola feeding sugared water to a hummingbird at a bird sanctuary.

Same as fig.19.

Kevin and myself with Mum at the family reunion.

Mum catching up with old friends.

Cooking jerk chicken at the family reunion.

Mum with her sister, Ms Eula Walker.

Group photo at the Rockland's Bird Sanctuary: Fayola, Kevin, myself, Safiya, Sally, Sharon, Marian, Gina, Magda, Lorna and a local guide.

Playing dominoes at the reunion.

Kevin, Sally, Gina and Steadman relaxing in Jamaica.

Friends and family on the veranda at our home in St Mary.

Some family members.

Family members.

205

At the Rockland's Bird Sanctuary, near Montego Bay, Jamaica, April 2015.

Myself and Sharon.

Fayola and Kevin.

Sharon, myself and Kevin.

Lorna.

Aunt Eula is the youngest of my maternal aunts.

Myself.

Young cousins, Ziah and Ophelia.

Jamaican flowers.

A drink prepared by the barman in Rastafarian colours – red, gold and green.

Bird of Paradise flower.

Red hibiscus flower.

Holiday resort – Runaway Bay, Jamaica.

Same as fig. 42.

Same as fig. 42.

Same as fig. 42.

Dunns River Falls.

Ochio Rios, Jamaica. Climbing Dunns River Falls in Ochio Rios is a popular tourist activity.

A view from the veranda of our family home in Jamaica.

A view from the hill.

A view of the Caribbean sea with sunset.

(Reproduced with the permission of Dr Dorothy Francis)

Appendix 4: A celebration of International Women's Day at Stoneygate Baptist Church, 2015

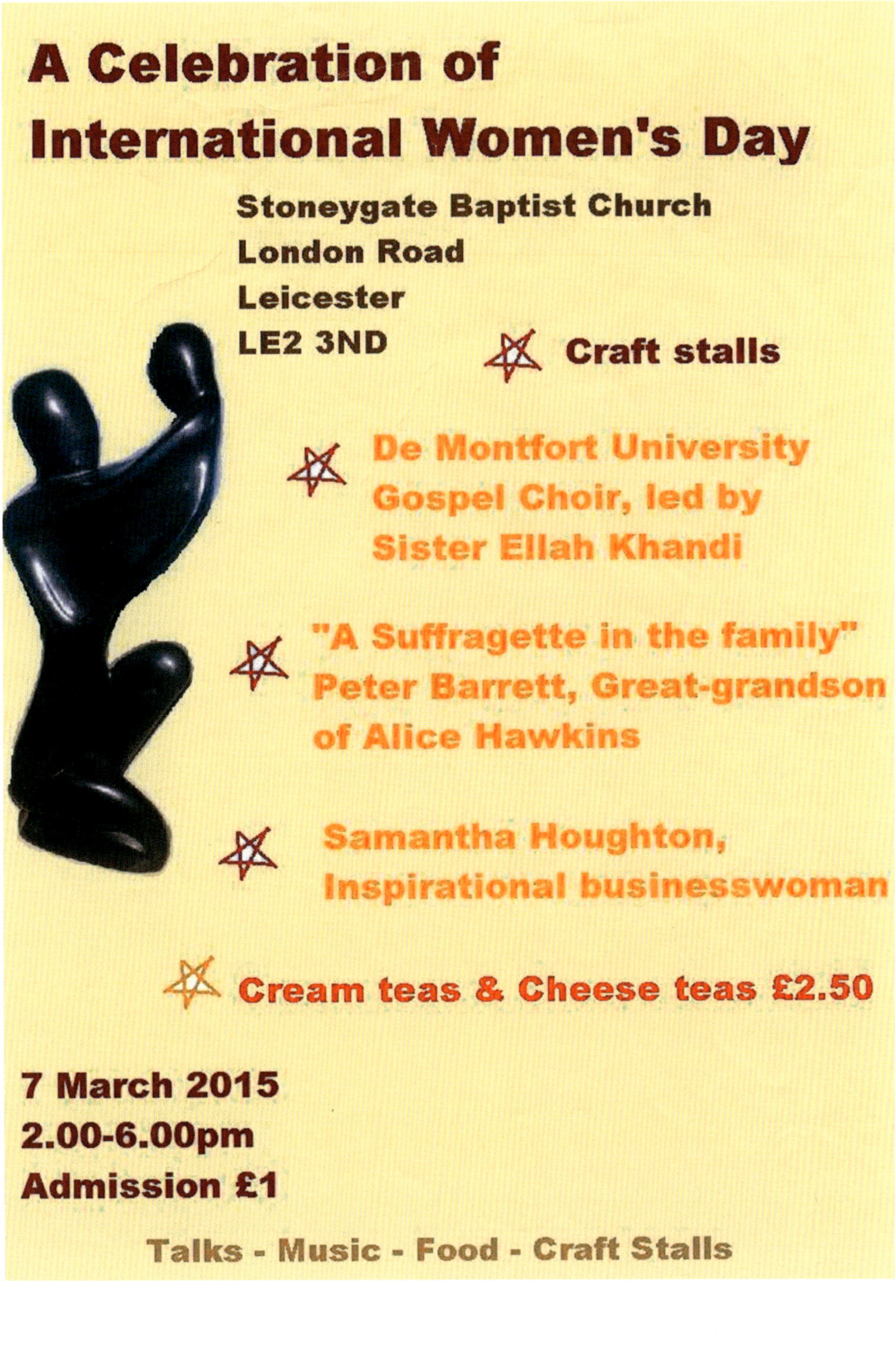

A Celebration of International Women's Day

**Stoneygate Baptist Church
London Road
Leicester
LE2 3ND**

✖ **Craft stalls**

✖ **De Montfort University Gospel Choir, led by Sister Ellah Khandi**

✖ **"A Suffragette in the family" Peter Barrett, Great-grandson of Alice Hawkins**

✖ **Samantha Houghton, Inspirational businesswoman**

✖ **Cream teas & Cheese teas £2.50**

**7 March 2015
2.00-6.00pm
Admission £1**

Talks - Music - Food - Craft Stalls

Stoneygate Baptist Church, London Road, Leicester. Kevin and myself have worshipped here since 1992.

The interior of the church. The event was a celebration of International Women's Day in March 2015.

Guests at the International Women's Day Celebration.

Alice Hawkins was a prominent suffragette in Leicester. Her great-grandson Peter Bennett attended the event to talk about her contribution to women's suffrage.

Peter Bennett acted as a consultant on the film 'Suffragette' which was released to critical acclaim in late 2015 and featured women who like Alice Hawkins fought for universal suffrage.

Peter Bennett and Dorothy Brawn – presenting at Stoneygate Baptist Church on the theme of female suffrage.

Peter Bennett, great-grandson of Alice Hawkins.

Dorothy Brawn – presents talk with Peter and dresses as a suffragette in Edwardian costume to illustrate the talks.

Dorothy congratulating Dorothy Brawn on her presentation.

213

Speaking at the International Women's Day event, March 2015.

Sharing a joke with a member of the De Montfort University Gospel Choir.

De Montfort University Gospel Choir performing at the International Women's Day event.

Kevin, Fayola and Safiya serving cream teas at the Stoneygate Baptist Church, International Women's Day celebration.

(Photographs by the editor)

Fayola, Safiya and myself serving cream teas at the Stoneygate Baptist Church, International Women's Day celebration.

⟨Photograph⟩
A 7 ft bronze statue of Leicester suffragette Alice Hawkins

Leicester Mercury, Monday, February 5, 2018.

⟨**Article**⟩

On day statue of city suffragette is unveiled, hundreds join parade to celebrate legacy of movement in its centenary. Fiona Dryden reports

ON A MARCH TO REMEMBER ALICE'S EQUAL RIGHTS FIGHT

A 7ft bronze statue of Leicester suffragette Alice Hawkins was officially unveiled in Leicester's new market square today.

A cheer went up followed by applause when the 800lb sculpture, hidden under purple drapes, was revealed in front of hundreds of people who had gathered. A host of speeches took place to commemorate the special occasion. Among those who spoke was Peter Barratt, Alice's great-grandson, who said he was extremely proud of the woman who had contributed so much to the suffragette movement, standing up for women's rights, regularly addressing Leicester crowds in her battle to win equality for women through the right to vote, but also in their jobs.

Echoing her words, "deeds, not words", he said the "fight for equality continues". He was joined at the momentous occasion by daughter Kate Barratt, and Leicester West MP Liz Kendall, who helped unveil the statue created by sculptor Sean Hedges-Quinn. Kate said it was great to celebrate Alice's life in the centenary year that votes for some women were granted and in the place where Alice herself gave "many rousing speeches". Miss Kendall said she was "honoured to be part of this incredibly special day".

Ahead of the statue's unveiling a mass procession took place which wound its way from Humberstone Gate East to the Clock Tower, before heading to the new market square. Leading the procession was city councilor Elaine Pantling who played the part of Alice Hawkins. She was flanked by women and men carrying banners and gave an emotional rendition of the Women's Marseillaise before regaling the crowd with the true-to-life tale of the movement's golf course sabotage, when Alice and others wrote in large letters on the green: "No votes for women, no golf for men". Speaking afterwards, Coun Pantling said: "It's been an absolute privilege to walk in Alice's shoes".

Medical genetics student Jenny Antrobus, 21, who lives in Clarendon Park, was among those who watched the unveiling. She said: "I'm proud of what Alice achieved. It reinforces the message that some things are well worth fighting for and equality is one of them". City Mayor Sir Peter Soulsby thanked all those involved in creating and bringing the statue to Leicester.

Leicester Mercury, Monday, February 5, 2018.

Alice Hawkins (1863~1946)

Alice Hawkins was born in Stafford in 1863, and her family moved to Leicester in 1876. In 1886 Alice started work at the Equity Co-operative Boot and Shoe Manufacturing Society in Western Road as a shoe machinist. She joined the Independent Labour Party in 1894 and became involved in suffragette activities in Leicester after attending a meeting in Hyde Park, London in February 1907, when she was arrested for disorderly conduct outside the House of Commons. She was sentenced to 14 days in prison for this, the first of five terms of imprisonment she served for suffragette activities in both Holloway and Leicester Prison. They included another 14 days for breaking windows in the Home Office in November 1911.

In April 1907 she helped to found the Leicester Branch of the Women's Social and Political Union, speaking at many public meetings in Leicester and cycling out on Sundays to towns and villages to gather support for the cause. She was also involved in the formation of an independent trade union for women working in the boot and shoe trade in 1911. She and her husband Alfred had five children, and he fully supported her suffragette activities.

The suffragettes suspended their campaign at the start of World War I in 1914, and in 1918 the parliamentary vote was finally extended to women over 30 who were householders or the wives of householders. Alice Hawkins died in 1946 at the age of 83 and was buried at Welford Road Cemetery, Leicester in an unmarked grave. More recently a headstone marking her contribution to women's suffrage has been placed on her grave, and in February 2018, around the anniversary of the first votes for women, a statue of her was unveiled in the New Market Place in Leicester.

Bibliography
'Alice Hawkins Suffragette – a sister of freedom', http://www.alicesuffragette.co.uk (29 May 2018)
Jess Jenkins, *The Burning Question: the Struggle for Women's Suffrage in Leicestershire*; Leicestershire, Leicestershire County Council, 2012
Joyce Marlow, *Suffragettes: the Fight for Votes for Women*, London; Virago, 2015
Richard Whitmore, *Alice Hawkins and the Suffragette Movement in Edwardian Leicester*, London and Derby, Breedon Books Publishing Co Ltd, 2007

(written by Mrs Cynthia Brown)

The De Montfort University Gospel Choir

RAISING MONEY

PICTURE: CHRIS GORDON
GOOD VOICE: The De Montfort University Gospel Choir in Gallowtree Gate

WATCH A VERSION OF JINGLE BELLS SUNG ESPECIALLY FOR OUR READERS.
leicestermercury.co.uk

Gospel choir out entertaining shoppers

A GOSPEL choir has been entertaining Christmas shoppers to raise money for a community centre and place of worship.

Fifty singers, drawn from the community, De Montfort University and Emmanuel Apostolic Church, have been performing outside BHS, in Gallowtree Gate, Leicester, since December 10.

They have also performed at John Lewis, in Highcross, as well as in Melton, South Wigston and Oadby.

The choir is raising money towards transforming the former Aylestone Working Men's Club, in Middleton Street, off Saffron Lane, Leicester, into a community centre and place of worship.

The project is expected to cost about £400,000.

Choir leader Pastor Samuel Gapara, said: "The choir has gone down very well and people have been very generous. All the funds collected during the Christmas period in the city centre and special events will go towards this project.

"We need to raise money for refurbishment, as all the plumbing, electricity and lead from the roof were stolen."

Leicester Mercury, December 24, 2015.

Appendix 5: Dorothy's annual carnival party at her home, 2017

Kevin, Safiya and Magda.

Sharon, Fayola and Lewis.

My brother Steadman and his partner Gina.

Naomi and Talitha, two of my nieces.

Suzanne and Beverley, two of my friends.

Talitha with close family friends, Magda and Marcin from Poland.

A small sample of the food served at the party.

The party spills out into the garden under gazebos lit by candlelight.

Monica and Nelista, friends of many years.

Neighbours, Alison and Emma.

Martin and Cathy.

Shirley, Sally and Michelle. Members of the monthly book club started by myself, Sally and Beverly in 2003.

Guests enjoying the party in the garden.

Bernice, Nelista and Tony – good friends of the family. Nelista is Fayola's and Safiya's godmother.

Tony, Donna and Suzanne.

Richard, Safiya's piano teacher, and my friend Donna.

Enjoying the party.

Jo, Kevin, myself and Donna.

Taking a break with Kevin.

(Photographs by the editor)

Appendix 6: Dorothy's work and her business awards

⟨Photographs⟩

Dorothy's award as Leicestershire Business Woman of the Year, 2011.

With my award as Leicestershire Business Woman of the Year 2011 at the Jubilee Women Awards ceremony at Curve Theatre, 19 November 2010.

Mum and me with my Leicestershire Business Woman of the Year award.

Dorothy's awards as Jubilee Business Woman of the Year award, 2011.

Jubilee Business Woman of the Year, 2011.

Holding my Jubilee Business Woman of the Year award.

With my Business Woman of the Year 2014 award from the Leicester Asian Business Association (LABA).

Same as fig. 5.

Leicester Asian Business Association (LABA) – Women of Achievement Awards, 2014.

I was a judge for the Leicester Asian Business Association Women of Achievement Awards 2014 and am pictured here with my fellow judges.

Same as fig. 7.

Leicester Asian Business Association (LABA) – Women of Acheivement Awards 2014.

My company collects food and donations from clients and friends each year. Guests are invited to a party to create beautiful hampers which are given as Christmas presents to people in need.

225

With work colleagues outside our workplace at The Crescent in Leicester.

My place of work, Leicester.

AIMS: BUSINESSES SUPPORT COMMUNITY

SUCCESS: From left, Dorothy Francis, Tobias Gould and Rajinder Bhuhi, at the Wise event
PICTURE: BETH WALSH / LEBW20140312G-007_C

Wise choice of award winners

by **ISOBEL FRODSHAM**

An award ceremony and networking event was held at the University of Leicester yesterday for businesses supporting the community.

The Working In Social Enterprise (Wise) event celebrated the success of three business owners and their companies over the past year, and provided a networking opportunity for firms and students.

Social enterprises are defined as "local businesses which care about local people".

The winners of the event were Ben Dodd, co-founder of Green Fox, a green energy project, in Leicester; Mark Clark, managing director of Inside n Out, a community company working with ex-offenders in the city; and Greg Semple, founding member and CEO of Excluded, a not-for-profit record label in the city centre.

Inside n Out, a magazine which has been running for two years, specialises in helping ex-offenders learn social, enterprise and creative skills.

Mark said: "I think the award is particularly exciting. It's great we have had some impact as a community enterprise company working with the criminal justice system."

Tobias Gould is social enterprise development officer for Wise – an organisation supported by the university, the European Union, Voluntary Action Leicester and social enterprise body, Case.

He said: "Wise delivers support, one-to-one training, networking and student placements to our social enterprise businesses. This is the biggest networking event of our year."

'VOUCHER'

Dorothy Francis, chief of enterprise for Case, the lead agency for Wise, said: "Events like this allow businesses the chance to grow and develop skills.

"The winners receive a voucher which can be put towards gaining a new skill.

"It also allows them to network and increase their sales and business CV."

Tobias said: "When deciding on the winners, a set of guidance notes and rules apply. However, everyone is invited to take part.

"Those who win generally have a high average increase in turnover and job creation over the year."

Attendees included Neil Hodgkin, a keynote speaker for the event and manager for the Saffron Acres Jam company which works with local volunteers to harvest fruit and make jam.

He said the event was inspiring others to join in and work hard to achieve something.

He said: "The more our company grows, the more space we have, and therefore the more employment we provide."

Amalia Frigura, 21, studies media and communications at the University of Leicester and Siqi Liu, 21, studies mathematics there.

Both girls are on a placement with the social enterprise, Smarti Paints.

Smarti Paints is a craft company which specialises in teaching vulnerable people new skills, such as social interaction, social development and creativity.

Amalia said: "I work with Smarti Paints to help them promote themselves and I also write a blog.

"This is important for their target audience, many of whom are disabled and find accessibility a struggle."

Siqi said: "I help locating the target audience for Smarti Paints, and also help organise coffee mornings, painting sessions and uniform sessions, where the attendees can create their own uniforms."

For more information visit: www2.le.ac.uk

Leicester Mercury, Thursday March 13, 2014.

Incentive schemes should be shared by all workers

BUSINESS VOICE

I WAS interested to read that Next boss Lord Simon Wolfson has waived a bonus of almost £4 million in favour of sharing it among 20,000 employees who have been with the company for three years or more.

Lord Wolfson benefits from an incentive scheme linked to the value of the company's shares and has chosen to distribute his gains to qualifying employees who will each receive a bonus of around 1.5 per cent of annual salary.

In rewarding his staff in this way, Lord Wolfson is perhaps acknowledging that people work best for businesses that recognise and value them.

This is of particular interest to me because I work within the co-operative field where businesses are owned and controlled by their members or employees.

Co-operatives play a significant role in business – the United Nations estimates the livelihood of nearly 3 billion people, or half of the world's population, is made secure by co-operatively run enterprise.

All participants within co-operatives are on board with management decisions which leads to committed, engaged and productive staff who help their businesses towards improved productivity. The resulting profits are returned to the members or community.

An example of this style of working is the John Lewis Partnership that famously rewards all its employees or 'partners' with a bonus each year.

This was instigated by Spedan Lewis, the son of the original John Lewis, who felt that profits created by businesses should be paid to the workers that generate it, not just shareholders, as this aligns employees' interests with that of the business and provides incentive to deliver excellent services or products.

While the employees at Next are no doubt delighted to receive an additional 1.5 per cent of annual pay in their May pay packets, they might perhaps cast an envious eye over the bonuses of partners at John Lewis who last month took home 15 per cent – the equivalent of almost eight weeks' pay – and who receive a similar-sized share of profits every year.

Perhaps a sea change at Next will allow the incentive scheme to be shared among the workers each year instead of being ring fenced for just a few individuals?

Now that really would be a bonus.

■ *Dorothy Francis, right, is chief executive of the Co-operative and Social Enterprise Development Agency, based in Leicester.*

Leicester Mercury, Tuesday April 15, 2014.

Myself through the years.

Queen's Awards for Enterprise Promotion, 2016. Awards presentation, 20th June 2016, Leicester Town Hall.

Presentation of the Queen's Award crystal chalice by Jennifer, Lady Gretton, Lord Lieutenant of Leicestershire.

Colonel Murray Colville, Vice Lord Lieutenant of Leicestershire, reads aloud the Deed of Appointment from Her Majesty the Queen conferring the Queen's Award for Enterprise Promotion Lifetime Achievement Award on me.

With the Deed of Appointment which grants me lifetime rights to use the Queen's Award title.

The Deed of Appointment and the Queen's Award chalice.

A close up of the Queen's Award chalice.

Same as fig. 23.

Left to right: Her Majesty's Lord-Lieutenant of Leicestershire, Jennifer, Lady Gretton JP; Vice Lord Lieutenant, Colonel Murray Colville; myself; Lord Mayor of Leicester, Cllr Stephen Corrall; Ed Mayo, CEO of Co-operatives UK; Leicester City Mayor, Sir Peter Soulsby.

The event was attended by many friends and supporters including Sarah Shepherd of the Just Fair Trade shop with whom I have worked for over 20 years.

With members of Soft Touch, from left, Gill Brigden, Dorothy, Helen Pearson and Naomi Diamond. Soft Touch is an award winning company that uses arts, media and music activities as a tool to engage with and change the lives of disadvantaged young people, and is the first business that I registered more than 30 years ago.

With Toyin from Stoneygate Baptist Church.

With Kevin and Fayola.

These photos were taken on 4th July 2016 at Buckingham Palace at the reception for the Queen's Award for Enterprise Promotion where Dorothy was recognised with the Lifetime Achievement Award.

Posing outside Buckingham Palace before the Queen's Award reception.

Same as fig. 30.

The inner courtyard at Buckingham Palace and the entrance to the State Rooms.

Posing in the courtyard before entering the State Rooms.

With Kevin outside the entrance to the State Rooms.

Enjoying my own red carpet!

Dorothy's MBE Investiture at Buckingham Palace, 2017.

Arriving at Buckingham Palace for my MBE Investiture on 11th May 2017.

Same as fig. 36.

Fayola and me at Buckingham Palace, 11th May 2017.

On the occasion of my MBE Investiture.

Kevin and myself at my MBE Investiture.

Fayola, Kevin, me and Safiya at my MBE Investiture, posing with my medal.

Same as fig. 41.

At Buckingham Palace posing with my MBE medal.

Myself and Kevin with medal.

Same as fig. 44.

(Reproduced with the permission of Dr Dorothy Francis)

⟨Articles⟩

From CASE (Co-operative and Social Enterprise Development Agency)

1

December 1, 2010

Dorothy Francis receives Leicestershire Business Woman of the Year award

"Local business woman, Dorothy Francis, is our rock", says successful co-operative

Dorothy Francis, Chief Executive Officer of the Co-operative and Social Enterprise Development Agency (CaSE-da), is celebrating being voted Leicestershire Business Woman of the Year in recognition of almost 30 years of working in the co-op movement and her achievement in being at the helm of CaSE-da for 12 years and personally assisting to develop over 200 new co-operative and social enterprises.

Dorothy received her award in front of 800 people at the prestigious Jubilee Awards at Curve Theatre, Leicester on 19th November. The award ceremony was organised by the LeicestHERday Trust to recognise and thank the women who help enhance and change the lives of people in Leicestershire.

Dorothy won the Woman in Business category and was particularly singled out for her sixteen-year involvement with Shepshed Carers Co-operative who provide care to elderly and infirm people to allow them to live independently in their own homes.

When Dorothy first began working with Pauline Graves and Sarah Pollard, the founders of Shepshed Carers in 1994, the duo were running the business out of Pauline's dining room.

Thanks to their own hard work and help and support from Dorothy and CaSE-da, Shepshed Carers now operates across four locations, employs over 100 staff and has a turnover in excess of a million pounds.

They have even visited 10 Downing Street to offer advice to the Prime Minister on how to promote co-operatives to successfully replicate what Shepshed Carers does.

Their success is overwhelming but Sarah Poland lays a part of that success firmly at Dorothy's feet saying, "Dorothy is our rock. She has helped us from day one to be what we have become."

Sarah particularly cited the way that Dorothy has helped Shepshed Carers to develop and implement HR policies over the years. "We started as a co-operative of self employed individuals and then contracting arrangements meant that we had to change our legal structure so all members had to become employees. This brought with it a huge raft of HR and employment changes but Dorothy took us through this with ease. In fact the policies that she devised were so good that the local authority ended up adopting them! There are an awful lot of HR changes required to take a business from a two person enterprise to a multi-site co-operative employing over one hundred people but Dorothy has dealt with everything we have ever asked her and has always done to so cheerfully and professionally – she really is our "personal rock".

Dorothy is modest about her achievements saying "I have worked at CaSE-da, which is itself a co-operative, since 1985 and have been the CEO for 12 years but I have never lost my love of working with people to help them to achieve their dreams through setting up and running co-operatives and other social businesses. I consider myself fortunate to have spent so many years working with people who run businesses that not only trade for profit but also with the planet and people in mind. It's an honour to be recognised for doing something that I enjoy so much."

She continues, "CaSE-da's business is to ensure that those requiring advice and assistance to set up and run co-operatives receive the best possible service. We take great care to ensure that people we work with are properly trained and equipped to run solid and sustainable co-operative and social enterprises. I received help 27 years ago from Coventry Co-operative Development Agency to set up a co-operative business and that inspired me to enter this world of work – it's great to be able to give something back and to work with so many wonderful co-operative businesses."

A selection of some of the most successful women in the East Midlands were invited to the Jubilee Awards as guest speakers, including Sheila Lock, Chief Executive of Leicester City Council; Liz Kendall, Labour MP for Leicester West; Sandra Pollock, National Chair at CMI Women in Management; and Rajinder Bhuhi, Enterprise Learning Officer at the University of Leicester. Sandra Pollock said: "Women are good at business and women in business are good for Leicestershire and the UK economy. It's time that this was acknowledged and by recognising successful women we are showing what is possible."

2 Queen's Award for CASE CEO

Co-operative Entrepreneur granted Lifetime Achievement Award, 2016.

We are delighted to announce that Dorothy Francis, Chief Executive of CASE – the Co-operative and Social Enterprise Agency – received a Queen's Award for Enterprise Promotion on Thursday 21st April on the Queen's 90th birthday.

She is one of five people in the UK to receive the Enterprise Promotion award and is the only person to be granted the accolade of a Lifetime Achievement Award. The Award is made to people who have played an outstanding role in promoting enterprise skills and attitudes by giving time, effort and advice.

Dorothy earns the Lifetime Achievement Award for Enterprise Promotion for over 30 years of supporting co-operatively run businesses to establish and grow, primarily through her service at CASE where she has been the Chief Executive since 2000 having started work with the agency in the mid 1980s. CASE specialises in delivering advice, training and business growth for co-operatives and social enterprises in Leicestershire and the East Midlands. Dorothy has directly supported over 200 enterprises to start and develop and has worked with many more to realise and grow their potential. A number of these businesses have now traded for 25 years and more and have grown to provide numerous local jobs and win national and local awards.

Dorothy was nominated by her team at CASE for this award. Jane Avery, a friend and colleague, commented: "I have known and worked with Dorothy for over 30 years; her reputation amongst our clients is legendary and many of her clients become firm friends. Her commitment to helping local people to bring their business ideas and dreams to reality is second to none; she is skilled in nurturing co-operative entrepreneurship and is valued enormously by the people that she works with. She works tirelessly for CASE yet goes home and does more of the same, volunteering at her local church and sitting on the boards of co-operative and community groups."

One of the businesses that Dorothy is most closely associated with is Shepshed Carers Co-operative. Sarah Pollard, a director and founder member said, "This Award is so well-deserved! Dorothy helped us to set up our co-operative, spending hours with us to build our business skills and confidence. Twenty three years on we employ over 100 people and deliver services to more than 640 people but without her support we would never have started in business – she had faith in us from day one and helped us to achieve our dream."

Dorothy has worked with too many businesses to list; however of special note are Soft Touch Arts, which was the first business that she registered 30 years ago, and Leicester Wholefoods Co-operative which was the second, and she is delighted that they have both gone from strength to strength! She took part in Just Fair Trade's recent 20th birthday celebration at Leicester Cathedral having registered the business at the start of its journey and has been pleased to play a key part in the development of many other local co-operative and social enterprises including CKI Martial Arts, Eagle Care Alternatives, Somali Development Agency, Just Services, Complete Wasters, Corner Plot, Just Wood Leicestershire, Sunflower Nursery and Nifty Thinking, amongst many others.

Dorothy said "It is an honour to receive this award and I consider myself fortunate to be awarded for doing a job that I love. It is a pleasure to work with CASE to support passionate, enthusiastic people who run businesses that bring positive change to local communities. I am rewarded in knowing that I help to support sustainable co-operatives and other forms of social businesses that have a huge impact within communities in Leicestershire and further afield. I enjoy what I do and can't quite believe that I have been recognised in this way!"

The Award was conferred on 21st April and Dorothy will travel to a reception at Buckingham Palace in mid-July to meet other Award winners.

The Award itself will be presented in Leicester by Lady Gretton, the Leicestershire Lord-Lieutenant, at a date to be confirmed. The Award takes the form of an engraved crystal chalice and a ceremonial Grant of Appointment, which bears a copy of HM The Queen's and the Prime Minister's signatures.

3

No 1
The Crescent
King Street
Leicester
LE1 6RX

Press Release

Leicester Woman presented with Queen's Award for Enterprise Promotion

Co-operative and Social Enterprise Entrepreneur granted Lifetime Achievement Award

The Queen's 90th birthday on April 21st was a very special day for local woman Dorothy Francis as it was revealed that she had been chosen to receive a Queen's Award for Enterprise Promotion and additionally had been granted the annual Lifetime Achievement Award. Dorothy is the Chief Executive of Leicestershire based CASE (Co-operative and Social Enterprise Development Agency) and received the award for services to the social business sector.

The Award was conferred at a celebratory event at Leicester Town Hall on Monday 20th June. Guest of honour was Her Majesty's Lord-Lieutenant of Leicestershire, Jennifer, Lady Gretton JP who presented the Award, which takes the form of an engraved crystal chalice. Her Majesty's Vice Lord-Lieutenant, Colonel Murray Colville TD DL read the Deed of Appointment proclamation which conferred the title upon Dorothy. The presentation was followed by speeches of congratulations from the Lord Mayor of Leicester, Stephen Corrall; the Mayor of Leicester, Sir Peter Soulsby and Ed Mayo, the Chief Executive of Co-operatives UK.

Also in attendance were Dorothy's colleagues, family members and representatives from many of the co-operatives and social enterprises that Dorothy has worked with from 1986 to the present day. To complete the formalities Dorothy will attend an evening reception at Buckingham Palace in mid-July where she will be presented to the Queen and will meet other Queen's Award winners.

Dorothy is one of five people in the UK to receive the Enterprise Promotion award in 2016 and is the only person to be granted the accolade of a Lifetime Achievement Award. The Lifetime Achievement Award is made to people who have played an outstanding role in promoting enterprise skills and attitudes by giving time, effort and advice within their local communities. The Award was instituted in 2005 and Dorothy is the 11th person to hold this prestigious honour.

Dorothy earns the Lifetime Achievement Award for Enterprise Promotion for over 30 years of supporting businesses to establish and grow, primarily through her service at CASE where she has been the Chief Executive since 2000 having started work with the agency in the mid-1980's. CASE specialises in delivering advice, training and business growth for co-operatives and social enterprises in Leicestershire and the East Midlands. Dorothy has directly supported over 200 enterprises to start and develop and has worked with many more to realise and grow their potential so that they now provide numerous local jobs and win national and local awards.

Dorothy was nominated by her team at CASE who feel that her unflagging commitment deserves recognition. Jane Avery, a friend and colleague commented "Dorothy works quietly and modestly to develop enterprising skills in local people and has built up an outstanding reputation over the past 30 years. She is skilled in nurturing entrepreneurship and is valued enormously by the people that she works with. She works tirelessly for CASE but does not stop there as she uses her leisure time to mentor young people, sit on the boards of community groups and volunteers at her local church – she really is unstoppable!"

The first business that Dorothy registered was Soft Touch Arts in 1986 and she has worked with the enterprise throughout all stages of development over the past 30 years. Sally Norman, a director of Soft Touch and one of the founder members said, "In a business life-cycle there are peaks and troughs. We've faced tough trading conditions, had difficult issues to deal with and awkward contracts to negotiate and we've also celebrated the successes, growth and the triumphs of our company and of the young people that we work with. Throughout it all Dorothy has been the go-to person for advice, support and encouragement and Soft Touch Arts has benefited enormously from her commitment and dedication."

Sally's words are echoed by Keira Cornish of Just Services Co-operative, an advocacy support service for people with disabilities, who says "Dorothy's unwavering support equipped Just Services to conquer hurdles and tackle problems over the past 15 years and she has also been at our side to celebrate the good times and our triumphs. Knowing that Dorothy is always there has meant so much to our company; she has consistently inspired a belief that we can run our business successfully. Getting Just Services to this stage would have been much harder without Dorothy's guidance."

Dorothy said "It is an honour to receive this award in front of so many friends, family, colleagues and clients. I am humbled and uplifted by the letters and cards that I have received since the Award was announced in April and by how delighted people have been at my success. However my success comes via the attainments of the many businesses that I have been privileged to work with and I feel that my true reward is in knowing that I help to support sustainable social businesses that have a huge impact within communities in Leicestershire and further afield."

4

February 2017

Meet… Dorothy Francis, a co-operative community builder

Dorothy Francis is CED of CASE (Co-operative and Social Enterprise) development agency, a workers' co-op offering business advice, support and training to individuals and communities. Here she talks about the changes she has witnessed, how being a co-op has been integral to CASE's survival – and the dilemma of accepting an MBE as a woman of colour.

HOW DID YOU START IN THE SECTOR?

My introduction to co-operatives was through being a client of a Co-operative Development Agency (CDA), a support organisation for people setting up and running co-operatives. Some friends and I sought advice from Coventry CDA in the early 1980s on how to set up a bookshop selling literature for, and about, people of colour. I was very impressed by the service at Coventry CDA and knew that I wanted to work in a similar role once I'd gained business experience. A few years later a job came up at what was then Leicester and County CDA (now renamed CASE). I applied with the intention of staying two years and never left!

WHAT DO YOU DO AT CASE?

We do a lot of liaison work to deliver our service. We are a small organisation so partnership working is very important for synergy of services and to build relationships for joint bids and working together. I started as a business adviser and still operate within that role, meeting with new-start businesses and existing clients to help them establish, grow and develop their enterprises. As an agency we aim to maintain contact with our clients and I have worked with some businesses for over 30 years.

CASE is a workers' co-operative so all members take ownership of running the business. My role as CED is to be a figurehead and a point of contact. I undertake a number of functions within my job including bid writing and creating and delivering training courses – at the moment I'm running a programme to deliver training to women to help them enter business, employment or training.

Helping women to get into business is one of my driving passions; getting people of colour into the co-op movement is another.

WHAT IS CASE'S CO-OP DIFFERENCE?

At the start, what made us stand out was that Leicester was one of the few CDAs constituted as a co-operative. We wrote a set of rules (the 'Leicester Model Rules') to suit our needs and sold these to ICOM (the Industrial Common Ownership Movement, which merged with the Co-operative Union in 2001 to become Co-operatives UK) for other small co-ops to use.

We firmly believe that having a co-operative structure has allowed CASE to adapt to changes and has contributed to CASE's longevity.

WHAT IS THE BEST – AND THE HARDEST – PART OF YOUR JOB?

The best part is working with people and helping them develop their business ideas. Seeing a business flourish and knowing that CASE has played a part is a great feeling.

The hardest part is accessing the finance to keep CASE going. A lot of people think we are funded but we are not; we bid for contracts and seek work on the open market. It's a challenge, but we like challenges! This can also be a positive aspect when talking to clients because they know that we are also a small business and that we offer advice from the experience of running an enterprise, rather than from a purely academic basis.

HAS IT BECOME EASIER OR HARDER FOR ENTERPRISES TO DEVELOP?

In the UK it is relatively easy to set up in business. However there are fewer support agencies than there used to be so if people need additional help – for example if they come from disadvantaged communities, have a disability, are long-term unemployed etc – they may find it harder to set up due to the barriers they face. They may lack assistance to overcome obstacles in their way.

One of our roles at CASE is to smooth the path so that people who want to set up in business are able to do so more easily. CASE excels in assisting people from disadvantaged communities entering into business and we gain great job satisfaction from doing so.

We find that we are always busy as there is great interest in co-operative ways of working. We promote co-operative values and principles in the work that we do as it is the crux of the movement. More people are now aware of social businesses as a viable alternative and we find that we do not need to explain co-operatives and social enterprises as much as we used to.

WHAT DOES RECEIVING AN MBE MEAN TO YOU?

I am delighted to have been recognised for my work and it's a great honour to receive an MBE although I had to think long and hard about whether or not to accept. An MBE commemorates 'empire', and as a person of colour, with Jamaican heritage, that is not something that I particularly wish to celebrate.

I decided to accept after doing a lot of thinking and some informal consultation (without letting on to the real reason as I was sworn to secrecy!) I asked friends and family what they thought, in principle, and the overwhelming response was that people of colour should be recognised for what they do and should feel free to accept awards and honours. It was felt that when we turn down awards we also turn down opportunities for people of colour to be recognised for their achievements and contributions and to be seen as influential role models for other people – of any colour – within society.

I accepted as I feel it's not just an award for me, but for my community, my family and my colleagues, past and present, at CASE. The deciding reason why I accepted is that I knew that it would have tremendous significance for my mother and would contribute, in a small way, to repaying the courage and faith that she showed in leaving Jamaica to make a life in Britain so that her children could have a better future. I'm pleased to accept on her behalf and gratified that 33 years of doing a job that I love has been recognised in this way.

(Author: Rebecca Harvey) [3rd February 2017]
From *Co-operative News*

(Reproduced with the permission of Dr Dorothy Francis)

Appendix 7: 'Day trip to Rochdale'

Toad Lane view.

In front of the Toad Lane shop.

The Toad Lane shop.

Replica in Japan.

Drawing of Toad Lane shop in the nineteenth century.

Interior of shop mocked up as it would have looked on the opening night in 1844.

Advertising poster.

The co-op was proud that it did not use cheap 'sweated' labour in any of its processes.

(Reproduced with the permission of Dr Dorothy Francis)

Appendix 8: Account of Honorary Doctorate of Laws, Graduation Day

University of Leicester Degree Congregation, De Montfort Hall, Friday, July 20, 2018.

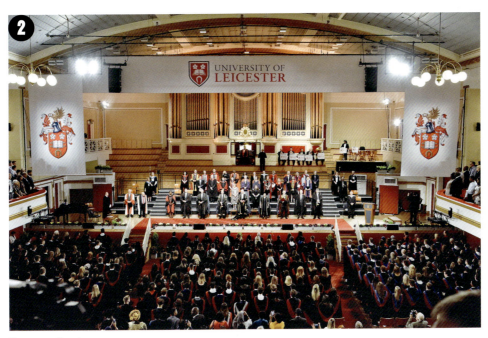

Same as fig. 1.

Listening to his oration.

Delivering my response to the oration by the public orator Mr Nigal Siesage.

Same as fig. 4.

With University of Leicester dignitaries following the ceremony.

With family and friends.

Posing with my scroll.

A very proud Kevin!

Selfie time with Fayola and Safiya.

With my sisters Sharon, Hortense and Lorna.

With my good friend, Nelista.

With my brother Steadman and cousin Trevor.

With family and friends.

257

Receiving Doctorate scroll.

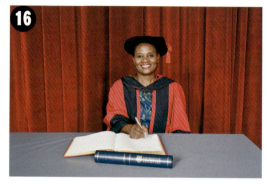

Signing the Honorary Doctorate register.

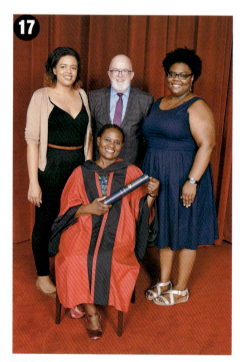

With Kevin, Safiya and Fayola.

Professor Kiyotaka Sato and myself.

(Reproduced with the permission of Dr Dorothy Francis. Nos. 1, 12 and 14: photographs by the editor)

Appendix 9: Dorothy's experience and 'Working together to end strip searching'

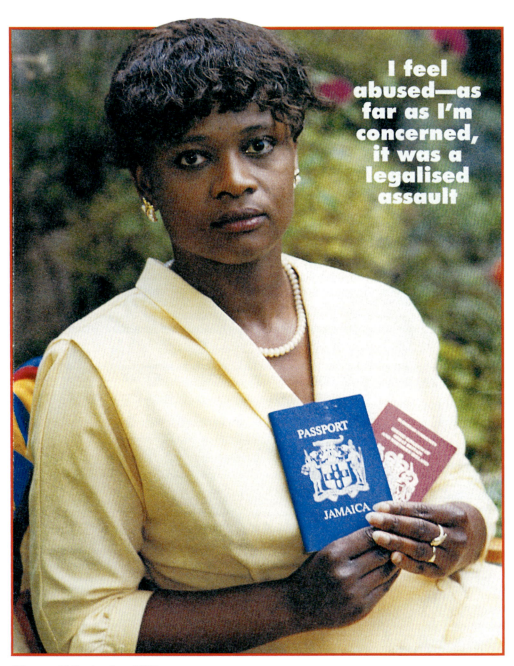

Woman, 13 September 1993.

1

27 March 1987

A letter from Keith Vaz BA (CANTAB), Solicitor (North Leicester Advice Centre, Leicester) to 'Chief Customs Officer, HM Customs and Excise, Heathrow Airport, London'.

Dear Sirs,

Re: Ms Dorothy Francis – 85 Wordsworth Road Leicester – 8.3.87 Flight No. BA292

I act for the above named who has informed me that she was on a flight from Jamaica to London on the above date.

On arrival at Customs, after she had gone through the area where excess duty is declared she was held at your offices for two and half hours and her baggage luggage and person was searched. Further, a number of items that belonged to her were damaged by your officers, who were apparently searching for drugs. My client has an impeachable record and deeply resents the fact that she was unlawfully held and subjected to indignities. She is also seeking compensation for the damage that was caused to her items.

I would be obliged if you could arrange for an investigator to be appointed to look into this case.

I look forward to hearing from you.

Yours faithfully,

KEITH VAZ
Solicitor

2

22 April 1987

A letter from HM Customs and Excise (Surveyor T4, Terminal Four, London Heathrow Airport, Hounslow, Middlesex) to Mr K. Vaz, Solicitor (North Leicester Advice Centre, Leicester).

Dear Sir

Re: Ms Dorothy Francis – Complaint

Thank you for your letter dated 27 March concerning the Customs treatment of Ms Francis on her arrival in the U.K, having flown from Jamaica on 8 March 1987. As the Customs manager in the Terminal I have called for full reports from the officers concerned.

As you are probably aware Customs operate a clearway system at London Airport whereby passengers with nothing to declare in excess of their allowances, or carrying other restricted items, walk through a Green Channel. Other passengers who are not sure or who have items that they know require a declaration to Customs pass through the Red Channel. Mrs Francis went into the Red Channel where due to the large numbers of fellow passengers also with goods to declare in front of her she unfortunately had a long wait before she was seen by an officer. The officer estimates that Ms Francis spent no longer than one and a half hours queuing and being dealt with by himself. This I do not seek to justify as reasonable and I can assure you that as the manager of Customs in this Terminal I will continue to strive for better and more efficient systems and accommodation, plus of course more staff to process the queuing passengers more quickly.

However Ms Francis was not unlawfully held as you allege for two and a half hours in private offices. She was in a public area whilst queuing and in the Red Channel where her baggage was examined except for the time when her person was searched. She was never under arrest and was dealt with at all times under Section 78 of the Customs and Excise Management Act 1979. The search of person is for many passengers a most distressing experience. Ms Francis was upset and the two lady officers took some time reassuring and explaining to her the reasons for the search and the fact that they would not touch her at all. I am satisfied that the strict procedural guidelines governing such searchers were adhered to. The officers who dealt with Ms Francis also apologised for the thoroughness of the examination and search and she did not complain to the duty senior officer who would have investigated any complaint at the time of the incident.

As regards compensation for the damaged items, of course a reasonable claim would be considered. The carvings were accepted as part of Ms Francis' allowances (£32) and the officer estimated a value of no more than £20. I would therefore make a without prejudice offer of £20 as fair and reasonable compensation for the damaged items which were damaged during the Customs examination.

Please convey my sincere apologies to Ms Francis for the distress caused to her but please also stress that in the efficient discharge of their duties my officers inevitably will inconvenience completely innocent travellers such as herself.

Yours faithfully,

R. Hawkes
Surveyor T4

3

July 1987

Woman's strip-search ordeal

A Leicester woman who was forced to partially strip and had personal possessions destroyed in a two-and-a-half hour search ordeal at Heathrow Airport has called a £20 compensation offer an "insult."

Now, Miss Dorothy Francis, aged 26, of Wordsworth Road, Knighton Fields, is threatening to take HM Customs and Excise Department to court unless more money is forthcoming.

Customs officers are given their powers of strip search under the Police and Criminal Evidence Act.

But before they can proceed with the search, you are within your rights to call in a magistrate or the senior Customs officer at the airport or port concerned to hear your case. They will decide if Customs officers have valid grounds to conduct a search.

Miss Francis says she was "singled out" by a Customs officer as she returned from a visit to her family in Jamaica in March.

She said: "All my souvenirs and presents were drilled through, the heels of my shoes were broken off and my suitcase was broken. They said they were looking for drugs, but I believe I was picked on because I was black and a woman.

"I was then partially strip-searched by two women Customs officers. It was a humiliating experience and the offer of £20 is insulting."

Her solicitor, East Leicester MP Mr. Keith Vaz, wrote to the Customs Office at Heathrow demanding an apology and compensation.

He said a letter came back offering an apology for damaging Miss Francis's possessions and offering £20 compensation.

"This was not satisfactory and I have written on behalf of Miss Francis asking for more money," he said.

Leicester Mercury, July 1987.

4

5 December 1987

Working together to end Strip Searching

REPORT OF A CONFERENCE
5 DECEMBER 1987

NEWS AROUND BRITAIN
Strip searching campaign
~a matter of urgency

Conference line-up shows the growing outrage at strip-searching: from left to right, Abena Simba-Tola, Susie Gramic, the leader of Southwark Council Anne Mathews (who chaired the meeting), republican ex-prisoner Briege Brownlee, Tracey Lambert of COHSE, Dorothy Francis and Jennifer McCarey.

1988 sees the launch of a co-ordinated national campaign to end strip searching. The campaign stems from the "Working together to end strip searching" conference held in London in December. Organised by the London Strategic Policy Unit, the conference brought together a variety of groups and individuals to discuss the future of the fight against strip searches.

While the scope of the conference covered all the areas where the British state uses strip searching, speakers like ex-Armagh prisoner Briege Brownlee and Isobel Anderson, sister of prisoner Martina Anderson, focussed on the strip searching of Irish Republican women prisoners. Isobel Anderson explained how the strip searching of Republican women must be seen in the context of British repression in Ireland, and how the ill-treatment of political prisoners is an essential part of the war in Ireland.

"Political oppression is a way of life in Ireland and it is becoming a way of life in Britain," she said. "Strip searching is part of this oppression and must be opposed." She added that the fight against the strip searching of Republican women prisoners could be part of a broad-based campaign against all strip searches.

WORKSHOPS

The conference featured a combination of panel discussion and workshops. Other speakers included representatives from Scottish and London anti-strip search groups, trade unionists, and a Black woman who had been strip searched at British Customs. Working within the Black community, the role of parliamentary action, Irish Republican women, the law, and the media were among the workshop topics. In the workshop on Irish Republican women there was much discussion about the danger of the strip searching of Republican women being marginalised in a broad campaign. It became clear it was up to activists around Irish issues to see that this does not happen.

At the conclusion of the workshops conference participants agreed unanimously to set up a campaign committee from Irish and Black organisations, trade unions and labour movement organisations, strip search campaigns, lesbian and gay groups, and any other interested groups who wish to give their support. The first meeting is **Feb 14, from 2-5pm at Hackney Town Hall, Mare Street, London E8**. The organisers urge groups to send representatives on to the meeting to carry on the campaign. Further information is available from Sheila Spurway on 01-222-7799.

STATEMENT

The conference also issued a statement calling for an immediate end to strip searching, saying that *"strip searching is used to degrade and humiliate. It is a technique of repression used systematically against Irish Republican women and it is now being increasingly used against Black and Asian women, Black youth, political activists, lesbians and gay men, and against people in prisons and at customs, in police custody, at military establishments and even in the streets. Strip searching must be ended as a matter of urgency."*

A report on the conference is available from Jacqui Kelly, LSPU, 7th Floor, Hampton House, 20 Albert Embankment, London.

Page 10 Troops Out, February 1988

London Strategic Policy Unit, *Working together to end Strip Searching: Report of a Conference 5 December 1987.*

Dorothy Francis
Strip searched at Customs

I was strip searched when I returned to England on 8 March, ironically enough, International Women's Day. I had returned from a five week stay in Florida and Jamaica and was totally unprepared for what happened to me on that day. When I arrived at Heathrow Airport I was carrying four extra bottles of rum which I decided to declare by going through the red channel. I queued for three-quarters of an hour in order to declare what I had. I approached a male customs officer who was at first quite friendly and chatty towards me, asking me where I'd been, had I had a nice holiday etc. In fact he was very friendly towards me until he asked me what I did for a living. I told him that I was a business adviser. Immediately his attitude towards me changed and he said: 'A business adviser, what's that?'. It quickly became very apparent that he thought that a young black woman had no right to be doing a professional job such as a business adviser in England and that he would quickly put me in my place.

He asked me to open my suitcases so that he could examine the contents. This was in full view of all the other passengers waiting to declare their items, which made it even more embarrassing because they were criminalising me before I had done anything, and by the way they were searching me it was as if they were expecting to find something on me. This was very humiliating. The customs officer found three wooden carvings in my suitcase which I had bought as souvenirs from Jamaica; they were head carvings to hang as plaques on the wall. He ordered one of his subordinates to take one away and drill holes through it with an electric drill. One of the officers drilled through the forehead, the nose, the mouth and each of the cheeks of the carving and rendered it totally useless. When I complained about this and said that I'd travelled 5,000 miles to buy them and they were now worthless, he said: 'Not at all, all you have to do is go to a hardware store, buy some plastic wood, fill in the holes, repaint it and they will be a good as new again'. He accused me time and time again of being hysterical, over-emotional, and of over-reacting, when in fact I was calm throughout and tried to act in a decent way even though they weren't treating me decently.

They took an hour to search my first suitcase and finally started on the second suitcase which had five locks. By this time the customs officer who was searching was getting increasingly irritated because it was quite obvious that he was expecting to find something on me and he hadn't so far. Even though I offered to open my suitcase for him so that he could search it he couldn't be bothered to wait for me to take the few seconds that it would have taken: he yanked at the suitcase, broke it open and one of the locks flew off.

At this stage I'd been there about 1½ hours, I was tired, hungry and just wanted to go home so I started to cry. He immediately assumed that I was crying because he was getting nearer to whatever he was looking for. So he searched with renewed vigour. They searched everything in the suitcase. They look clothing out of the suitcase, looked in pockets of clothing from the suitcase, felt the hems, unscrewed and opened every single container they could, including my lipstick, my contact lens case, my tampax, my vaseline, my shampoo, everything in sight. By the time they'd finished searching, the contents of my suitcase were scattered across the table. Everybody on the same flight as me was able to see every single item that was in my suitcase.

After nearly two hours of this, when they decided that they hadn't humiliated me enough, the customs officer demanded that I be strip searched. I said that they had no reason to do so as they had searched minutely every single item in my luggage and it was impossible for me to be carrying anything. Throughout all this I was never told why I was being searched. I assumed that because I'd left England to go to Florida and had then left there to go to Jamaica, they were searching me for marijuana as it's well known that marijuana is easily available in Jamaica. But I think that I would be a total idiot as a young black person to smuggle any marijuana back into this country. If they were looking for marijuana they would have had no need to feel the hems of my clothing or to look into my lipstick, or other such tiny containers, because, I think as we all know, marijuana is a bulky item and certainly it wouldn't be worth trying to smuggle it through in the hem of a dress. So, I don't really know why they wanted to search me.

They still demanded that I be strip searched and I refused, saying that if necessary they could frisk me but I certainly wasn't going to strip. I had come from a climate where, although it was March, it was 87 degrees and therefore I was wearing a thin pair of jeans and an equally thin tee-shirt. I said that it was impossible for me to have anything strapped under clothes so thin. But they took no notice and I was taken away into a small side office by two female customs officers who once again demanded that I strip.

By this time I was crying so much because I was so distressed that it was impossible for me to stand up unassisted. I think even the customs people, as inhumane as they are, realised just how upset I was and so I sat down on a chair for 10 minutes until I could compose myself to strip.

Throughout all this I asked them whether a strip search was necessary, but they told me that if I didn't submit to the search that I wouldn't be allowed to leave customs, which I later found out was totally incorrect. At no time did they inform me of my rights to see a senior customs official or to ask someone else to be brought in to decide whether or not I should be strip searched. I finally stood up, still crying, and because I was crying so much they said that I need not undergo a full strip search and needn't take off *all* my clothes. So they made me drop my lower garments to my ankles and raise my upper garments to shoulder level and hold them there. Although they said that in any way it was any less humiliating than a full strip search. In fact I would have preferred to take my clothes off totally rather than stand there with my jeans around my ankles and my tee-shirt hoisted up to my shoulders.

They wrote down my passport number, and I noticed that there were about 10 other numbers before mine. This indicated that another 10 people had been searched in that room alone and there were about another three or four rooms. They wrote down my passport number and paraded around my body and looked at me. They didn't touch me, but I don't think that made any difference. After walking around for about four minutes they said that I could put my clothes on and go. They offered me no apology. I found all my belongings across the room and I was just told to pack them up and go away. I was crying so much that I could not even see to put my goods away. By this time I'd been in customs about three hours. When I finally came out my friend, who'd been waiting for me, was going frantic with worry. He'd been putting my name across the tannoy system and asking everybody whether they'd seen me because he knew that I'd caught the plane in Jamaica, that it had been a direct flight and that I couldn't possibly have got off. He knew that the plane had landed three hours previously and that I hadn't emerged from customs. Thankfully that friend was there because if he hadn't been I don't know what would have happened.

When I finally emerged from customs and saw him there I was so relieved and so weak that I just collapsed onto the floor and had to be carried out of Heathrow Airport by him. He could get no sense out of me at all, because I was so incoherent and couldn't describe what had happened.

My experience compared to some of the people here today might seem insignificant in that I was only strip searched once. Some people have said to me since then that I made a lot of fuss over that one incident. I would argue, however, that it doesn't matter whether I was strip searched once or 100 times. My basic human rights were violated. I was mistreated, mishandled, abused and harassed. Strip searching is an attack against women and especially an attack against black women and in my case, I can only presume, an attack against a Jamaican (although I've lived here for the last 21 years I'm a Jamaican citizen by birth and still carry a Jamaican passport). When I asked the customs officer who searched me why he'd done it so extensively and said to him: 'You've racially and sexually humiliated me for 2½ hours, you find nothing on me and you give me no explanation as to why', he just shrugged this shoulders and said 'Well what do you expect if you come off a flight from Jamaica carrying a Jamaican passport'. So I can only assume that if I'm black, a woman and Jamaican I can expect that kind of hassle and harassment every time I come through customs. Thank you for listening.

(Reproduced with the permission of Dr Dorothy Francis)

Appendix 10: The Windrush scandal (Extracts from the *Leicester Mercury*)

1

Friday, April 27, 2018

Ashworth criticises 'inhumane treatment' of immigrants
MP holds meeting over the Windrush scandal

By Dan Martin, Politics Correspondent

A public meeting is to be held in Leicester today for anyone who may have been affected by the Windrush scandal.

Leicester South MP John Ashworth has convened the meeting in the wake of the Home Office threatening to deport immigrants who came to the UK from the Caribbean to settle at the invite of the British Government between 1948 and 1971. It will take place at St Peter's Church Hall, St Peter's Road, Highfields, at 1.30pm today.

Mr Ashworth has been assisting his constituent Rolston Knight, who came to the UK from Curacao as a two-year old and settled in Aylestone. The 60-year-old was granted a UK passport in 1974 but was told he was not British when he attempted to renew it in 2011 so he could apply for jobs. Mr Ashworth said: "I have already contacted local organisations who may know of people affected and I am holding a public meeting on Friday to give people caught up in this scandal an opportunity to meet with me."My constituents need to know that I totally disagree with the Government's immoral and inhumane treatment of them."

Mr Knight, whose inability to work drove him to depression and alcoholism, told the Mercury he was now cautiously optimistic he would get a new passport following a series of apologies made by Prime Minister Theresa May and Home Secretary Amber Rudd over how the Windrush Generation has been treated. Mr Knight, who has a British wife and two grown-up British children, was however told he would have to pay £1,500 to confirm his immigration status and apply for naturalisation in a country he has lived and worked in for the best part of 60 years. He said those fees had eventually been waived after it emerged he and others were facing large bills to confirm their British citizenship. He said: "It was a lot of money which I don't really have. I'm glad I don't have to pay anything. I think, I hope, things will be sorted out for me very soon. There has been a lot of pressure on the Government."

Ms Rudd has spoken of her "bitter regret" at failing to grasp the scale of the Windrush scandal sooner. The Home Secretary, who has faced calls to resign over the crisis, told MPs she had become aware there was a "potential issue" over the "past few months".

But she said: "I bitterly, deeply regret that I didn't see it as more than individual cases that had gone wrong that needed addressing. I didn't see it as a systematic issue until very recently." Ms Rudd and her predecessor Mrs May have come under intense pressure after it emerged long-term residents who arrived in the decades after the Second World War were having their immigration status challenged – despite being in the country legally. As a result of the disclosures, the Home Office launched a major review to check whether anyone had been incorrectly deported.

Ms Rudd told the Commons Home Affairs committee that so far 7,000 out of around 8,000 records dating back to 2002 had been checked with no wrongful removals discovered so far. A dedicated helpline set up last week has received more than 1,300 calls about potential Windrush cases, with 91 appointments booked and 23 cases resolved so far.

Leicestermercury.co.uk/politics

2

Wednesday, June 27, 2018

News

Moving speech highlights human cost of immigration department's failings 'How my parents helped put this country back on its feet'

Councillor George Cole told how he had witnessed first-hand the dedication and commitment members of the Windrush generation have showed and the repercussions of the recent scandal he had seen. He told fellow city councillors: "I witnessed my mother and my father and countless other people from the Windrush generation working seven days a week, treading through snow and ice, wind and rain to put this country back on its feet, I've seen that for myself."

He went on to describe the direct impact the scandal has had on his own family. "Following my mother's retirement, she went to live in the Caribbean, believing that as a British citizen she can travel to the United Kingdom as and when she needs to, now, at the age of 85, she finds that every time she wants to come to the United Kingdom, to say goodbye to a dead relative, or someone dying in the family, she has to go to the British authorities in Jamaica to be treated like a criminal, then she has to pay a large sum for a visa to gain entry to a country that she gave the best years of her life to, to rebuild that country – the country that she entered in 1956 as a British citizen from the Commonwealth. "It hurts, it really hurts to see what is happening to her and countless others for no reason other than the colour of her skin."

3

Friday, August 10, 2018

News
What is the Windrush scandal?

The Windrush generation arrived in the UK between 1948 and 1971 from Caribbean countries. After the ship Windrush brought the first group in 1948, about 500,000 people had moved to the UK from a Caribbean country by 1971. The Home Office did not keep a record of those granted leave to remain, meaning it is hard for Windrush arrivals to prove they are here legally. Landing cards belonging to Windrush migrants were destroyed in 2010. Those without documents are now being told they need them to continue working, get NHS treatment, or remain in the United Kingdom.

Victim of Windrush scandal: It means so much to get my British passport.
By Dan Martin, Politics Correspondent

Rolston Knight's seven-year wait for a British passport is finally over. The 60-year-old, one of the Windrush Generation, has now been confirmed as a citizen of the country in which he has lived since he was a toddler. "It's been such an effort to get it, I don't dare let it out of my sight," said Rolston after the tiny Burgundy travel document dropped through his letterbox this week. "It means so much to me, it's silly, really, but it does."

Rolston has lived in Leicester for 58 years. He came across to the UK with his family from the Dutch Caribbean Island of Curacao in 1960, at first to London but them to Aylstone. He went to school in the city, made friends in the city, married a British woman – Delria – and raised a British family here. Rolston was given a British passport in 1974, at age 16, and all was well until he tried to renew it in 2011 so he could apply for jobs. The Home Office refused his application, telling him it did "not appear" he was a British Citizen.

His case emerged earlier this year when the Government came under fire for its treatment of members of the Windrush Generation, who found their citizenship questioned despite having lived here for decades. His plight was taken up by Leicester South MP John Ashworth's office, which has guided him through the process of applying for citizenship and his passport. The father-of-two said: "I've always known I was British, but I haven't felt it. I don't like to dwell on it now, but it feels like we have been picked on. I totally understand the need to control immigration – it is crucial – but people like me have been here all our lives nearly. I do feel a little bitter, a bit let down, but that's because there are still people in the limbo that I was in."

After Rolston's passport renewal was refused he lost his job and spent years out of work unable to apply for another position. He started to drink too much, gambled and fell into depression and became suicidal. He said: "It wasn't good. I couldn't see any light at the end of the tunnel. Now I feel like I'm getting my confidence back. I feel I've got some dignity and the best bit is I've got a job." Rolston, who worships at Leicester Central Seventh Day Adventist Church, off London Road, where he volunteers helping the homeless, has secured work as a warehouse operative for DHL at Magna Park. He said: "I've only just started but I'm loving it. I work with a great team in the chilled unit. It just feels fantastic to be earning again, not stuck at home watching telly. I've had enough of that. That's the most important thing. Now I've got a passport I should really use it. I don't have the money yet and it might take a while to save up but when I do I'm going to have a holiday in Curacao."

He thanked Mr Ashworth's team, saying "I don't think this would have been sorted without them. I had to fill in a 60-page form to get a citizenship certificate. It was complicated and I was desperate not to make a single mistake just in case it meant I got rejected. His staff took me through it. It really feels like a new start for me and my family." Mr Ashworth said: "I was pleased I was able to help Mr Knight, although it is a disgrace he found himself in this situation. I am delighted Mr Knight has now received his passport, but he should not have had to go through this process, especially as he was issued with a British passport in 1974. I have assisted approximately 10 people from the Windrush Generation with difficulties they have faced in proving their right to stay. All but two have been resolved and my office is continuing to assist these people."

Leicestermercury.co.uk

Appendix 11: Ethnicity and religion in the UK, Coventry and Leicester

[1981 Census]

Leicester: Country of Birth: Caribbean, 1981

Map 1

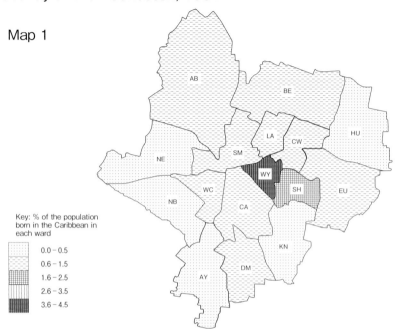

Table 1   Caribbean population in each ward (1981)

Ward	Total ward population	Total born in the Caribbean	% of ward total
Aylestone	18,614	48	0.3
Belgrave	22,398	163	0.7
Charnwood	15,863	210	1.3
De Montfort	16,983	145	0.9
Evington	19,599	183	0.9
Humberstone	18,415	55	0.3
Knighton	15,797	73	0.5
Latimer	14,072	128	0.9
Newton	20,438	68	0.3
North Braunstone	17,644	90	0.5
St. Margaret's	13,950	94	0.7
Spinney Hill	17,234	356	2.1
The Abbey	27,597	190	0.7
The Castle	10,149	74	0.7
Westcotes	13,361	89	0.7
Wycliffe	14,130	584	4.1
TOTAL	276,244	2,550	0.9

Source: Rooney, Yvonne &O'Connor, Henrietta, *The Spatial Distribution of Ethnic Minority Communities in Leicester, 1971, 1981 & 1991: Maps and Tables*, Leicester: the Centre for Urban History/ the Ethnicity Research Centra, University of Leicester, 1995, pp.33-34.

[1991 Census]

Leicester: Country of Birth: Caribbean, 1991

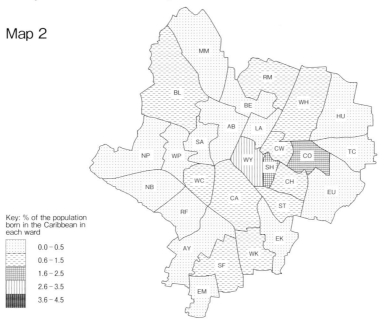

Map 2

Key: % of the population born in the Caribbean in each ward
- 0.0 – 0.5
- 0.6 – 1.5
- 1.6 – 2.5
- 2.6 – 3.5
- 3.6 – 4.5

Table 2   Caribbean population in each ward (1991)

Ward	Total ward population	Total born in the Caribbean	% of ward total
Abbey	8,538	41	0.5
Aylestone	9,898	28	0.3
Beaumont Leys	15,626	126	0.8
Belgrave	10,649	43	0.4
Castle	8,429	75	0.9
Charnwood	9,292	116	1.2
Coleman	8,980	149	1.7
Crown Hills	9,597	138	1.4
East Knighton	7,821	13	0.2
Evington	8,516	37	0.4
Eyres Monsell	9,115	10	0.1
Humberstone	8,705	39	0.4
Latimer	7,953	28	0.4
Mowmacre	7,014	10	0.1
New Parks	10,302	34	0.3
North Braunstone	8,710	27	0.3
Rowley Fields	9,746	43	0.4
Rushey Mead	11,470	81	0.7
Saffron	11,290	80	0.7
St. Augustines	9,619	45	0.5
Spinney Hill	10,033	168	1.7
Stoneygate	9,247	94	1.0
Thurcourt	9,975	48	0.5
Westcotes	8,844	64	0.7
Western Park	11,194	59	0.5
West Humberstone	9,877	105	1.1
West Knighton	8,584	57	0.7
Wycliffe	11,501	362	3.1
TOTAL	270,525	2,120	0.8

Source: Rooney, Yvonne & O'Connor, Henrietta, *op. cit.*, pp.35-36

[2001 Census]

African-Caribbean, 2001, Leicester

Map 3

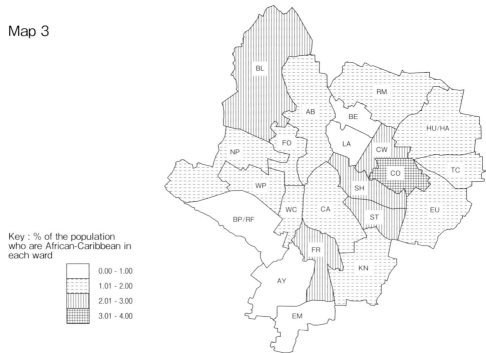

Table 3 African-Caribbean population in each ward (2001)

	Abbreviations	Wards	Population	Caribbean Population	%
1	AB	Abbey	12,713	184	1.45
2	AY	Aylestone	10,801	101	0.94
3	BL	Beaumont Leys	13,838	292	2.11
4	BE	Belgrave	10,297	99	0.96
5	BP/RF	Braunstone Park & Rowley Fields	16,614	166	1.00
6	CA	Castle	13,465	232	1.72
7	CW	Charnwood	10,664	319	2.99
8	CO	Coleman	12,099	383	3.17
9	EV	Evington	9,788	121	1.24
10	EM	Eyres Monsell	11,229	69	0.61
11	FO	Fosse	10,735	137	1.28
12	FR	Freemen	9,983	241	2.41
13	HU/HA	Humberstone & Hamilton	11,893	142	1.19
14	KN	Knighton	16,265	170	1.05
15	LA	Latimer	11,583	79	0.68
16	NP	New Parks	16,022	204	1.27
17	RM	Rushey Mead	15,134	192	1.27
18	SH	Spinney Hills	21,249	630	2.96
19	ST	Stoneygate	17,068	458	2.68
20	TC	Thurncourt	9,936	130	1.31
21	WC	Westcotes	8,653	122	1.41
22	WP	Western Park	9,892	139	1.41
		City of Leicester (Total)	279,921	4,610	1.65

Table 4   Black or Black British population in each ward (2001), Leicester

Ward	Total ward population	Caribbean		African		Other Black		Black or Black British	
		population	%	population	%	population	%	population	%
AB	12,713	184	1.45	56	0.44	12	0.09	252	1.98
AY	10,801	101	0.94	40	0.37	20	0.19	161	1.49
BL	13,838	292	2.11	281	2.03	47	0.34	620	4.48
BE	10,297	99	0.96	56	0.54	23	0.22	178	1.73
BP/RF	16,614	166	1.00	107	0.64	18	0.11	291	1.75
CA	13,465	232	1.72	468	3.48	31	0.23	731	5.43
CW	10,664	319	2.99	214	2.01	58	0.54	591	5.54
CO	12,099	383	3.17	152	1.26	47	0.39	582	4.81
EV	9,788	121	1.24	141	1.44	23	0.23	285	2.91
EM	11,229	69	0.61	40	0.36	7	0.06	116	1.03
FO	10,735	137	1.28	105	0.98	18	0.17	260	2.42
FR	9,983	241	2.41	72	0.72	19	0.19	332	3.33
HU/HA	11,893	142	1.19	37	0.31	13	0.11	192	1.61
KN	16,265	170	1.05	118	0.73	14	0.09	302	1.86
LA	11,583	79	0.68	57	0.49	8	0.07	144	1.24
NP	16,022	204	1.27	53	0.33	21	0.13	278	1.74
RM	15,134	192	1.27	94	0.62	22	0.15	308	2.04
SH	21,249	630	2.96	757	3.56	74	0.35	1,461	6.88
ST	17,068	458	2.68	349	2.04	44	0.26	851	4.99
TC	9,936	130	1.31	37	0.37	7	0.07	174	1.75
WC	8,653	122	1.41	145	1.68	21	0.24	288	3.33
WP	9,892	139	1.41	53	0.54	6	0.06	198	2.00
Total	279,921	4,610	1.65	3,432	1.23	553	0.20	8,595	3.07

Table 5 Ethnicity in the UK and Leicester (2001)

Ethnic Group	UK		Leicester		Coventry	
	Population	%	Population	%	Population	%
White	54,153,898	92.1	178,739	63.9	252,643	83.98
British	50,366,497	85.67	169,456	60.54	235,632	78.32
Irish	691,232	1.2	3,602	1.29	10,401	3.46
Other White	3,096,169	5.27	5,681	2.03	6,610	2.2
Mixed	677,117	1.2	6,506	2.3	5,163	1.72
White & Black Caribbean	——	——	2,841	1.01	2,453	0.82
White & Black African	——	——	539	0.19	271	0.09
White & Asian	——	——	1,908	0.68	1,605	0.53
Other Mixed	——	——	1,218	0.44	834	0.28
Asian or Asian British	2,331,423	4.0	83,751	29.9	33,910	11.27
Indian	1,053,411	1.8	72,033	25.73	24,177	8.03
Pakistani	747,285	1.3	4,276	1.53	6,169	2.05
Bangladeshi	283,063	0.5	1,926	0.69	1,741	0.58
Other Asian	247,664	0.4	5,516	1.97	1,823	0.61
Black or Black British	1,148,738	2.0	8,595	3.1	5,412	1.8
Caribbean	565,876	1.0	4,610	1.65	3,314	1.1
African	485,277	0.8	3,432	1.23	1,679	0.56
Other Black	97,585	0.2	553	0.2	419	0.14
Chinese	247,403	0.4	1,426	0.51	2,183	0.73
Other Ethnic Group	230,615	0.4	904	0.32	1,537	0.51
Total	58,789,194	100	279,921	100	300,848	100.0

Table 6 Religion in the UK, Leicester and Coventry (2001)

Religion	UK		Leicester		Coventry	
	Population	%	Population	%	Population	%
Christian	42,079,000	71.6	125,187	44.7	196,346	65.26
Buddhist	152,000	0.3	638	0.2	784	0.26
Hindu	559,000	1.0	41,248	14.7	7,757	2.58
Jewish	267,000	0.5	417	0.2	222	0.07
Muslim	1,591,000	2.7	30,885	11.0	11,686	3.88
Sikh	336,000	0.6	11,796	4.2	13,960	4.64
Other religion	179,000	0.3	1,179	0.4	733	0.24
No religion	9,104,000	15.5	48,789	17.4	45,314	15.06
Religion not stated	4,289,000	7.3	19,782	7.0	24,046	8.0
Base	58,789,000	100	279,921	100	300,848	100.0

Table 7   African-Caribbean population in the towns in England (2001)

Local authority	Population	%	Local authority	Population	%
Birmingham	47,831	4.9	Luton	7,653	4.2
Lambeth	32,139	12.1	Merton	6,976	3.7
Lewisham	30,543	12.3	Greenwich	6,755	3.2
Brent	27,574	10.5	Leeds	6,718	0.9
Croydon	26,065	7.9	Harrow	6,116	3.0
Hackney	20,879	10.3	Westminster	5,613	3.1
Haringey	20,570	9.5	Bristol	5,585	1.5
Southwark	19,555	8.0	Tower Hamlets	5,225	2.7
Newham	17,931	7.4	Sheffield	5,171	1.0
Waltham Forest	17,797	8.2	Bromley	4,637	1.6
Enfield	14,590	5.3	Leicester	4,610	1.7
Ealing	13,507	4.5	Kirklees	4,203	1.1
Wandsworth	12,665	4.9	Barnet	4,113	1.3
Sandwell	9,403	3.3	Kensington & Chelsea	4,101	2.6
Nottingham	9,189	3.4	Camden	3,635	1.8
Redbridge	9,126	3.8	Slough	3,470	2.9
Wolverhampton	9,116	3.9	Barking & Dagenham	3,434	2.1
Manchester	9,044	2.3	Coventry	3,314	1.1
Islington	8,550	4.9	Hillingdon	3,275	1.3
Hammersmith & Fulham	8,534	5.2	Reading	3,181	2.2

[2011 Census]

Table 8 Ethnicity in Leicester and 'England and Wales' (2011)

Ethnic group	England and Wales	Leicester		Coventry	
	%	population	%	Population	%
White: UK	80.5	148,629	45.1	211,188	66.63
Irish	0.9	2,524	0.8	7,305	2.30
Other White	4.4	15,066	4.6	15,385	4.85
Gypsy or Irish Traveller	0.1	417	0.1	151	0.05
Mixed: White and Black Caribbean	0.8	4,691	1.4	3,672	1.16
White and Black African	0.3	1,161	0.4	943	0.30
White and Asian	0.6	3,388	1.0	2,388	0.75
Other Mixed	0.5	2,340	0.7	1,227	0.39
Asian or Asian British: Indian	2.5	93,335	28.3	27,751	8.76
Pakistani	2.0	8,067	2.4	9,510	3.00
Bangladeshi	0.8	3,642	1.1	2,951	0.93
Other Asian	1.5	13,181	4.0	3,728	2.42
Black or Black British: Caribbean	1.1	4,790	1.5	3,317	1.05
African	1.8	12,480	3.8	12,836	4.05
Other Black	0.5	3,315	1.0	1,611	0.51
Chinese	0.7	4,245	1.3	3,728	1.18
Other Ethnic Groups: Arab	0.4	3,311	1.0	2,020	0.64
Any other ethnic group	0.6	5,257	1.6	3,319	1.05
Total	100.0	329.839	100.0	316,960	100.0

Table 9 Religion in Leicester and England (2011)

Religion	England	Leicester		Coventry	
	%	population	%	Population	%
Christian	59.4	106,872	32.4	170,090	53.66
Buddhist	0.5	1,224	0.4	1,067	0.34
Hindu	1.5	50,087	15.2	11,152	3.52
Jewish	0.5	295	0.1	210	0.07
Muslim	5.0	61,440	18.6	23,665	7.47
Sikh	0.8	14,457	4.4	15,912	5.02
Other religions	0.4	1,839	0.6	1,641	0.52
No religion	24.7	75,280	22.8	72,896	23.0
Religion not stated	7.2	18,345	5.6	20,327	6.41

Table 10   African-Caribbean population in the towns in England (2011)

Local authority	Population	%	Local authority	Population	%
Birmingham	47,641	4.4	Islington	7,943	3.8
Croydon	31,320	8.6	Hammersmith & Fulham	7,111	3.9
Lewisham	30,854	11.2	Harrow	6,812	2.8
Lambeth	28,886	9.5	Leeds	6,728	0.9
Brent	23,723	7.6	Bristol	6,727	1.6
Hackney	19,168	7.8	Bromley	6,609	2.1
Waltham Forest	18,841	7.3	Sheffield	5,506	1.0
Haringey	18,087	7.1	Tower Hamlets	5,341	2.1
Southwark	17,974	6.2	Barking & Dagenham	5,227	2.8
Enfield	17,334	5.5	Leicester	4,790	1.5
Newham	15,050	4.9	Kirklees	4,626	1.1
Ealing	13,192	3.9	Hillingdon	4,615	1.7
Wandsworth	12,297	4.0	Barnet	4,468	1.3
Sandwell	11,382	3.7	Westminster	4,449	2.0
Manchester	9,642	1.9	Trafford	3,802	1.7
Wolverhampton	9,507	3.8	Bradford	3,581	0.7
Redbridge	9,064	3.2	Camden	3,496	1.6
Luton	8,177	4.0	Derby	3,405	1.4
Merton	8,126	4.0	Wycombe	3,382	2.0
Greenwich	8,051	3.1	Hounslow	3,381	1.3
			Coventry	3,317	1.0

Appendix 12: Maps of Jamaica with the Caribbean Sea; Coventry and Leicester in the UK

1 The Caribbean Islands and flag of Jamaica

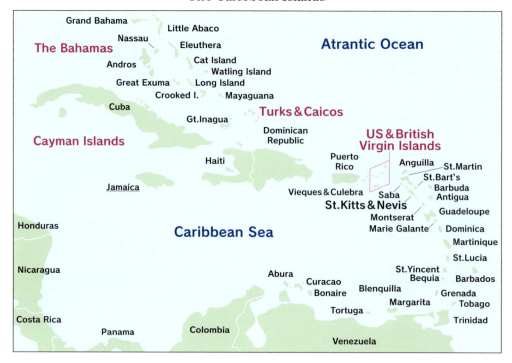

The Caribbean Islands

Flag of Jamaica

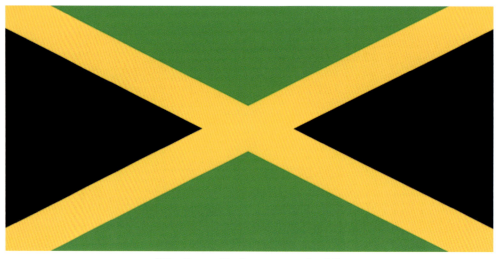

(The Cross, black, green, and gold)

2 Jamaica and its population

Parishes of Jamaica (2011 census)

Parish	Population

Cornwall County

Parish	Population
Hanover	69,533
Saint Elizabeth	150,205
Saint James	183,811
Trelawny	75,164
Westmoreland	144,103

Middlesex County

Parish	Population
Clarendon	245,103
Manchester	189,797
Saint Ann	172,362
Saint Catherine	516,218
Saint Mary	113,615

Surrey County

Parish	Population
Kingston Parish [1] [2]	89,057
Portland	81,744
Saint Andrew [1]	573,369
Saint Thomas	93,902
Jamaica	2,697,983

[1] The parishes of Kingston and Saint Andrew together form the Kingston and St. Andrew Corporation.
[2] The parish of Kingston does not encompass all of the city of Kingston. Most of the city is in the parish of St. Andrew.

3 Dorothy's life in Coventry

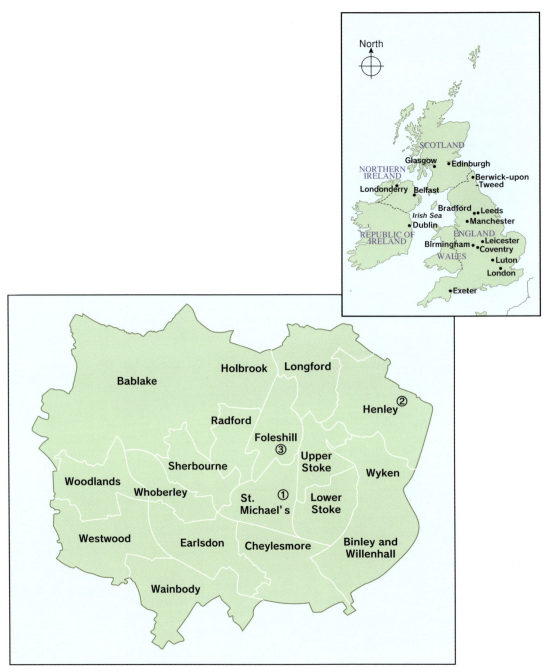

① Dorothy first lived in St Michael's ward for a few months after she came to Coventry in 1966. At that time she was five.
② Dorothy moved to Henley Green, in the Henley ward on the outskirts of Coventry, when she was six. She lived there for eight years.
③ Dorothy moved to the Foleshill ward, north of St Michael's, in 1975.

4 Leicester in the UK

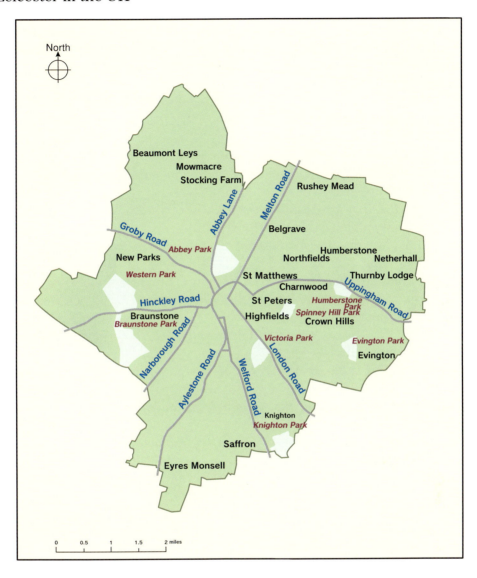

IV Appendices

Appendix 13: Select bibliography and websites

African-Caribbeans, mainly in the Caribbean Islands (including Jamaica)

○ Adams, L. Emilie, *Understanding Jamaican Patois: An Introduction to Afro-Jamaican Grammar, with a Childhood Tale*, by Llewelyn 'Dada' Adams, Kingston: LMH Publishing Ltd, 1991.

○ Asserate, Asfa-Wossen, *King of Kings: The Triumph and Tragedy of Emperor Haile Selassie I of Ethiopia*, London: Haus Publishing Ltd, 2015 (Translated by Peter Lewis; originally published in German in 2014).

○ Barrett, Leonard E. *The Rastafarians*, Boston: Beacon Press, 1997.

○ Barringer, Tim & Modest, Wayne (eds.), *Victorian Jamaica*, Durham, North Carolina: Duke University Press, 2018.

○ Blair, Teresa, P, *A-Z of Jamaican Patois (Patwah): Words, Phrases and How We Use Them,* Bloomington, Indiana: AuthorHouse, 2013.

○ Blaisdell, Bob (ed.), *Selected Writings and Speeches of Marcus Garvey*, New York: Dover Publications, Inc, 2004.

○ Bogdanov, Vladimir, Woodstra, Chris, Erlewine, Stephen Thomas & Bush, John (eds.), *All Music Guide to Hip-Hop: The Definitive Guide to Rap & Hip Hop*, San Francisco: Backbeat Books, 2003.

○ Boyd, Paul C., *The African Origin of Christianity, Vol. II: Its Place in Modern R.E.*, London: Karia Press, 1991.

○ Bradley, Lloyd, *This Is Reggae Music: The Story of Jamaica's Music*, New York: Grove Press, 2001.

○ Campbell, Horace, *Rasta and Resistance: From Marcus Garvey to Walter Rodney*, London: Hansib, 1985.

○ Clarke, Peter B., *Black Paradise: The Rastafarian Movement,* Wellingborough: The Aquarian Press, 1986.

○ Cohen, Abner, *Masquerade Politics: Explorations in the Structure of Urban Cultural Movements*, Berkeley: University of California Press, 1993.

○ Dabydeen, David & Samroo, Brinsley Samatoo (eds.), *India in the Caribbean*, London: Hansib/University of Warwick, 1987.

○ Gordon C., *The Reggae Files: A Book of Interviews*, London: Hansib, 1988.

○ Headley, Krissey, *Jamaican Patois: Story Come to Bump*, Independently published, 2017.

○ Hill, Robert A., *Dread History: Leonard P. Howell and Millenarian Visions in the Early Rastafarian Religion*, Chicago, Kingston & London: Frontline Distribution International, 2001.

○ Katz, David, *Solid Foundation: An Oral History of Reggae*, revised ed., London: Jawbone Press, 2012.

○ Klepeis, Alicia Z., *Jamaica (Exploring World Cultures)*, New York: Cavendish Square, 2019.

○ Larkin, Colin, *The Virgin Encyclopedia of Reggae*, London: Virgin Books, 1998.

○ Livesay, Daniel, *Children of Uncertain Fortune: Mixed-Race Jamaicans in Britain and the Atlantic Family, 1733-1833*, Williamsburg, Virginia: Omohundro Institute of

Early American History and Culture and Chapel Hill: the University of North Carolina Press, 2018.

○ Mack, Douglas R.A., *From Babylon to Rastafari: Origin and History of the Rastafarian Movement*, Chicago & London: Research Associates School Times Publications, 1999.

○ Mckenzie, Everal Emanuel, *Jamaica Tonics – Aphrodisiac Foods and Herb Culture: Tonic and Herbal Recipes from Jamaica*, New York: Blue Mountain Media, 2006.

○ Masouri, John, *The Story of Bob Marley's Wailers: Wailing Blues*, London & New York: Omnibus Press, 2008.

○ Meyer, Laure, *Black Africa: Masks, Sculpture, Jewelry*, Paris: Terrail, 1992.

○ Miller, Errol (ed.)*, Education and Society in the Commonwealth Caribbean*, Mona, Jamaica: Institute of Social and Economic Research, 1991.

○ Miller, Kei (ed.), *New Caribbean Poetry: An Anthology*, Manchester: Carcanet Press Limited, 2007.

○ Morgan, Philip D. & Hawkins, Sean, *Black Experience and the Empire*, Oxford: Oxford University Press, 2004.

○ Murrell, Nathaniel Samuel, *Afro-Caribbean Religions: An Introduction to Their Historical, Cultural, and Sacred Traditions*, Philadelphia: Temple University Press, 2010.

○ Nettleford, Rex (ed.), *Jamaica in Independence: Essays on the Early Years*, Kingston: Heineman Caribbean, 1989.

○ Poupeye, Veerle, *Caribbean Art*, London: Thames and Hudson, 1998.

○ Rogoziński, Jan, *A Brief History of the Caribbean: From the Arawak and Carib to the Present*, revised ed., New York: A Plume Book, 2000.

○ Romain, Gemma, *Connecting Histories: A Comparative Exploration of African-Caribbean and Jewish History and Memory in Modern Britain*, London: Kegan Paul, 2006.

○ Sewell, Tony, *Garvey's Children: The Legacy of Marcus Garvey*, 2nd ed., London & Basingstoke: Macmillan Education Ltd, 1990.

○ Sherlock, Philip & Bennett, Hazel, *The Story of the Jamaican People*, Kingston: Ian Randle Publishers and Princeton: Markus Wiener Publishers, 1998.

○ Shim, Jermel, *The Long Road to Progress for Jamaica: The Achievements and Failures in the Post-colonial Era*, Parker, Colorado: Outskirts Press, 2018.

○ Sloat, Susanna (ed.), *Caribbean Dance from Abakua to Zouk: How Movement Shapes Identity*, Gainesville: University of Florida, 2005.

○ Small, Stephen, *Racialised Barriers: The Black Experience in the United States and England in the 1980s*, London & New York, Routledge, 1994.

○ Solow, Barbara & Stanley, Engerman (eds.), *British Capitalism and Caribbean Slavery: The Legacy of Eric Williams*, Cambridge: Cambridge University Press, 1987.

○ Spring, Chris, *African Art in Detail*, London: British Museum Press, 2009.

○ Stephenson, Martha, *Jammin' Jamaican Recipes: Recreate Delicious Jamaican Dishes in Your Kitchen!*, CreateSpace Publishing, 2018.

○ Timm, Birte, *Nationalists Abroad: The Jamaica Progressive League and the Foundations of Jamaican Independence*, Kingston: Ian Randle Publishers, 2016.

○ Troeder, Werner, *Reggae: From Mento to Dancehall*, Kingston: LMH Publishing Limited, 2011.

IV   Appendices

○ Williams, Eric E., *Capitalism and Slavery*, Chapel Hill, North Carolina: The University of North Carolina Press, 1944.

○ Williams, Eric E., *Documents of West Indian History Vol. 1: 1492-1655 from the Spanish Discovery to the British Conquest of Jamaica*, Port of Spain, Trinidad: PNM Publishing, 1963.

○ Williams, Eric E., *From Columbus to Castro: The History of the Caribbean 1492-1969*, New York: Harper & Row, 1970.

○ Zuke, Ras, *The Rastaman Vibration*, Naples, Florida: Far-Eye Productions, 2002.

African-Caribbeans, mainly in the UK

○ Ackah, William & Christian, Mark (eds.), *Black Organisation and Identity in Liverpool: A Local, National and Global Perspective*, Liverpool: Charles Wootton College Press, 1997.

○ Adams, Norman W., [Jah Blue], *A Historical Report: The Rastafari Movement in England*, London: GWA Works, 2002.

○ Bauer, Elaine & Thompson, Paul (eds.), *Jamaican Hands Across the Atlantic*, Kingston and Miami: Ian Randle Publishers, 2006.

○ Beckford, Robert, *Jesus Is Dread: Black Theology and Black Culture in Britain*, London: Darton, Longman & Todd, 1998.

○ Benyon, John (ed.), *Scarman and After: Essays Reflecting on Lord Scarman's Report, the Riots and their Aftermath*, 1984 (1995).

○ Benyon, John & Solomos, John (eds.), *The Roots of Urban Unrest*, Oxford: Pergamon Press, 1987.

○ Bourne, Stephen, *Black in the British Frame: Black People in British Film and Television 1896-1996*, London & Washington, D. C.: Cassell, 1998.

○ Bousquet, Ben & Douglas, Colin, *West Indian Woman at War: British Racism in World War II*, London: Lawrence & Wishart, 1991.

○ Brinkhurst-Cuff, Charlie (ed.), *Mother Country: Real Stories of the Windrush Children*, London: Headline Publishing Group, 2018.

○ Home Office, *The Brixton Disorders 10-12 April 1981: Report of an Inquiry by the Rt. Hon. The Lord Scarman, O.B.E*, London: Her Majesty's Stationary Office, 1981.

○ Chamberlain, Mary, *Narratives of Exile and Return*, New Brunswick, New Jersey: Transaction Publishers, 2005.

○ Chamberlain, Mary (ed.), *Caribbean Migration: Globalised Identities*, London and New York: Routledge, 1998.

○ Chamberlain, Mary, *Family Love in the Diaspora: Migration and the Anglo-Caribbean Experience*, New Brunswick, New Jersey and London: Transaction Publishers, 2006.

○ Chuck, D., *Fight the Power: Rap, Race, and Reality*, Edinburgh: Payback Press, 1997.

○ Collins, Wallace, *Jamaican Migrant*, London: Routledge & Kegan Paul, 1965.

○ Connolly, Michelle, Roberts, Kenneth, et al. (eds.), *Black Youth in Liverpool*, Culemborg, Netherlands: Giordano Bruno Culemborg, 1992.

○ Craven, Anna, *West Africans in London*, London: Institute of Race Relations, 1968.

○ Dabydeen, David and Wilson-Tagoe, Nana, *A Reader's Guide to Westindian and Black British Literature*, London: Hansib, 1988.

IV **Appendices**

○ Dabydeen, David, John Gilmore & Cecily Jones (eds.), The *Oxford Companion to Black British History*, Oxford: Oxford University Press, 2007.

○ Donnell, Alison (ed.), *Companion to Contemporary Black British Culture*, London: Routledge, 2002.

○ Ellis, June (ed.), *West African Families in Britain: A Meeting of Two Cultures*, London, Henley & Boston: Routledge & Kegan Paul, 1978.

○ Foner, Nancy, *Jamaica Farewell: Jamaican Migrants in London*, Berkeley: University of California Press, 1978.

○ Fryer, Peter, *Staying Power: The History of Black People in Britain*, London, Pluto Press, 1984.

○ Glass, Ruth, *Newcomers: The West Indians in London*, London: Centre for Urban Studies and George Allen & Unwin Ltd, 1960.

○ Gmelch, George, *Double Passage: The Lives of Caribbean Migrants Abroad and Back Home*, Ann Arbor: The University of Michigan Press, 1992.

○ Gordon, Paul & Newnham, Anne (eds.), *Different Worlds: Racism and Discrimination in Britain*, 2nd ed., London: The Runnymede Trust, 1986.

○ Goulbourne, Harry, *Caribbean Transnational Experience*, London: Pluto Press, Kingston: Arawak Publications, 2002.

○ Gundara, Jagdish S. & Duffield, Ian (eds.), *Essays on the History of Blacks in Britain: From Roman Times to the Mid-Twentieth Century*, Aldershot: Avebury, 1992.

○ Hall, Stuart, *Familiar Stranger: A Life Between Two Islands*, London: Allen Lane, 2017.

○ Haynes, Aaron, *The State of Black Britain*, Vols.1-2, St. John's, Antigua: Hansib Caribbean, 1996, 1997.

○ Harris, Roxy & White, Sarah (eds.), *Changing Britannia: Life Experience with Britain*, London: New Beacon Books Ltd, 1999.

○ Hill, Clifford S., *Black and White in Harmony: The Drama of West Indians in the Big City, from a London Minister's Notebook*, London: Hodder & Stoughton, 1958.

○ Hill, Clifford S., *West Indian Migrants and the London Churches*, London: Oxford University Press, 1963.

○ Hintzen, Percy C., *West Indian in the West: Self-Representations in an Immigrant Community*, New York & London, New York University Press, 2001.

○ Institute of Race Relations, *How Racism Came to Britain*, London: Institute of Race Relations, 1985.

○ James, Winston & Harris, Clive (eds.), *Inside Babylon: The Caribbean Diaspora in Britain*, London & New York: Verso, 1993.

○ Kay, Jackie, Procter, James & Robinson, Gemma (eds.), *Out of Bounds: British Black & Asian Poets*, Newcastle upon Tyne: Bloodaxe Books Ltd, 2012.

○ Markham. E. A. (ed.), *Hinterland: Caribbean Poetry from the West Indies & Britain*, Northumberland: Bloodaxe Books Ltd, 1989.

○ McLeod, Mike, *Ethnic Trade and the Inner Cities: West Indian Business Links with the Caribbean*, Policy Paper in Ethnic Relations, No.20, Coventry: Centre for Research in Ethnic Relations, University of Warwick, 1990.

○ Morgan, Phillip D. & Hawkins, Sean (eds.), *Black Experience and the Empire*, Oxford:

IV Appendices

Oxford University Press, 2004 (2009).

○ Newham Monitoring Project, *Forging a Black Community: Asian and Afro-Caribbean Struggles in Newham*, London: Newham Monitoring Project, 1991.

○ Olusoga, David, *Black and British: A Forgotten History*, London: Macmillan, 2016.

○ Owusu, Kwesi & Ross, Jacob, *Behind the Masquerade: The Story of Notting Hill Carnival*, London: Arts Media Group, 1988.

○ Owusu, Kwesi (ed.), *Black British Culture & Society: A Text Reader*, London and New York: Routledge, 2000.

○ Parsons, Gerald, 'Filling a Void? Afro-Caribbean Identity and Religion', in Parsons, Gerald (ed.), *The Growth of Religious Diversity: Britain from 1945*, Vol.1: *Traditions*, London: The Open University, 1993, pp. 243-273.

○ Patterson, Sheila, *Dark Strangers: A Sociological Study of the Absorption of a Recent West Indian Migrant Group in Brixton, South London*, London: Tavistock Publications, 1963.

○ Paul, Kathleen, *Whitewashing Britain: Race and Citizenship in the Postwar Era*, Ithaca & London: Cornell University Press, 1997.

○ Peach, Ceri, *West Indian Migration to Britain: A Social Geography*, London: Oxford University Press, 1968.

○ Pearson, David, *Race, Class and Political Activism: A Study of West Indians in Britain*, Farnborough, Hampshire: Gower, 1981.

○ Phillips, Mike, *London Crossings: A Biography of Black Britain*, London & New York: Continuum, 2001.

○ Phillips, Mike & Phillips, Trevor, *Windrush: The Irresistible Rise of Multi-Racial Britain*, London: HarperCollins, 1998.

○ Pilkington, Edward, *Beyond the Mother Country: West Indians and the Notting Hill White Riots*, London: I.B. Tauris & Co Ltd, 1988.

○ Plummer, John, *Movement of Jah People: The Growth of the Rastafarians*, Birmingham: Press Gang, 1978.

○ Pryce, Ken, *Endless Pressure: A Study of West Indian Life-styles in Bristol*, Bristol: Harmondworth: Penguin, 1979.

○ Sewell, Tony, *Keep On Moving – the Windrush Legacy: The Black Experience in Britain from 1948*, London: Voice Enterprises Ltd, 1998.

○ Wambu, Onyekachi (ed.), *Empire Windrush: Fifty Years of Writing About Black Britain*, London: Phoenix, 1999.

○ Wambu, Onyekachi (ed.), *Hurricane Hits England: An Anthology of Writing about Black Britain*, New York: Continuum, 2000.

Leicester in general

○ Adam, Rosalind (ed.), *Jewish Voices: Memories of Leicester in the 1940s and 50s*, Leicester: Writing School Leicester Ltd, 2009.

○ Bonney, Richard, *Understanding and Celebrating Religious Diversity: The Growth of Diversity in Leicester's Places of Religious Worship since 1970*, Leicester: University of Leicester, 2003.

○ Brown, Cynthia, *Leicester Voices*, Stroud: Tempus, 2002.

Ⅳ Appendices

○ Burrell, Kathy, *Moving Lives: Narratives of Nation and Migration among Europeans in Post-War Britain*, Aldershot: Ashgate, 2006.

○ Daahir, Jawaahir, et al. (eds.), *Somalia to Europe: Stories of Somali Diaspora*, Leicester: Leicester Quaker Press, 2011.

○ Davis, Vernon, *Leicester Celebrates: Festivals in Leicester Past & Present*, Leicester: Leicester City Council Living History Unit, 1996.

○ England, Steve, *Magnificent Mercury: History of a Regional Newspaper: The First 125 Years of the Leicester Mercury*, Leicester: Kairos Press, 1999.

○ Haq, Tim & Law, Bill (eds.), *Belgrave Memories: 1945 to 2005*, Leicester: Contact Cultures, 2007.

○ Herbert, Joanna, *Negotiating Boundaries in the City: Migration, Ethnicity, and Gender in Britain*, Aldershot: Ashgate, 2008.

○ Herbert, Joanna, 'Immigration and the Emergence of Multicultural Leicester', in Rodger, Richard & Madgin, Rebecca (eds.), *Leicester: A Modern History*, Lancaster: Carnegie Publishing Ltd, 2016, pp.330-346.

○ Hyde, Colin, Vadnerkar, Smita & Cutting, Angela (eds.), *Parampara continuing the Tradition: Thirty Years of Indian Dance and Music in Leicester*, Leicester: Leicester City Council Living History Unit, 1996.

○ Jewson, Nick (ed.), *Migration Processes and Ethnic Divisions*, Leicester: Centre for Urban History/Ethnicity Research Centre, University of Leicester, 1995.

○ Jordan, Christine, *The Illustrated History of Leicester's Suburbs*, Derby: Breedon: Books Publishing, 2003.

○ Kuepper, W. G., Lackey, G. L. & Swinerton, E. N., *Ugandan Asians in Great Britain: Forced Migration and Social Absorption*, London: Croom Helm, 1975.

○ Lalani, Z. (compiled), *Ugandan Asian Expulsion: 90 Days and Beyond Through the Eyes of the International Press*, Tampa, Florida: Expulsion Publications, 1997.

○ Leicestershire Multicultural Archive Project, *Highfields Remembered: Memories of How a Community Developed from the First World War to Present Day*, Leicester: Leicestershire Multicultural Archive Project, 1996.

○ Marett, Valerie, *Immigrants Settling in the City*, Leicester: Leicester University Press, 1989.

○ Marett, Valerie, 'Resettlement of Ugandan Asians in Leicester', *Journal of Refugee Studies*, Vol. 6, No. 3, 1993, pp.248-259.

○ Martin, John & Singh, Gurharpal, *Asian Leicester*, Stroud: Sutton Publishing, 2002.

○ Nicholson, Julia, *Traditional Indian Arts of Gujarat*, Leicester: Leicestershire Museums, 1988.

○ Rodger, Richard & Madgin, Rebecca (eds.), *Leicester: A Modern History*, Lancaster: Carnegie Publishing Ltd, 2016.

○ Rooney, Yvonne & O'Connor, Henrietta, *The Spatial Distribution of Ethnic Minority Communities in Leicester, 1971, 1981 & 1991: Maps and Tables*, Leicester: Centre for Urban History/Ethnicity Research Centre, University of Leicester, 1995.

○ Sato Kiyotaka (ed.), *Life Story of Mrs Claire Wintram: A Jewish Woman and Her Identity*, Tokyo: Research Centre for the History of Religious and Cultural Diversity, Meiji University, 2010.

Ⅳ　Appendices

- Sato Kiyotaka (ed.), *Mrs Jasvir Kaur Chohan: Life Story of A Sikh Woman and Her Identity*, Tokyo: Research Centre for the History of Religious and Cultural Diversity, Meiji University, 2011.
- Sato Kiyotaka (ed.), *Mr Sarup Singh, MBE and Mrs Gurmit Kaur: Life Stories of A Sikh Artist and His Wife*, Tokyo: Research Centre for the History of Religious and Cultural Diversity, Meiji University, 2012.
- Sato Kiyotaka (ed.), *Life Story of Mr Jaffer Kapasi, OBE: Muslim Businessman in Leicester, and the Ugandan Expulsion in 1972*, Tokyo: Research Centre for the History of Religious and Cultural Diversity, Meiji University, 2012.
- Sato Kiyotaka (ed.), *Life Story of Mr Terry Harrison, MBE: His Identity as a Person of Mixed Heritage*, Tokyo: Research Centre for the History of Religious and Cultural Diversity, Meiji University, 2013.
- Sato Kiyotaka (ed.), *Life Story of Mr Andrejs Ozolins, a Latvian, and His Wife Mrs Dulcie Ozolins*, Tokyo: Research Centre for the History of Religious and Cultural Diversity (Meiji University), 2014.
- Sato Kiyotaka (ed.), *The Life Story of Mr Ramanbhai Barber, MBE, DL: the President of the Shree Sanatan Mandir in Leicester*, Tokyo: Research Centre for the History of Religious and Cultural Diversity, Meiji University, 2015.
- Sato Kiyotaka (ed.), The *Life Story of Mrs Nilima Devi, MBE: an Indian Classical Dancer in Leicester*, Tokyo: Research Centre for the History of Religious and Cultural Diversity, Meiji University, 2016.
- Seliga, Joseph, 'A Neighbourhood Transformed: the Effect of Indian Migration on the Belgrave Area of Leicester, 1965-1995', *The Local Historian*, Vol. 28, No. 4, 1998, pp.225-241.
- Singh, Gurharpal, 'A City of Surprises: Urban Multiculturalism and the "Leicester Model"', in Ali, N., Kalra, V. S. & Sayyi, S. (eds), *A Postcolonial People*, London: Hurst & Company, 2006, pp.291-304.
- Smith, Michael, *The Story of Belgrave: the Life and Death of a Leicestershire Village*, Birstall: Birstall Local History Society, 2013.
- Vershinina, N., Barrett, R. & Meyer, M., *Polish Immigrants in Leicester: Forms of Capital Underpinning Entrepreneurial Activity*, Leicester: De Montfort University, 2009.
- Walker, Penny (ed.), *We are South Highfields: Life in Our Area, Past and Present*, London: Near Neighbours, 2012.
- Wheatley, Ken, *More Memories of Leicester*, Elland, West Yorkshire: True North Books, 2000.

[Pamphlets, newspapers and other sources]
- *Survey of Leicester, 1983: Initial Report of Survey*, Leicester: Leicester City Council and Leicestershire County Council, 1984.
- *Survey of Leicester, 1983: Ward Tables*, Leicester: Leicester City Council and Leicestershire County Council, 1988.
- *Embracing the Present, Planning in the Future: Social Action by the Faith Communities of Leicester*, Leicester: Leicester Faiths Regeneration, 2004.

IV Appendices

- *20th Anniversary Brochure for Leicester Council of Faiths*, Leicester: Leicester Council of Faiths, 2006.
- *The Diversity of Leicester: A Demographic Profile*, Leicester: Leicester City Council, 2008.
- *Leicester Migration Stories: Making Histories*, London: Runnymede, 2012.
- At Home in Europe, *Somalis in Leicester*, New York: Open Society Foundations, 2014.
- *Leicester Mercury*, 1987, 2014, 2017, 2018.

African-Caribbeans in Leicester
[Books and Articles]

- Afrikan Caribbean Support Group Research Project, African Caribbean People in Leicestershire, *Education Matters: African Caribbean People and Schools in Leicestershire*, by Lyle, Stephen, Benyon, John, Garland, Jon and McClure, Anna, Scarman Centre for the Study of Public Order University of Leicester, 1996.
- Afrikan Caribbean Support Group Research Project, African Caribbean People in Leicestershire, *Summary of the Final Report*, by Benyon, John, Dauda, Bola, Garland, Jon, Lyle, Stephen, and the Afrikan Caribbean Support Group, Scarman Centre for the Study of Public Order University of Leicester, 1996.
- Afrikan Caribbean Support Group Research Project, African Caribbean People in Leicestershire, *Final Report*, by Benyon, John, Dauda, Bona, Garland, Jon, Lyle, Stephen, and the Afrikan Caribbean Support Group, Scarman Centre for the Study of Public Order, University of Leicester, 1996.
- Afrikan Caribbean Support Group Research Project, African Caribbean People in Leicestershire, *Community Experiences and Opinions*, Centre for the Study of Public Order, University of Leicester, 1994.
- Afrikan Caribbean Support Group Research Project, African Caribbean People in Leicestershire: *First Interim Report*, University of Leicester, Centre for the Study of Public Order, 1992 (revised edition, updated January 1993).
- Aucott, Shirley, *Women of Leicester 1850-2000*, Leicester City Council, 2000.
- *Black Elders in Leicester*, Leicester: Social Services Department, Leicestershire County Council, 1986.
- Brown, Cynthia, 'Immigrant Communities in Leicester', *Women's History Notebooks*, vol.32, Summer 1996.
- Byron, Margaret, *Post-War Caribbean Migration to Britain: The Unfinished Cycle*, Aldershot: Avebury, 1994.
- Calabash! *Traditional Caribbean Remedies, Memories & Stories*, Leicester: Leicester City Council, 2008.
- Chessum, Lorna, *From Immigrants to Ethnic Minority: Making Black Community in Britain*, Aldershot: Ashgate, 2000.
- Highfield Rangers Oral History Group and the Sir Norman Chester Centre for Football Research University of Leicester, *Highfield Rangers: An Oral History*, Leicester: Leicester City Council Living History Unit, 1993.
- *Highfields Remembered*, Leicester: Leicestershire Multicultural Archive Project, 1996.
- Moore, Valerie & Roberts, Bead (eds.), *Sharing Leicester Caribbean Memories: Carib-*

IV Appendices

bean Calabash, Leicester: Leicester Adult Education College, 2001.

○ Sato, Kiyotaka (ed.), *Life Story of Mrs Elvy Morton: First Chair of the Leicester Caribbean Carnival*, Tokyo: Research Centre for the History of Religious and Cultural Diversity, Meiji University, 2010.

○ O'Connor, Henrietta, *The Spatial Distribution of Ethnic Minority Communities in Leicester, 1971, 1981 & 1991: Analysis and Interpretation*, Leicester: Centre for Urban History and the Ethnicity Research Centre, University of Leicester, 1995.

○ Rooney, Yvonne & O'Connor, Henrietta, *The Spatial Distribution of Ethnic Minority Communities in Leicester, 1971, 1981 & 1991: Maps and Tables*, Leicester: Centre for Urban History and the Ethnicity Research Centre, University of Leicester, 1995.

○ Twine, France Winddance, *A White Side of Black Britain: Interracial Intimacy and Racial Literacy*, Durham, North Carolina: Duke University Press, 2011.

[Unpublished Paper]

○ Earle Robinson, The Development of Caribbean Organisations in Leicester: A Case Study, A Professional Study Course Paper for the Graduate Diploma in Community Education, Leicester: Department of Social and Community Studies, Leicester Polytechnic, 1980.

British Co-operative movement

○ Aves, Ernest, *Co-operative Industry*, London: Methuen & Co., 1907.

○ Bailey, Jack, *The British Co-Operative Movement*, London: Hutchinson, 1955.

○ Barou, N., *The Co-operative Movement in Labour Britain*, London: Victor Gollancz Ltd, 1948.

○ Birchall, Johnston, *Co-op: the People's Business*, Manchester & New York: Manchester University Press, 1994.

○ Birchall, Johnston, *The International Co-operative Movement*, Manchester: Manchester University Press, 1997.

○ Black, Lawrence, *Consumerism and the Co-operative Movement in Modern British History: Taking Stock*, Manchester: Manchester University Press, 2009.

○ Bonner, Arnold, *British Co-operation: The History, Principles, and Organisation of the British Co-operative Movement*, Manchester: Co-operative Union Ltd, 1961.

○ Burton, Alan, *The British Consumer Co-operative Movement and Film 1890s-1960s* Manchester: Manchester University Press, 2005.

○ Cole, G.D.H., *A Century of Co-operation*, Manchester: Co-operative Union Ltd, 1945.

○ Cole, G.D.H., *The British Co-operative Movement in a Socialist Society: A Report Written for the Fabian Society*, London: Allen & Unwin, 1951.

○ Flanagan, Desmond, *1869-1969: A Century Story of the Co-operative Union of Great Britain and Ireland*, Manchester: Co-operative Union Ltd, 1969.

○ Gaffin, Jean & Thoms, David, *Caring & Sharing: The Centenary History of the Co-operative Women's Guild*, Manchester: Co-operative Union Ltd, 1983.

○ Gurney, Peter, *Co-operative Culture and the Politics of Consumption in England, 1870-1930*, Manchester & New York: Manchester University Press, 1996.

○ Hall, F. & Watkins, W. P., *Co-operation: A Survey of the History, Principles, and Organ-*

IV   Appendices

isation of the Co-operative Movement in Great Britain and Ireland, 2nd ed., Manchester: Co-operative Union Ltd, 1937.

○ *Leicester: A Souvenir of the Forty-Seventh Co-operative Congress. Whitsuntide, 1915, including Some Aspects of Co-operation in the Midlands*, Manchester: Co-operative Wholesale Society Limited, 1915.

○ Redfern, Percy, *The New History of the CWS,* London: J.M. Dent & Sons Limited, 1938.

○ Richardson, Sir William, *The CWS in War and Peace 1938-1976: The Co-operative Wholesale Society Limited in the Second World War and Post-war Years*, Manchester: Co-operative Wholesale (publisher), 1977.

○ Robertson, Nicole, *The Co-operative Movement and Communities in Britain, 1914-1960: Minding Their Own Business*, Farnham: Ashgate, 2010.

○ Scott, Gillian, *Feminism and the Politics of Working Women: The Women's Co-operative Guild, 1880s to the Second World War*, London: UCL Press Limited, 1998.

○ Svendsen, Gunnar Lind Hasse & Svendsen, Gert Tiggaad, *The Creation and Destruction of Social Capital: Entrepreneurship, Co-operative Movements and Institutions*, Cheltenham: Edward Elgar, 2004.

○ Webb, Beatrice Potter, *The Co-Operative Movement in Great Britain*, London: Swan Sonnenschein, 1891.

○ Yeo, Eileen, 'Culture and Constraint in Working-Class Movements, 1830-55', in E. and S. Yeo (eds.), *Popular Culture and Class Conflict 1590-1914: Explorations in the History of Labour and Leisure*, Brighton: Harvester Press, 1981.

○ Yeo, Stephen, 'Working-Class Association, Private Capital and the State in the late Nineteenth and Twentieth Centuries', in Parry, Noel, Rustin, Michael and Satyamuti, Carole (eds.), *Social Work, Welfare and the State*, London: E. Arnold, 1979.

○ Yeo, Stephen, *Who was J.T.W. Mitchell?*, Manchester: CWS Membership Services, 1995.

Websites

○ BBC – Leicester – Abolition – The Long Road to Freedom
  (www.bbc.co.uk/leicester/content/articles/2007/03/05/...)
○ International Slavery Museum, Liverpool
  (www.liverpoolmuseums.org.uk/ism/slavery)
○ Leicester Caribbean Carnival [Images & Videos]
  (www.leicestermercury.co.uk./all-about/leicester-caribbean-carnival)

Appendix 14: Message from Dr Dorothy Francis, MBE

I am honoured that Professor Sato chose to write a book about my life as part of his 'Memory and Narrative' series, and would like to thank him for the painstaking work that he has devoted to editing many hours of oral narrative, gathering additional information, reproducing photographs and talking to a range of people who added different dimensions to the story. The book has taken a number of years to produce as Professor Sato resides in Japan and is only able to visit the UK for a few weeks each year on vacation from his position at Meiji University and the narrative was gathered during these visits.

Professor Sato's first 'Memory and Narrative' book told the life story of Mrs Elvy Morton who is credited as the originator of Leicester Caribbean carnival. Mrs Morton travelled to England when she was in her 20s and the book covers the travails and triumphs of her life over the subsequent half a century. Having heard her story Professor Sato wished to tell the story of an individual who arrived in the UK as a small child to compare Mrs Morton's experience to that of someone growing up in England as a newly arrived immigrant. He was guided to me by a mutual friend who was aware that I had arrived from Jamaica aged five. Professor Sato's original intention was to write a chapter about my experiences; however our first meeting produced enough material for at least three chapters as we talked into the evening and the initial chapter soon became a book!

Writing the book has been an interesting process as it has caused me to revisit many experiences, good and bad, that have shaped my life and it has been intriguing to consider the influence of the incidents and how they fashioned me to become the person that I am. I came to England before my sixth birthday yet remember the migration with clarity and that journey to a new life and the adjustments of living in a new country remains engraved on my mind. Some of the reminiscences are very personal and even painful to recount but I chose to share them in the context of providing an honest account. So many of the stories relate to the blatant and casual racism that was rampant in the 1960s and '70s and which coloured everyday life for immigrant communities who faced signs in guest houses and pubs reading 'No blacks, dogs or Irish'. It is hard to tell the story of these years without making reference to the hardships and prejudices that we faced as newly arrived communities and which, to some extent, is still the story of immigrants to the UK today. However the book also allows me to recount happy stories such as the many white British people who extended the hand of friendship to help my parents settle into their new lives in England and who shielded them from some aspects of racism. I also recall adventures into English food, social life and customs and recollect a childhood which consisted of freezing cold winters in a house bereft of central heating but offset by seemingly endless days of summer playing games and roaming the countryside, and these summertime memories always bring a smile to my face.

I grew up in Coventry and attended university in Birmingham before moving to Leicester in my mid-20s. At the time of writing I have lived in Leicester for 33 years so I think that Leicester has claimed me as her own! I enjoy living in Leicester and believe it to be one of the greatest cities in the UK. I have been privileged to work amongst local communities for more than three decades and am pleased to have been instrumental in helping hundreds of people to achieve their ambition of setting up in business. My reward is in doing a job that I love and helping others to achieve their goals, but I am delighted that my work has been recognised by a number of honours including the Queen's Award for Enterprise Promotion Lifetime Achievement Award, Companionship of the Chartered Management Institute, an MBE for services to enterprise and the communities of Leicestershire and an Honorary Doctorate of Laws for services to the co-operative movement. These awards are the icing on the cake for a career spent in the promotion of co-operative principles, self-determination and community engagement and they inspire me to greater efforts.

I have come on a long journey, both geographically and in terms of life experience, and the writing of the book offered opportunities for personal introspection and engaging discussions with my family regarding their memories of the time. My family are my roots; their love keeps me grounded and their support allows me to flourish and grow. I would not be where I am without their encouragement and belief and am pleased to use this opportunity to say thank you to my mother, Orinthia Francis, née Walker; my sisters Hortense, Sharon and Lorna; my brother Steadman and my cousin-brother Trevor. Thank you for believing in me.

I would like to thank my cousins in Jamaica and the USA who love me like a sister and rejoice in supporting me; Milo, Dean, Marva, Patrick, Junie, Peaches, Jacynth and Erica – your love means so much to me. Thank you also to your mother, Aunt Eula, who is a second mother to me. I send my love to my nieces and nephews who are the future: Velma, Sharla, Cory, Naomi, Talitha, Joseph, Samuel, Grace, Varli, K'Mayiah, Riyon, Keelen, Joshua and Jordan; I love you all and hope that you achieve all that you aspire to reach.

Thank you to my colleagues and friends at the Co-operative and Social Enterprise Agency (CASE) where I have worked for many years as a co-owner. CASE is a co-operative that is committed to changing lives and communities through co-operatives and social business. It is owned and controlled by people who are passionate about their work and it is a pleasure to work with such dedicated people.

The writing of this book consumed many hours in terms of recordings, editing and discussion and at times made me a virtual recluse as I worked towards deadlines. I owe apologies to my husband and children for the many hours that I was closeted away from their company but also owe them thanks for their encouragement, critique and endless cups of tea that kept me going! Thank you to my husband Kevin Hudson; your love is a constant in my life and your faith and belief in me sustains me to reach new heights. My daughters, Fayola and Safiya, you are my joy and delight and it is a pleasure to be the mother of such bright, hardworking, dedicated and kind young women. You bring happiness to my life and inspire me to work harder each day so that I may in turn inspire you.

The unifying theme within Professor Sato's 'Memory and Narrative' series is that of ordinary people who strive to achieve extraordinary change in their own lives, that of their families and the communities around them. They have all, without exception, applied their skills, dedication and passion to promoting education, developing goodwill and harmonising communities. The books celebrate the capacity of people to work for change to build a better society. I am delighted to be amongst the ranks of such wonderful people and I hope that you will enjoy my contribution to this series as much as I have enjoyed writing it.

Dorothy Francis
Leicester
August 2018